BUSINESS PLANNING FOR SCIENTISTS AND ENGINEERS

Fourth Edition

by

(585) 594-0025

Jenny C. Servo, Ph.D.

Cover design by Loren Clapp
Book design, figures, and tables by Adrienne Stiles and Melody Ossola

Online Companion -
Technical design and programming by Justin Craig-Kuhn
Graphic design and layout by Adrienne Stiles and Melody Ossola
Promotional website design and programming by Peter Lazarski

Quantity orders need to be placed with ©DAWNBREAKER® (585) 594-0025.

ISBN 0-9772843-0-1

Acknowledgments

This edition of the business planning book was funded internally. My goal in this update was not only to incorporate new information on licensing, complex technology platforms, operational plans, and financials, but also to take advantage of the capabilities that the internet enables to enhance motivation and learning. I thoroughly enjoyed working with Melody Ossola and Adrienne Stiles on this manuscript, as well as with Justin Craig-Kuhn on the design of the companion website.

The first edition of *Business Planning for Scientists and Engineers* was part of an evolving vision that started at the US Department of Energy (DOE). The need for assistance by companies approaching Phase III was recognized in the late 80's by Dr. Sam Barish. DOE championed a pilot project to provide commercialization assistance to companies that had received Phase II funding through the US Department of Energy's Small Business Innovation Research (SBIR) program. It has been Dawnbreaker's privilege to develop the Commercialization Assistance Program (CAP) and to become part of this vision.

The second edition of the book (1995) was funded by Virginia's Center for Innovative Technology. Thanks to Cathy Renault we had the opportunity to modify the first section of the book making it a useful guide for companies working on their own. The information in Section III was updated last years as part of a separate effort conducted for NIST's Advanced Technology Program (ATP) and has been updated again in this current edition. I would like to thank Rosalie Ruegg and Dr. Robert Sienkiewicz from ATP for that opportunity.

Thanks to Dr. Walter Polansky and Dr. Robert Berger the third edition was a substantive revision of the workbook (Section II) in which all activities were re-examined, the process streamlined, and more complete explanations provided.

Re-writing a book is always a difficult task and requires that many sets of eyes examine the modifications made - for only in this way can you assure that the changes made are indeed improvements. I would like to thank the members of the Dawnbreaker team for the time spent in editing and reviewing the materials. Gretchen Bird, Eva Patry, and John K. Servo provided invaluable comments which assured that the changes made had the desired impact. I would also like to thank the thousands of Principal Investigators from SBIR-, EM-, and ATP-funded companies with which Dawnbreaker has worked over the past fifteen years. Your questions have helped clarify what needed to be explained and pointed the way to the conceptualization of the revised workbook.

I would like to give particular thanks to Paul Hauler who for many years has been my mentor and my friend. Paul's guidance and expertise on business planning have contributed importantly to Dawnbreaker, as well as to the many companies with which he has worked through Dawnbreaker's Commercialization Assistance Program.

BUSINESS PLANNING FOR SCIENTISTS AND ENGINEERS

SECTION 1: Commercialization

Chapter 4: Sponsors: Potential Funding Sources

Chapter 5: Commercialization Strategies

Chapter 6: Licensing

SECTION 2: The Workbook

Tables

Figures

Section 1 | Commercialization

Introduction

" Ideas won't keep. Something must be done about them. When the idea is new, its custodians have fervor, live for it, and if need be, die for it."

- Alfred North Whitehead, English mathematician and philosopher

Chapter 01

Our experience with business planning probably echoes that of most small companies. You need the plan when you have the least resources available to develop it.

Prelude

Business Planning for Scientists and Engineers is a combination text/workbook intended for use by scientists or engineers actively engaged in developing a product or technology to commercialize. Whether you are just starting a company or have been in business for 5, 10, or 15 years, a business plan will increase the likelihood of successfully achieving your goals.

Parents and company founders alike have many things in common. Both love their offspring and find it difficult to be objective about them. In addition, one can become a parent or a company founder without specialized training or licenture. Anyone with an idea can start a company and try to reenact the Horatio Alger story. It is that ease of entry which probably accounts for the high mortality rate of small business. On average, only 1 in 3 companies makes it past the 4 year mark.[1, 2] Only 9% of companies with less than 20 employees last longer than 10 years. Business planning, a cohesive, transformational process, can help the technology entrepreneur acquire specialized, on-the-job training, while at the same time yield a document (business plan) that will assist with obtaining external financing and which will serve as a valuable internal guide.

66% of small businesses close their doors within the first 4 years

The first edition of *Business Planning for Scientists and Engineers* was developed for use in the Commercialization Assistance Program offered by the U.S. Department of Energy. The second edition modified the manuscript further to make it easier for individuals such as yourself to use in developing a business plan on their own. The third edition contained revised workbook with internet references added throughout. After reflecting upon the common misconceptions which advanced technology firms make, as well as those factors which businessmen and women take for granted the materials were substantively revised. Special emphasis was placed upon the development of operational plans and strategic thinking. The fourth edition expands the discussion of intellectual property and financials, and provides the option of various on-line support tools that complement the activities in the workbook.

What Makes this Book Unique?

Although there are many books on the market which indicate the desired contents of a business plan, there are none which clearly indicate how to find the needed information, while keeping yourself honest about the market potential.

The most basic requirements for business plan development are time and human resources. Our experience with business planning probably echoes that of most small companies. You need the plan when you have the least resources available to develop it. After all, time spent in developing the business plan competes with time you could use to meet development milestones, sell your product/service, or do other productive work. Business matters always seem to be more urgent and pressing than developing the plan. However, business planning is also important. In Chapter 7 attention is given to project planning in an effort to increase the likelihood that you successfully make it through this program and emerge with a completed business plan.

Business planning is usually described as a linear process. However, experience clearly indicates that it is iterative in nature. It starts with the plan the entrepreneur already has in his or her head. When asked, any entrepreneur can tell you what his technology or product is, who he thinks will buy it, how many he will sell, and what the cost of development or production will be. However, these answers are usually conjecture. For the most part, little data collection has actually gone into verifying the assumptions that this information represents. That initial plan, however, is important as it contains a myriad of hypotheses that need to be tested. We refer to that initial plan as a *Mind Map*. It represents the entrepreneur's starting point and the drum to which he or she is marching. Through a gradual process of adding more facts, that plan begins to shift. One organizing theme throughout this book is to move *from conjecture to certitude, from intuition to facts*. This is done in an iterative fashion as each new element of information that you uncover has implications for the rest. The Dawnbreaker® business planning process will accelerate the rate at which initial assumptions change.

A mind map is the set of untested hypotheses and assumptions entrepreneurs have about their business. It is their marching orders, their first plan.

Business Planning for Scientists and Engineers is not intended to be an academic treatise, but a useful document that will guide you through the business planning process. The Workbook, Section II, assumes that the company is developing a technology or product and does NOT have a business plan in hand. However, the workbook can also be used in an alternative fashion by individuals with existing plans that need to be revitalized or strengthened. See Section II for a discussion of how the workbook may be used in an alternate fashion by those having completed preliminary work. The sections of the book which cover financing options and commercialization strategies will be useful reading for experienced and novice entrepreneurs alike. This book specifically addresses an audience of scientists and engineers.

The business planning process turns conjecture into certitude.

Intended Audience - Scientists and Engineers

No, the title is not an oxymoron - Scientists and engineers can become excellent business planners. The title is intended to highlight unique problems shared by technologists. Scientists and engineers typically develop a business that reflects their expertise or research interests. Most commonly the technology entrepreneur hails from a university, a Federal laboratory, or the R&D/Manufacturing area of a large company. The technology or product that they wish to commercialize has been the focus of their research passion for many years. Therefore, scientists and engineers tend to approach entrepreneurship with a *"technology in search of a marketplace"* mindset. This approach is contrasted with that of a person from marketing and sales who has spent years interfacing with customers and has been immersed in their desires, wishes, and complaints. The latter are more likely to approach entrepreneurship from the perspective of a *"Need in search of a solution."* This common starting point results in common problems for technology entrepreneurs.

On many occasions, people have asked *"Why do you have a special program for technologists? Isn't business planning the same whether it's for a Mom & Pop store or a high tech enterprise?"* The answer is an unqualified *"No." Technology entrepreneurs face unique and difficult issues clustered in three areas:*

» Financing
» Sizing Markets
» Intellectual Property

Financing

By definition, research and development is risky and oftentimes fails. R&D is also expensive, requiring sophisticated measurement and calibration devices, special environments, specialized equipment, adherence to special codes, and skilled personnel. High risk and expensive! That's not a formula which gives investors a "warm feeling." In fact it sends them running - away! Most investors prefer to wait until technical risk has been decreased before they consider backing an enterprise based on a new technology. The result: a common problem for technology entrepreneurs is scarcity of financing particularly during the initial R&D phase. More often than not, this need leads the technology entrepreneur to develop his core technology through "Science-for-hire" arrangements with various Federal government research programs such as the Small Business Innovation Research Program (SBIR) or the Small Business Technology Transfer Program (STTR). Such programs spawn valuable R&D initiatives. Without them many technology firms would not survive the initial gestation period when resources are most scarce

Technology entrepreneurs often fund high risk R&D through "science-for-hire" performed under government contracts.

Once the R&D phase is complete, the technology entrepreneur must find partners and funding mechanisms to support engineering, manufacturing, marketing, sales, and distribution. This leads the entrepreneur down a path of choices that requires that he or she become familiar with the pros and cons of a wide range of equity and debt financing methods - with a heavy emphasis on equity.

Science-for-hire is a phrase applied to those situations in which a scientist is hired to conduct research and development activities for another entity.

One can readily see the difference in financing issues faced by technology entrepreneurs and "Mom & Pop" shop owners. The latter do not have to finance the risky, expensive R&D phase. Neither do most "Mom & Pops" deal with equity, but instead place a heavier emphasis on the use of debt financing. Although equity financing is sometimes used, it is uncommon for retail stores to have to consider the pros and cons of private placement, venture capital, limited partnerships, or initial public offerings to grow their businesses.

Sizing Markets

Another unique problem faced by scientists and engineers is how to size the market. Because technology entrepreneurs start the development of their business from an R&D perspective, more often than not they deal with new or emerging markets. It is, therefore, difficult to determine the rate at which a new technology will be accepted and the rate at which it will replace other approaches to solving the same problem. The rate of acceptance is dependent upon many factors including new legislation, the enforcement of existing legislation, the number of competitors, approval from organizations such as FDA or U/L, drastic reductions in product pricing, the amount of training required by the customer before he can use the device, the amount of capital invested in alternative approaches, the size of the installed base of complimentary equipment, and breakthroughs in other, synergistic technologies. The many factors which effect the rate at which emerging markets will blossom creates market risk. Again, investors do not wish to provide significant financing while market risk is high. They would rather wait until preliminary customer acceptance is demonstrated before making significant investments.

Market risk and technical risk keep private sector investors away. Most wait until risk is reduced before providing capitalization.

The complexity of the process involved in sizing the market for emerging technologies also differentiates business planning for technology entrepreneurs from "Mom & Pop" stores or routine services. Someone, for example, who is setting up a veterinary hospital can draw upon data provided by professional associations regarding population density and the number of veterinary offices in an area that can be supported by such a population. One can also turn to professional associations for determining the range of services required, pricing, hours, etc. When setting up a "Mom & Pop" grocery store, entrepreneurs can walk into their competitors' shops and look at their merchandise, look at their advertising and promotional materials, determine who their suppliers are, and look at population density and demographics to determine the location of their store. By contrast, with advanced technology firms, one needs to build a hypothetical construct to determine the market size for products such as electric cars, fuel cells, and virtual reality, and then must predict a rate of growth based on a set of relevant data and some assumptions.

A method that is commonly used to size emerging markets is a market build-up method. This is a forecasting method that calls for identifying all potential buyers in each market and estimating their potential purchases.

Intellectual Property

When you create a business from an R&D perspective, you develop a technology/product that most often is novel, useful, and nonobvious--three criteria which determine patentability. Patents, as well as other forms of intellectual property (trade secret, copyright, and trademark), are valuable assets and ones that may be required by potential investors as a prerequisite for financing. The technology entrepreneur, therefore, needs to become conversant with issues of intellectual property, needs to develop a strategy for appropriately protecting their inventions, and determine how to finance this aspect of their business. Some forms of intellectual property protection are expensive and involve complicated processes. Again, "Mom and Pop" stores do not typically concern themselves with such issues.

Common Problems, Common Solutions

Although technology entrepreneurs share common problems, their training and experience in graduate research and the scientific method provide useful frames of reference that they can draw upon in the process of business planning. Research skills, coupled with the ability to put in long hours of work, the willingness to learn new things, and tenacity make scientists and engineers well suited for the task of business planning. We do not mean to imply by this statement that only scientists and engineers can develop business plans. There are many people that have not had the benefit of such training who have voracious appetites to learn and are outstanding business planners. Likewise, there are scientists and engineers who consider such tasks beneath them and who close their mind to new experiences. However, after having worked with hundreds of technology entrepreneurs, small business owners, and independent inventors, we conclude that those who find joy and challenge in learning new things, who have a tremendous capability for work, and who are undaunted by the complexities of business do very well as technology entrepreneurs. It is to such people that this book is directed!

Chapter 1 Endnotes

[1] Holland, Robert. Planning Against a Business Failure. ADC Info #24, October 1998.

[2] Headd, Brian. Redefining Business Success: Distinguishing Between Closure and Failure. Small Business Economics, 21, 51-61, 2003

Of Plans and Planning

"Plans are nothing. Planning is everything."

- Dwight D. Eisenhower

Chapter 02

Business planning is often a painful process. To be successful, it requires that the theory builder be willing to part with a perspective that he or she may hold that upon examination may not coincide with the evidence at hand.

The Process of Business Planning

Technology entrepreneurs typically approach business planning as a necessary evil, a "ticket" required to play the capitalization game. However, a more appropriate way for you, as a technology entrepreneur, to view business planning is as a form of theory construction or model building. These paradigms are familiar to scientists/engineers and make the transition to business planning easier. At the outset, a scientist's view of his or her business contains numerous assumptions and hypotheses. Through the application of a systematic process, these hypotheses must be tested and discarded as deemed fit. Important variables must be isolated, and the discovery of lawful relationships among them must proceed rigorously. Just as a good scientific theory is fertile and guides scientific inquiry, a good business plan will focus an entrepreneur's resources and guide the manner in which business plan development is carried out. Theories are nets that we weave to capture reality--so it is with business planning. Business planning is the business counterpart of scientific theory construction and embodies the scientist's understanding of the business world in which the technology exists and can develop. It is a process by which "Conjecture is turned into certitude" and "Intuition is replaced by facts."

Business planning is like theory construction

Business planning is often a painful process. To be successful, it requires that the theory builder be willing to part with a perspective that he or she may hold that upon examination may not coincide with the evidence at hand. In most cases, the outcome of good, strategic business planning requires a change...a modification in the technology, the product, the team, the direction, or the assessment of the opportunity.

Just as a scientist strives to observe, explain, predict, and control the phenomenon of interest, he or she must do the same in the business planning process. The scientist as business planner must observe the world in which the potential business opportunity exists. The most important variables which he must understand are customers, competitors, market size, financial resources, risks, human resources, and technology/product. The business planner must gather sufficient information to explain the behavior of those variables so that adequate predictions can be made about their probable interaction. Strategies then need to be developed to maximize the likelihood that the course of development can be controlled in the desired fashion; that is, the creation of a commercially viable business. Somewhat different approaches will be required than the methods with which you are accustomed, since in business you are dealing with a dynamic system which is frequently difficult to predict and manage.

Business Planning Process

- Conduct Research in a systematic fasion
- Expect changes in
  - Product/service concept
  - Definition of market
  - Pricing
  - Assessment of competition
  - Understanding of costs
  - Commercialization strategy

The scientist should expect the business planning process to require as much time and effort as conducting a master's thesis. This process, however, needs to be entered into by a team. Since the team will execute the plan, it is important that team be involved with its development and take "ownership." Now is the time to begin coalition building, a skill that you will need throughout the business development process. As the driver of this process, you will be required to learn about the variables of importance: customers, competitors, market size, financial resources, risks, and human resources. Although you will not be expected to become an expert in all of these areas, you must understand them so that you can be effective in coalition building and in modifying your perspective, as appropriate. In this endeavor, the most successful scientist/entrepreneurs are those who continue to learn and develop in new directions. Becoming a successful technology entrepreneur is an obtainable goal and a transition that we have seen countless scientists successfully make.

Variables

» Customers » Competitors » Markets

» Money » Human Resources »Products, technology

The team you develop must be multi-disciplinary!

Business Plans and Business Planning

It is obvious to any scientist or engineer that, failure to apply appropriate methodology when conducting experimental research, will result in invalid conclusions. The resulting technical paper will be flawed as it is only as good as the research which precedes it. The same relationship holds true between business planning and the development of a business plan. A business plan is merely a document. However, just as a good technical paper summarizes the results of rigorous scientific research, a good business plan can only be developed after rigorous business research. Rigor is no less important in the realm of business than it is in the physical sciences.

Although this appears to be a truism, there is the tendency for technologists to approach business planning as a writing exercise rather than as a research endeavor. In other words, when confronted with the need for cash flow, many give into the financial imperative and hurriedly package available information in a manner which seems plausible. With little research and with, at best, a sample business plan to follow, the technologist applies him- or herself for several days and "Voila,.... a business plan!" What the unsuspecting entrepreneur doesn't understand, however, is that this document is just as invalid as a technical paper based on scientific hypotheses and assumptions masquerading as empirical facts. The impression created when such a makeshift plan is given to a qualified investor is that the scientist doesn't understand his market, his costs, or the risks. This is frequently the case when a business plan is produced in this fashion. Rigorous research on customers, competitors, markets, and the financial resources required to meet objectives for growth is necessary before developing a valid business plan, just as it is a prerequisite for good science!

A business plan is only as good as the research which precedes it!

Why this dichotomy? Why do brilliant scientists approach their technology with tremendous rigor but approach business planning in a very casual, unsophisticated way? Is it because they don't care about the business issues? Is it because they don't understand the business planning process? or is it because they don't have the time?

Table 2-1: Timeline for business planning process and plan development

weeks

1-3	4-8	9-12	13-16	17-20
commercialization strategy	customer	confirm strategy	draft plan	write final draft
mission	market research	operation plans	feedback	package plan
vision	industry analysis	finances	reevaluation	disseminate
product	competitors			
	reevaluation			

The premise of this book is that, in most cases, this dichotomy is the result of a lack of time and resources coupled with a lack of understanding of the business planning process. However, rest assured that business planning can be taught and scientists such as yourselves can master this process and produce excellent business plans, which will serve you well.

Timetable for Developing a Business Plan

You have undoubtedly picked up this book as you are in need of a business plan. The information and methods included in this book will help you to realize that goal in a 20 week period. We have worked with hundreds of scientists and engineers in the same position as you. They are strapped for time, strapped for resources, and need to develop a good business plan while fulfilling all the other tasks required to keep their business enterprise growing. A 20 week period allows adequate time for conducting the research, analyzing the information gathered, testing the preliminary hypotheses, and developing a good business plan. The pace will be far from easy. Expect busy weekends, late nights, joy, exhaustion, bewilderment, frustration, and finally satisfaction with a job well done. Table 2-1 is an advanced organizer which schematically represents the various tasks that you will accomplish during this 20 week period. This information will be elaborated upon in Section II: the Workbook.

Develop a good business plan in 20 weeks, while meeting your other obligations.

Who should Develop the Business Plan?

Because the founder of a small company is overextended, it is not uncommon for the founder to look for someone else to develop the business plan for him. If money is available, the most common first preference is to hire a consultant. When funds are tight, the founder often seeks to involve someone else to develop the plan on "spec"; that is, to invest their time in exchange for a job or equity position in the firm.

As the leader of your firm, you should be directly and intimately involved with business planning.

No matter how appealing these options may seem, you must develop the business plan yourself. As the leader of your firm, you must be directly and intimately involved. Business planning is a transformational process and, if you are not involved, you will fail to grow with your business. If you are serious about developing a good business plan, you must begin by setting aside time on a weekly basis to complete various tasks associated with the business planning process.

Leverage your time by appropriately involving others.

To say that you should be involved does not mean that you should proceed without help. Quite the contrary; in order to be able to add this activity to an already busy schedule, you must look for ways to leverage your time. This is accomplished by appropriately involving others. More than likely you have already seen good examples of this to use as a frame of reference.

Table 2-2: Sources to involve in various tasks associated with business planning process

SKILLS	SOURCES OF ASSISTANCE
Hypothesizing	You, management team
Data gathering	State programs, RTTC, students, consultant
Review & synthesis	You, management team, board
Decision making	You, management team
Strategizing	You, management team, board
Number crunching	You, management team, accountant, state program, consultant, SCORE
Re-evaluation	You, management team, board
Writing	You, management, board
Editing	You, editor

Earlier we used the analogy of a master's thesis. This is actually a good process to reference when looking at how to leverage your time in business planning. When in graduate school you probably worked for a professor who was responsible for many of the conceptual aspects of the research with which you were involved. The professor also mapped out the methodology, was involved with the synthesis of information, and made most pertinent decisions. Others performed the more routine tasks associated with data gathering, literature searches, and editing. Others who have worked in an apprenticeship programs have doubtless seen a similar division of labor. This same conceptual framework can be applied to business planning. The principal cognitive skills required are listed in Table 2 - 2 as well as sources to consider involving with selected tasks. This model is elaborated upon in the Workbook and is provided here as an advanced organizer.

300 person hours of cumulative effort!

The individuals who should be involved with each of these skills depends on the size of your company and how your firm is structured. If you are a sole proprietor, you will be responsible for accomplishing most of these activities on your own and periodically involving other trusted or reasonably priced resources. If you are on your own, remain undaunted. We have mentored many individuals who have developed extremely good plans and accomplished the research on their own while still fulfilling the primary objective of their business. If you have a management team, make sure that they are intimately involved with this process as they must take ownership of the results. If all members of the team are not involved, the transformation of your management team will be uneven and conflicts may develop and/or linger.

The development of a good business plan will take approximately 300-person hours. However, if you leverage your time wisely, the time spent will not all be yours.

Table 2 - 2 includes a summary of the variety of players that you can and should involve with business planning. Notice that the greatest use of external sources will be with data gathering tasks. You will need to gather information about customers, markets, competitors, and industries and contrast that information with the assumptions and hypotheses currently in your mind map. Also notice the use of the term outsider in combination with most skills. An outsider is someone who lacks a vested interest in your company and who possesses a variety of business skills and insights. As this enterprise is your baby, it is important to involve an objective third party to help keep you honest. Such outsiders also play a key role in your on-the-job training, as a wisely selected entity will have skills and experiences that you can draw upon to learn more about business planning.

Why do I Need a Business Plan?

A business plan has both an internal and external value to a company. Although most companies develop a business plan to obtain financing (external value), many companies develop a business plan exclusively to act as an internal guide.

Business plans have internal and external value.

Internal Value of a Business Plan

Most companies run lean. They operate on the Grizzly Principle --that is, if you stop running, the grizzly bear will get you. You have to keep moving forward in order to survive. The business landscape is dotted with safe havens where you can stop momentarily (large contracts) - before you quickly move on. In this grizzly, entrepreneurial environment, it is common that people fail to communicate adequately. Everyone is running, more or less, in the same direction. As new people join the organization, they must jump in and learn to run alongside the others fairly quickly. The direction in which people are running is not necessarily correct. In the absence of sound strategic planning, the direction in which people are running may prove to be apocalyptic.

A sound strategic business plan not only draws together the efforts of this team but assures that everyone is moving downfield together in the best possible direction. The value of a business plan as an internal document is that it can:

(a) provide the mission for the staff, educating them regarding the company's past, present, and future goals,

(b) identify strengths, weaknesses, opportunities, threats, and trends,

(c) communicate expectations and priorities,

(d) provide the basis for measuring performance against specific milestones, as well as

(e) provide a framework for making intelligent management and financial decisions.

"Grizzly Principle"- You have to keep moving forward to survive.

External Document

When drafting a business plan it is important to be mindful of the audience to which the plan is directed. If your goal is to raise external funding, it will be directed to equity investors, potential strategic allies, or debt financing institutions. Each of these potential audiences has somewhat different concerns. An equity investor is interested in the return on investment (ROI) that would result from an investment in your firm, while a potential strategic ally looks at the leveraging advantage your opportunity would provide his/her existing business. By contrast, a debt financing institution will want to thoroughly understand your collateral. All investors will be interested in cash flow, accounts receivable, and other signs of corporate stability and market acceptance.The business plan is the vehicle which demonstrates the likelihood that they will realize an acceptable, reasonable return if they invest in your company.

So What Format do I Follow?

To familiarize you with the end product, we have included two versions of a business plan outline on the following pages. When looking at this, please keep in mind that any business plan is only as good as the research which precedes it. If you merely package the hypotheses and assumptions that you currently have using this format, you miss the point. A good business plan requires good business planning. Therefore, before you begin to draft a business plan, go to Section II: the Workbook and begin the process of business planning.

Why two business plan outlines? The first is a heuristic to provide you with an overall look at the structure of the document. When used as a selling tool, the purpose of the business plan is to create a logical case for investment. The plan starts in Section 2 by stating this is who we are and what we have. Sections 3-5 constitute the market assessment, a key component of any business plan. The purpose of the market assessment is to demonstrate that you have had first hand experience with your customers and that there are enough of them who are ready, willing, and able to buy your product, technology, or service. Sections 7 - 10 indicate how your company will realize this opportunity. It is a set of operational plans for each functional area. Section 11, the Contingencies section, indicates that, recognizing that any business is fallible, you have thought through responses to various impediments that may arise. Section 12, the Financials, depends on everything that has gone before. Revenue streams are identified and costs are clarified for each functional area. This section is the numerical statement that articulates how you will grow the company and provide a return on investment (ROI) for yourself and your investors.

The second outline provides more detailed elements of a good business case. *The items in italics are topics to be addressed in whatever sequence seems most appropriate within that particular section.*

Business Plan Outline (General)

1. Executive Summary
2. Company & Technology
3. Industry Overview
4. Customers
5. Market
6. Competitors
7. Marketing/Sales Plan
8. R&D Plan
9. Manufacturing/Engineering Plan
10. Human Resource Plan
11. Contingencies
12. Financial
13. Appendices
14. References

This is a general heuristic model. Note that a good plan contains a market assessment and functional plans for realizing the opportunity.

Figure 2-1

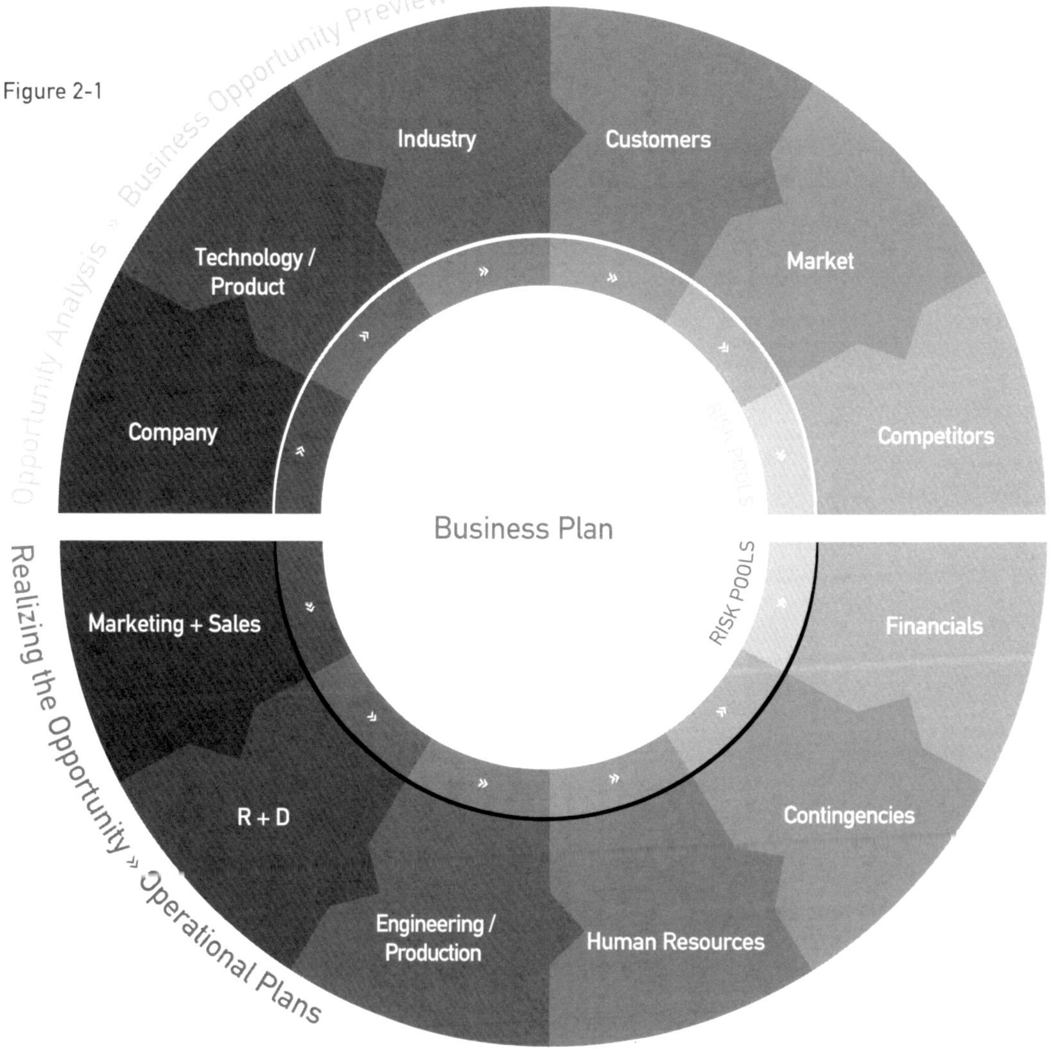

Business Plan Outline (Detailed)

Cover Page
Table of Contents

1. Executive Summary

2. Company & Technology

2.1 Brief company introduction
- *Mission*
- *Location, size, history*
- *Overview of company capabilities*
- *Customers & past performance*

2.2 Technology
- *Brief description*
- *Applications*

2.3 Product/Service
- *Brief description*
  - 2.3.1. Intellectual property status

2.4 Commercialization strategy - brief overview

3. Industry Overview

3.1. Industry definition and description
- *New products and developments within the industry*
- *Major players within the industry, factors driving dynamics*

3.2. Legislation and policies driving the industry
- *Future and historical trends*

4. Customers

4.1 Customers & end-user
- *Need addressed by the technology/product/service*
- *How the need is currently filled?*
- *Features, Advantages, and Benefits; Price point*
- *Who has the need? - Differentiate between end-users and customer needs*
- *Distribution channels used by customers and end-users*

4.2 Buying behavior
- Decision makers
  - *Who makes the decision to buy*
  - *Who influences the purchase decision*
  - *Characterization of decision makers*
- Basis for purchase decisions
  - *Frequency of purchase decisions*
  - *Basis for purchase decisions*

5. Market

5.1. Market definition
- 5.1.1. Primary market
- 5.1.2. Secondary markets

5.2. Market size and trends - Primary market
- *Current total and served-available markets*
- *Predicted annual growth rate*

6. Competitors

6.1. Indirect competitors

6.2. Direct competitors
- *Who are they?*
- *Strengths and weaknesses*
- *Market share of competitors*

6.3. SWOT analysis

7. Marketing / Sales Plan

7.1. Opportunity statement

7.2. Marketing & sales objectives

7.3. Current customers (if appropriate)

7.4. Potential customers
- *Customers targeted for intensive selling efforts*
- *How other customers will be identified and qualified*
- *Product features emphasized and contrasted with competitors*

7.5. Pricing
- *Basis for targeted price point*
- *Margins & levels of profitability at various levels of production & sales*

7.6. Sales Plan
- *Sales force analysis (reps, distributors, direct)*
- *Sales expectations for each salesperson & each distribution channel*
- *Margins given to intermediaries*
- *Service and warranties*
- *Organizational chart for sales/marketing staff, indicating planned growth for 3 - 5 years*

7.7. Advertising
- *Year 1- Detailed Marketing Communications plan*
- *Years 2-5 (general)*

7.8. Sales/Marketing Budget
- *Assumptions*

8. R&D Plan

8.1. R&D Objectives

8.2. Milestones and current status
- *What remains to be done to make the product marketable?*

8.3. Difficulties and risks

8.4. Staffing

8.5. R&D Budget
- *Assumptions*

9. Manufacturing/Engineering Plan

9.1. Objectives

9.2. Use of Subcontractors

9.3. Quality control

9.4. Staffing

9.5. Manufacturing/Engineering budget
- *Assumptions*

10. Human Resource Plan

10.1. Staffing Objectives

10.2. Organizational structure - phased over 3-5 years

- *Introduction of management team*
- *Key individuals to be recruited and plans for doing so*
- *Board of Directors, Advisory Board*
- *Incentives for commitment*

10.3. Human Resource Budget

- *Assumptions*

11. Contingencies

11.1. Potential Risks

- *Impact and responses*

12. Financials

12.1. Financial Objectives

- *Commercialization strategy (elaborated)*
- *Use of funds*
- *Terms and conditions of any previous financing arrangements*

12.2. Plans for obtaining investors or strategic alliance

- *Profile of investor or partner sought*
- *Leveraging advantage for investor/partner*
- *Detailed plans for obtaining investor/partner*
- *Costs and time associated with securing investor/partner*

12.3. Pro Forma Profit & Loss statements

12.4. Pro Forma Cash Flow projections

12.5. Pro Forma Balance Sheet

12.6. Alternative return scenarios

- *Exit scenarios*

This detailed outline is included as a preview of the end product. It is organized in a way that builds a logical business case, both for internal and external use.

Appendices

*In the first draft of the business plan, place the budget for each functional area at the conclusion of the relevant planning section. This is recommended to increase the likelihood that you build your financials from the bottom-up, as opposed to generating numbers from plugging in ratios to spreadsheet programs. The financials must be clearly tied to the objectives, activities, and costs associated with implementation of your plans. In the final version of the plan, however, the budgets for each functional area should be removed from the planning section, consolidated, and included only in section 12 of the business plan.

The Scope of a Business Plan

To be useful, a business plan must have great specificity; for only in the presence of specific information can one ascertain customer needs and develop strategies, costs, and realistic financial goals. The requirement for specificity demands that the entrepreneur limit the scope of a business plan. For example, suppose that you have developed a rich technology platform that has diverse applications in the automotive, computer, and chemical industries. Furthermore, suppose you wish to pursue different commercialization strategies with each application--licensing to the automotive industry, equity financing to manufacture a component for use in the computer industry, and a joint venture with a large firm in the chemical industry. The question is should you develop one business plan or three? In order to make the business planning process productive and manageable, the answer is "Three", one around each of the three different applications. If, conversely, you tried to tackle all three concurrently, the information would be kept at the macro level - resulting in a superficial, misleading treatment of the opportunities. Technology rich companies are better served developing plans around lines of business, strategic business units, or product lines aimed at similar markets.

Scope also refers to time. Business plans usually have a five year horizon although in some industries the timespan will be shorter (software) and with others (pharmaceuticals) it will be longer. In other words, the document reflects a course charted for a five year period. The operational plans for the first year are usually expressed in great detail and in a more general fashion for years two through five. On an annual basis (at a minimum), the business plan should be revisited and course adjustments made in light of new information acquired during the realization of the first year's goals and objectives. To facilitate ease of updating a plan, an on-line companion is available which allows the entrepreneur the ability to readily update assumptions and generate new strategies and financials.

Business plans have a five year horizon.

Commercialization Plans vs Business Plans

Many times companies confuse business plans with commercialization plans. They are not the same, even though they do have a direct bearing on one another. A commercialization plan is a strategic statement of how you will bring one or more technologies to market. It is an overview, a macro, strategic statement. Many times commercialization plans also include a detailed analysis of which applications and which markets are likely to mature first. By contrast, a business plan is detailed and charts a clear, specific path to realize financial reward around well-defined opportunities. Each business plan will tie back to the commercialization plan. In summary, a commercialization plan is macro, the business plan is micro; a commercialization plan is global, a business plan is specific; a commercialization plan encompasses a whole technology, a business plan is tied to lines of business. If you are developing a commercialization plan as part of an SBIR or STTR proposal, this will have very specific meaning. Please consult the guidelines provided by the Agency.

A commercialization plan is a strategic, macro statement of how you plan to commercialize a technology. It is NOT a business plan.

Prospectus vs Business Plan

Confusion often arises between a business plan and a prospectus. A prospectus is a stylized, public disclosure document developed in accordance with the guidelines of the Securities and Exchange Commission. Whereas a business plan has both internal and external value, a prospectus is developed specifically for an audience of unqualified and qualified investors. "Buyer beware" is the message that this document must portray. The focus of the document is full disclosure of financials, money requested, how it will be used, risk, and the management team. It does not require that you address the market, customers, or operational plans in the fashion described in the business plan. A business plan is an important document for companies wishing to go public. It is frequently a necessary document to interest and involve viable underwriters.

A prospectus is a stylized disclosure document. It is NOT a business plan.

The focus of this book is neither commercialization plans, nor prospectus. They are mentioned here only to clarify the differences between these documents. In this document we have also added a variation of business planning referred to as a Licensing package vs business play. This is a concept developed by Dawnbreaker and consists of a set of external and internal documents (3 in total) used with a licensing strategy. The outline for a licensing package is provided separately in Chapter 6.

Summary & Conclusions

A business plan is the result of a rigorous planning process. As in science, the document produced is only as good as the research which precedes it. To merely package the information that you currently have without first testing your hypotheses and assumptions would be tantamount to writing a conclusive technical paper based on the hypotheses and assumptions that precede rigorous scientific inquiry. The purpose of this book is to walk you through a systematic process for conducting business research and producing an excellent business plan at the end. In the process of planning you must involve others to leverage your time. In addition, you will find that in growing a business you must become skilled at coalition building and in engaging others to share in your dream. Chapter 3 introduces terminology that we will be using throughout when describing the commercialization process.

Building a Commercialization Team

" ...in crucial things, unity - in important things, diversity."

- Inaugural address of President George Bush

Chapter 03

What is Commercialization?

Terminology

Commercialization has become THE issue of importance, particularly for advanced technology firms which rely heavily on government funding for their R&D. If taxpayer money is being used to support private sector R&D, it must yield a benefit for the public. But how is that benefit to be demonstrated? The score card takes into account various things including the creation of new jobs, the generation of new tax revenue, and improved quality of life - all resulting from the successful commercialization of the technology. So what is commercialization? It is nothing less than a sweeping, macro term that is applied to one result and the multitude of tasks involved with realizing it. That result is sales, putting the product/process into the market place and making money with it, either from increased savings and/or profitability.

Commercialization is the process of turning a concept into a product, process, or service which is sold in the marketplace.

It is true that there are various degrees of commercialization. One can argue that they have commercialized if they sell only one copy of a product to one customer or millions of copies of a product to multiple customers. Both have commercialized, that is, in both situations a concept has been taken and turned into a product or process which has been sold in the marketplace. This debate stresses the importance of developing metrics for the success of new products. Cooper, in his work with Fortune 500 companies used three metrics: (1) return on investment (ROI) where the investment is the total amount spent from concept development up to and including product launch, (2) the average payback period, and (3) the average market share attained in the defined target market. [1] As a benchmark, in a study of 203 new product launches from Fortune 500 companies, using the median, 50% of new products achieved a 33% ROI or better, half had a payback period of two years or less, and 50% had a market share in excess of 35%. However, the odds of success are not high. Within the Fortune 500 companies studied, for every 7 new product ideas, 4 entered development, 1.5 were launched, and only 1 succeeded.[2] Cooper's work also indicated that the probability of success did vary with product type, with the success rate being the greatest for both low and highly innovative products (as opposed to those classified as moderately innovative)."Highly innovative products" are defined as new-to-the-world products and innovative new product lines to a company; while "low innovate products" are defined as repositioning existing products and product modifications that achieve cost reductions.

Cooper analyzed the reasons for product success and failures and found that the single largest cause for failure (24%) was "Poor marketing research" defined as failure to adequately speak with end-users and customers to determine their needs. There was too little "voice-of-the-customer" making it into new product considerations. Other problems included, technical problems (16%) often in scale-up, or over-engineering products as opposed to providing customers with the degree of technical performance that they have requested. Other problems include insufficient marketing effort (14%), usually associated with the assumption that the product is so good that it will sell itself. "In 22% of the failure projects, no detailed market study was done at all, but in hindsight was considered a critical error of omission."[3] Cooper concludes that if you want to fail; (1) omit a market study or conduct a superficial one, (2) don't invest in a test market or have a formal product launch, and (3) avoid a detailed financial analysis.

By contrast, success is associated with an iterative process in which the voice of the customer is pulsed, and market and financial analysis are conducted. The marketing, sales, and financial considerations occur in and around various parts of the product development process. Table 3-1 lists the sequence in which these are conducted in successful product launches. By contrast, companies that slight some of these steps are more likely to fail.

Table 3-1: Key Activities in the New Product Process (Cooper)

Step 1:	Initial Screening
Step 2:	Preliminary Market Assessment
Step 3:	Preliminary Technical Assessment
Step 4:	Detailed Market Study
Step 5:	Predevelopment business/financial analysis
Step 6:	Product Development
Step 7:	In-House Product tests
Step 8:	Customer test of products
Step 9:	Trial sell
Step 10:	Trial production
Step 11:	Precommercialization business analysis
Step 12:	Production start-up
Step 13:	Market Launch

To introduce discipline into the new product development process, Cooper developed what is referred to as a stage-gate model. The term stage refers to gathering information concurrently that relates to customers, markets, competitors, and product differentiators. Cooper defines six stages: (1) Discovery, (2) Scoping, (3) Building the Business Case, (4) Development, (5) Testing and Validation, and (6) Launch. By contrast a gate, is a go/no go decision point – where the decision can be made to kill the project or to let it advance to the next stage. Each gate is associated with deliverables, evaluation criteria, and approved action. Within a large company, the stage-gate model is implemented within the firm. In other words, the decision makers reside within the company that is developing the new product. However, with small businesses that rely on external funding to mature a technology, much of the stage-gate model is implemented with the involvement of people and processes that are external to the company.

Given the language that has arisen around the Small Business Innovation Research (SBIR) process, instead of talking about this process as product development, throughout this chapter it is referred to as the commercialization process.

The tasks involved with commercialization, as well as the resources consumed in the process, are multiple. Although the commercialization process can be described in many ways, we will borrow from the work of Robert Cooper (Cooper, 2001).

Cooper's model describes a new product development process when self-contained within a medium or large firm. This model differs markedly from the perspective of small, technology-driven companies that tend to view the process in the following fashion:

» Concept development
» Technology / product development
» Market Launch (Commercialization)

There are three major reasons for the differences in perspective between large and small companies. First, large companies are multi-functional, whereas at the outset, small technology firms are not. The small tech-driven companies therefore tend to look at issues only related to technology. Secondly, government funding sources which support R&D initiatives tend to discuss the commercialization process in this fashion. As they fund R&D, they have historically spoken about commercialization as the last step in a linear process, rather than a concurrent, iterative activity. Thirdly, large firms tend to put in decision gates to determine if they should continue to spend money, whereas small firms usually do not and simply turn to the outside for financing.

Figure 3-1: Stage Gate Model

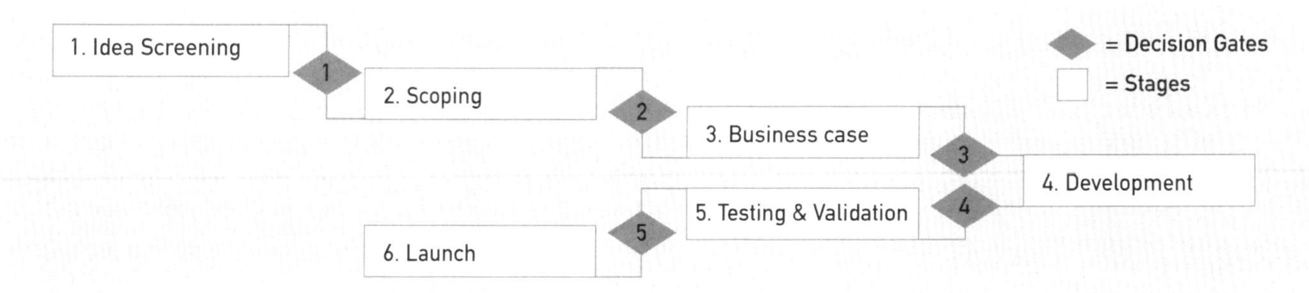

Figure 3-2: Comparison of Large Company and Technology Entrepreneur's Gate Keepers

Large Company INTERNAL FINANCING	**Entrepreneur** EXTERNAL FINANCING
Step 1: Initial screening	**Step 1: Initial screening (Concept)**
Step 2: Preliminary market assessment	**Step 2:** Preliminary market assessment
Step 3: Preliminary technical assessment	**Step 3:** Preliminary technical assessment
Step 4: Detailed market Study	**Step 4:** Detailed market Study
Step 5: Predevelopment business/financial analysis	**Step 5:** Predevelopment business/financial analysis
Step 6: Product development	**Step 6: Product development**
Step 7: In-House product tests	**Step 7:** In-House product tests
Step 8: Customer test of products	**Step 8:** Customer test of products
Step 9: Trial sell	**Step 9:** Trial sell
Step 10: Trial production	**Step 10:** Trial production
Step 11: Precommercialization business anlaysis	**Step 11:** Precommercialization business anlaysis
Step 12: Production start-up	**Step 12:** Production start-up
Step 13: Market launch	**Step 13: Market launch**

To put the cost of commercialization into perspective, in Cooper's sample, R&D spending accounted for less than 40% of a firm's total expenditure for product innovation.

The purpose of Figure 3 - 2 is to reflect that small technology companies tend to focus on activities related to their technology (enboldened in Figure). However, when they go outside for financing - it is these outsiders who require that they attend to other business issues such as market research, competitive analysis, and the like. It is often the requirement for outside financing and the investor's need for a well articulated business plan which spurs the growth of the business maturity of small, technology firms. Without the potential investors' demand for a good business case, many technology-driven firms would be slow to add appropriate attention to issues regarding markets, industry trends, and financing options.

In passing, let us interject at this point that small companies often commercialize by teaming with other firms, rather than assuming the responsibility for all of the steps between product development and market launch. These different strategies for commercialization will be described in Chapter 5.

Perspectives in the Commercialization Process

Let's examine the commercialization process again, but this time from the perspective of the types of players with which one becomes involved as the technology/product shifts from concept development to market launch. Concept development is initiated in many settings: universities, government R&D labs, small businesses, and large corporations. Technologies tend to be basic in nature and involve finding solutions to fundamental problems. Concept development is usually accomplished by a small, fairly homogeneous group of scientists, engineers, and technicians. With the exception of large corporations, funding for concept development tends to come from the entrepreneur herself, government agencies, and foundations. Grant writing is the accepted mechanism for procuring funds from these external sources. Proposal acceptance tends to be based upon:

- the scientific and technical merit of what is proposed;
- the credentials of the parties executing the work;
- the availability of facilities and equipment needed to conduct the research.

As one moves to the stage of Technology/Product Development, the vantage point required for success must shift. What is now required is an emerging sensitivity to the commercial marketplace as well as to various sources for obtaining private funding. As scientists tend to be highly specialized, it is at this point that the staff needs to begin diversification. Although scientists can be sensitive to the marketplace, this is often not the case. Hiring an extra pair of "eyes" with a different perspective is not only useful, but essential at this point.

Figure 3-3: Required commercialization resources as a function of development phase

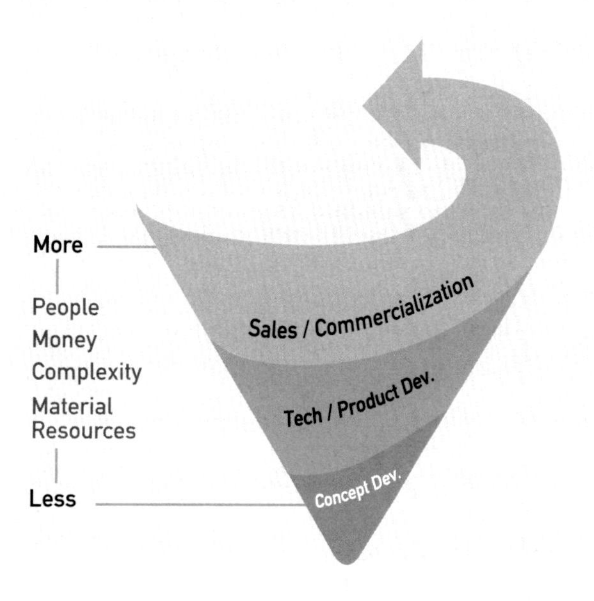

During the transition from technology to product development, the staff must rigorously examine various alternatives and dismiss those which do not have a high likelihood of yielding additional monies on a timely basis needed for product development. This examination requires that the scientists reach beyond the intended use of the technology and entertain other applications, many of which may be quite distant from the initial use of the technology. It is often difficult for scientists who have conceptualized the technology in one fashion to break with their original paradigm and view the technology from a different vantage point. Although many applications are possible, in order for the business enterprise to survive, the selection process must focus on those applications for which there is the greatest market need, as well as the greatest likelihood of finding investment dollars. Grant monies may continue to be a viable source for product development. However, the scientist must begin to develop a total business perspective, rather than one based solely on the technology. This perspective will lead the management team to focus on the commercial viability of the product, rather than only the technical merits of the technology. As the delight for the scientist comes from the technology, this transition is often difficult.

For the technology entrepreneur the shift from Technology/Product Development to commercialization is the most difficult. The number of people, resources, and dollars required, as well as the overall complexity, increases exponentially. Although the scientist contributes greatly during the technology development phase, the amount of time, effort, and resources required to transform the technology into a viable commercial product/process is many times greater than that which the scientist has already invested. Successfully moving along the commercialization continuum requires, above all, great skill at coalition building.

This coalition is built among a large informal cast of players referred to as Inventors/Scientists, Gatekeepers, Champions, Sponsors, and Stakeholders. This is the commercialization team. It evolves informally over time and includes both people inside and external to your organization. They are recognized by the role they play and not by the existence of any formal relationship with your company.

The responsibility for knitting together the commercialization team rests with the company's management team. The latter refers to those employees in your organization who play a management role and who represent the key functional areas (technology, marketing, finance, and administration). In many entrepreneurial companies, it is not uncommon at the outset to have one person play all of these roles. However, as the organization continues to grow, different people usually become assigned to each of these functions.

Players in the Commercialization Process

Borrowing from the literature on product innovation, a great deal is known about the cast of players required to move an idea from conception to successful commercialization.

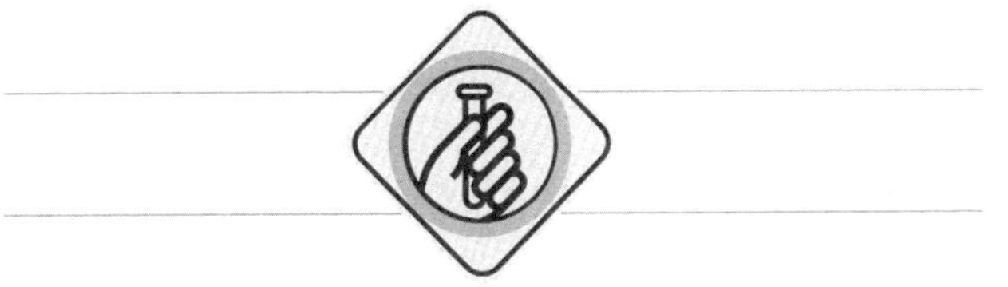

Inventor/scientist

Inventors/Scientists like to reduce the idea to practice; in fact they savor it. For inventors and scientists alike, the challenge is in solving the problem, in putting the solution into a tangible form. More likely than not, their inventions are not initially in a marketable form.

Gatekeeper

Another important role is that of a *Gatekeeper*. The term "technology gatekeeper" was initially applied, however, the intent is more broad. A gatekeeper is anyone who has cutting-edge information. Such a person could be a scientist, lawyer, accountant, or market research firm — in short, anyone who can provide you with specialized information quickly. The information the gatekeeper provides serves as the context in which the technology needs to grow. It also can apply to external certificate bodies, such as the FAA, FCC, EPA, that may need to certify your product before it can be used.

Champion

A *Champion* is a person with status or clout who advocates on behalf of another. Champions, in fact, provide legitimacy to an inventor. They serve as a bridge, a translator between the more unconventional inventor and the more traditional parts of an organization or society. Without champions, few products go forward. They are the unsung heroes of any great invention. Many champions are necessary in the evolution of a product. However, the 'initial champion' must be the scientist himself or herself. In other words, in order to go forward the scientist must also assume this role and forge a coalition, involving this cast of players. For the sake of this discussion, you should assume that all champions (other than the 'initial champion') are individuals outside your organization who can be influential in bringing you and your technology/product to the attention of others. This is usually done informally.

Sponsor

A *Sponsor* has resources (money, equipment, or human resources) and applies them towards the development of an idea. A sponsor usually has higher status within an organization and a proven track record. Some organizations have evolved specifically to play the sponsorship role. Banks, small business associations, angels, venture capitalists, and the like all act as sponsors. They all share the weight of financial responsibility and are very cautious about investing the funds with which they are charged. Return on Investment (ROI) is clearly the motivating force. The phrase "I'm from Missouri, prove it to me" definitely applies to sponsors. They cannot afford to be blinded by the "Gee whiz" aspect of an invention. Much to the disappointment of the inventor, the technology is initially taken as a given. What they want to know is who will buy the product, what is the competition like, and who are you, anyway? "Conjecture must be turned to certitude." They must be convinced there are people who will buy the product in a timely fashion, and that you can manage the enterprise.

Stakeholder

A *Stakeholder* is anyone who will be affected by the innovation. He is often the forgotten player. Stakeholders should be approached during the process of collecting market research.

Table 3-4: Stakeholder Mapping

1. Identify the Stakeholders.
2. How do you think they will be affected by this product/process?
3. How will they perceive the impact of this product/process?
4. List what you know about the stakeholders.
5. If you don't know anything about them, find out what you can.
6. What is the stakeholder's view of this product/ process likely to be? Why do you say that?
7. What will the stakeholders gain from this new product/process?
8. If the stakeholders have considerable power, identify people that the stakeholders respect ("influencers").
9. How can you minimize risk and maximize reward for the stakeholders?
10. If stakeholders do not have a lot of power, involve them in the development of the idea early on, especially if they are gatekeepers.
11. Listen to stakeholders' input and modify the product/ process so that it is more adaptable to the environment.
12. If stakeholders have a lot of power, include their influencers in the product/ process at an early stage. Try to have the influencers become your champions.

The users of the old technology or product are stakeholders. How readily will they embrace a new technology which may make obsolete a technology in which they have invested heavily? What can you do to minimize their resistance and involve them with the new? A technique called stakeholder mapping is described below to address these issues.

Although this cast of players is described as unique, one individual may play multiple roles. For example, a person may simultaneously be an inventor, champion, and sponsor. However, oftentimes these roles are discrete. Another important item to remember is that multiple players are required in each category. In other words, you will need many gatekeepers, champions, and sponsors to realize the successful commercialization of a product or technology. The successful entrepreneur is one who can locate these other players and involve them as part of the commercialization team. Coalition building is key!

Coalition building involves bringing in champions, sponsors, and stakeholders and making them a part of your vector of support.

Looking for Champions

Generally, you should look for champions before you look for potential sponsors. Again, keep in mind that potential sponsors are potential investors. They reside within corporations, utilities, government, universities, banks, and venture capital firms in geographically diverse locations. As you may only have one opportunity to present your business opportunity to a potential sponsor, it would be to your advantage to know as much as possible about that organization and the players beforehand. You can leverage your effectiveness in this process by developing champions internal to those organizations. A champion who knows your work, knows you, and thinks well of what you can do can help maintain your presence in the other organization. Champions leverage your opportunity for success by helping you become more sensitive to the potential sponsor's needs. Such considerations must be made early so that your technology will evolve in a way that is desirable to potential sponsors.

Where to look for champions for your technology

Some people look for champions at the top of an organization. We recommend that you delay doing this until you "have your act together."

R & D, manufacturing

Although many consultants advise against approaching R&D departments, when looking for a technology champion your first task is always to gather information about the current or historical interest in the technology you are working on. For example, if you believe that company X should be a good potential licensee for your technology, you need to probe this. Lack of knowledge may result in alot of wasted time. For example, if you don't know that Company X invested millions of dollars in studying this approach previously and then abandoned it, you may find a very cool reception. If however, you can determine that this is a current interest, you may find greater interest, as R&D departments of many large firms are outsourcing more of their research and development activities.

One of the best ways to find contacts within R & D or Manufacturing is to look through Association Membership Directories or by scanning Conference and Convention Proceedings. The Encyclopedia of Associations, found in the reference section of most libraries, is a very useful resource for finding the names of associations that deal with your area of interest. Another resource that can be consulted is the Directory of Conventions that list upcoming conventions. Generally speaking, the first potential champions to be approached should be within the technology area. The scientist/inventor is best equipped to make the initial contact.

Another way to begin developing champions is through people exchange programs. Many universities and federal labs are beginning to encourage this by offering their services as consultants and/or inviting employees from the company in which they are interested to work within their organization for a period of time.

Where to look for champions for your products.

New product development, engineering, and marketing divisions.
In addition to the sources mentioned above, another useful source to regularly review is the local paper. New product introductions and/or technological advancements are commonly announced in local media. Subscribe to the paper in those cities in which companies of interest are headquartered. You can obtain many names in this manner. Another useful source is Dialog, which is an information provider. Dialog has an SDI service (Selected Dissemination of Information) which can be used to automatically send you updates of information on topics of interest. (There is a fee for service.) Dialog can electronically scour local newspapers and technical newsletters worldwide to provide you with information of interest. For a small company, the easiest way to obtain access to this service is through your university library. For larger companies, it is best to train someone within marketing to be facile with various electronic databases. He can initiate SDI services from his terminal.

When you approach potential champions, initial discussions should be general. You will be most successful if you do not approach them with the intent of selling, but with the intent of defining a potential customer's need. In order to be successful, you need to be viewed as a potential ally as quickly as possible, rather than as an outsider.

Another point to keep in mind is that when you do seek a sponsor, you will be competing for dollars that managers could spend internally on development projects. Your project has to represent a clear opportunity rather than a distraction; moreover, becoming involved with your project must be a benefit to everyone involved, as well as to the corporation. If you have SBIR Phase II funding, the fact that you bring development dollars with you is of great advantage. Likewise, if you have accomplished considerable development on a needed technology, that too is advantageous.

Looking for Sponsors.
Potential sponsors are brought into the picture at a later time, when your business opportunity is clarified. Champions can be helpful in telling you who the potential sponsors are within their organization. They will not refer to them as sponsors, so you will need to inquire who is responsible for making decisions about strategic partnerships, joint ventures, and licensing.

Other portals that you can approach directly are:

New Business Development Areas.
Some of the larger companies have departments devoted specifically to new business development and /or venture development. In the past large corporations tended to acquire smaller, high tech firms in an effort to obtain the desired technology. However, the clash between the culture of the small entrepreneurial company and the larger Fortune 500 companies frequently proved damaging. The glacial speed with which decisions are made in large corporations and the cumbersome accounting procedures often knock the wind out of zestful,

fleet, entrepreneurial teams. To address this issue, some large companies have established their own venture capital funds, to help encourage promising technology along.

Submitted Ideas Offices.
Many large organizations have departments established specifically to deal with ideas submitted from outside the company. Kodak, for example, has a Submitted Ideas office to handle such inquiries. In such organizations, this is the portal the company wishes you to approach. However, you will have the greatest luck in finding a champion if you attempt to gain access to the organization at multiple levels.

Legal Departments.
Many people who are responsible for licensing or corporate acquisitions work within the legal department of an organization. Although, some companies have separate departments for licensing, many will be a subset of the legal department. Call the general information number for the company of interest and ask them to direct you to this department. Ask them who is responsible for "Licensing, Corporate Acquisitions, and the like." Some receptionists won't know what these terms mean, and you may need to describe the concept. Four or five phone calls will usually get you to the right place. Another source that can be consulted for the names of people responsible for licensing is the Membership Directory for the Licensing Executive Society. This directory lists members by company name.

Vice Presidents of various divisions.
In the business section of most libraries one can find numerous directories which list the names of Vice Presidents of the major functional units of an organization. The most commonly used are Dun and Bradstreet's Million Dollar Directory, Standard and Poor's Register of Corporations, Directors and Executives, and Moody's Manual. Although some people begin by making contact at the top, we have found it better to make initial inquiries lower in the organization. In this way, by the time you get to the top you know more about the organization and its needs and can make a better impression with decision makers.

As you can surmise, within large organizations decisions regarding funding involve numerous people and are made with great caution. Any potential sponsor will have to convince others that your opportunity is a better one in which to invest than others and that minimal risk is involved. In order to do this successfully, you must provide the potential sponsor with the information that is needed to convince others. The typical vehicle for doing so is a business plan, which includes your compilation of the information that best represents the opportunity your technology represents to the potential investor. When seeking a sponsor within an established company, the NIH (Not Invented Here) factor is quite high. The best way to combat this tendency is to introduce the new technology to the organization early in its development and involve others with its growth and development. NIH is usually more pronounced when the technology is introduced into another organization later in its development.

In summary, you will be most successful in obtaining sponsorship funds if you bear in mind that potential sponsors:

» **must be able to justify the expense to others,**

» **look to minimize risk,**

» **look to maximize return,**

» **live in highly dynamic environments**

Summary and conclusions
Commercialization is a lengthy process involving many players. It unfolds in a fortuitous, somewhat unpredictable fashion. The true challenge waiting for the technology entrepreneur is to learn how to communicate effectively with this diverse cast of players. The glue that binds is the entrepreneur!

Chapter 3 Endnotes

1 Cooper, Robert G. Winning at New Products: Accelerating the process from idea to launch. Basic Books, 2001.

2 Booz-Allen & Hamilton. New Product Management for the 1980's (New York: Booz –Allen & Hamilton, Inc. 1982)

3 Cooper, Robert G. Winning at New Products: Accelerating the process from idea to launch. Basic Books, 2001, page 27.

Sponsors: Potential Funding Sources

" Without champions and sponsors, commercialization doesn't happen-
they are the unsung heroes."

Chapter 04

It is imperative that technology entrepreneurs thoroughly familiarize themselves with different funding mechanisms

Advanced technology firms have a voracious appetite for money as commercialization is an expensive endeavor. It is therefore, imperative that technology entrepreneurs thoroughly familiarize themselves with different funding mechanisms. The scientist shouldn't approach financing by asking "Which type of funding do I prefer", but should assume that at different points in the life cycle of their business they may need to utilize a wide variety of financing methods to nurture and sustain their business. The questions to consider then are:

1) How do the available financing methods vary as a function of the stage of technology/product development?

2) In what sequence should the technology entrepreneur consider different financing options?

3) How do you keep various financing options available to your firm as you increase commitments to other creditors? and

4) How do your personal goals and aspirations interact with the available alternatives?

Financing is a key variable, which shapes the business planning process.

The purpose of this chapter is to briefly introduce alternative methods of financing.

A reasonable question to ask is 'Why start with a discussion of financing methods, rather than waiting until the business plan has been developed and then selecting one?' The reason is simple - financing is a key variable which shapes the planning process. It interplays with every strategic consideration that you make. Therefore, due to its fundamental importance in shaping the planning process, an introduction to various methods of financing or capitalizing your firm will be made.

Generally speaking, there are five broad categories of financing which may be used to capitalize your firm: *sweat equity, science-for-hire, debt, equity, and profit.* The order of introduction reflects the general sequence in which start-ups tend to utilize them. Each of these broad categories will be discussed briefly, and then elaborated upon later in this chapter.

The term *sweat equity* implies the use of uncompensated time and the lending of one's own resources to nourish the business during its earliest phases. Periodically when cash flow wanes, it is not uncommon for founders to delay compensation for their work until a later time. Thus, the use of sweat equity is a method which many technology entrepreneurs use to give birth to their business and also to sustain it during periods of financial difficulty.

The phrase *science-for-hire* refers to Research and Development activities conducted for another party on a contractual basis. Depending on the nature of the agreement, the technology entrepreneur may retain rights to the intellectual property developed during the performance of the contract and/or grant. Many technology entrepreneurs support the preliminary development of a technology through participation in Federally funded R&D programs. This is an important vehicle for financing start-ups, as nascent R&D is difficult to finance with any other type of funding.

Without federally funded science-for-hire programs, many small technology firms would not survive. Private sector investors prefer to wait until technology and market risks are reduced, before investing their funds.

Figure 4-1: Methods for financing the small high tech firm

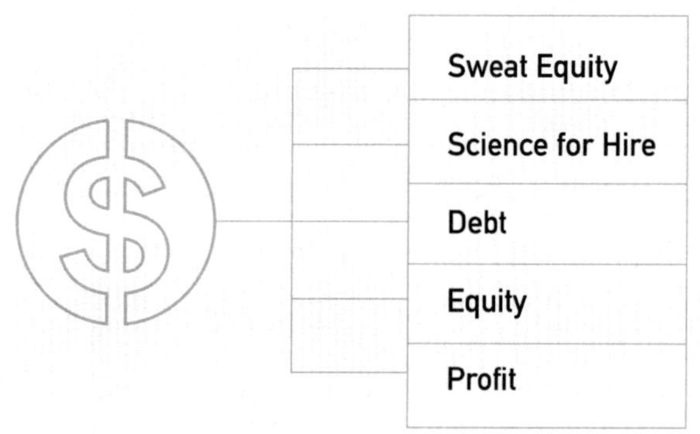

Debt financing refers to the borrowing of money with the promise of full repayment of the principal with interest. There are a variety of vehicles that can be used for debt financing including secured and unsecured loans, promissory notes, bonds, leases, supplier credit, and other debentures. Debt gives its owner the right to be repaid the investment with interest irrespective of the success or failure of the business venture. Debt financing can be considered when an individual or a company has sufficient collateral.

Equity financing is speculative in nature as the financier is not guaranteed repayment of the money invested. This is high risk capital and therefore commands hefty compensation commensurate with the degree of risk taken. Vehicles used for equity financing include the receipt of stock through the investment of venture capital, business angels, and investment bankers. The return on an equity investment is dependent upon the success of the business. One reaps a large financial reward if the company is successful and no reward if the company fails. Equity financing is subordinate to debt financing which means that in the case of bankruptcy, debt financing

arrangements must be honored before any payment to equity investors may be made. Business angels are recognized as providing the most lenient terms and for making smaller equity investments than, institutional investors.

Equity financing is subordinate to debt financing.

When making decisions regarding the capitalization of your firm with debt or equity, many things need to be considered. The preliminary choice of debt or equity has IRS implications, as taxation is handled differently with these two methods of financing. Interest paid on the repayment of a debt is tax deductible. However, dividends paid on equity investment must be paid with after-tax dollars. This debt-equity decision also raises control issues. For example, the most common evidence of an equity investment is the issuance of common stock. The owners of common stock have voting rights which gives them a say in the management of your company. Debt can also be changed to equity. A good discussion of these two methods of capitalization can be found in a Desk Book for Setting up a Closely Held Corporation by Robert Hess (1985).

As your company grows and becomes successful you will accumulate more profit that can be used to fund various business functions rather than needing to rely so heavily on external sources of capital.

What do You Want to be When You Grow-up?

The sources of financing which will be available to your firm can be anticipated by reflecting upon the vision for your company. Three prototypical visions exist, with distinguishing hallmarks are noted in Table 4-1 (Hisrich & Peters, 1989). These prototypes are referred to as:

» **Life-style firms**

» **High-potential venture, and**

» **Foundation company**

If your intent is to develop a company that will remain fairly small, allow you to pursue your technical interests, and support you and a few others, yours is more aptly described as a *life-style company*. Such a company sees itself as having revenues of $2-3 million within five years and of employing 30-40 people at the most. Such a company is NOT of interest to the venture capital or investment banker community, as their purpose in making an investment is to realize a large return through involvement with fast growth companies. You may however, find local business angels to be amenable to small investments if you have a good business plan and a good team. Life-style firms are best served by pursuing science-for-hire arrangements, strategic alliances, and debt financing, once sufficient collateral has been obtained.

Although it is important to recognize if you are a life-style company, it is not recommended that you label yourself as such when talking with external audiences.

At the other extreme is the *high-potential venture*. Such a firm envisions revenues of $30+ million in 5 to 7 years and anticipates *going public* as a means of cashing out and creating value for its investors. A company founder who selects this path, must anticipate that he or she will be stretched to the limits of their capabilities; will need to involve a multi-disciplinary team early in the company's life; must become facile with different financing options; and masterful at coalition building. As if that is not enough, the technology entrepreneur who aspires to creating a high-potential venture must also plan to potentially step aside when the company goes public if he or she is unable or unwilling to redirect their energies to investor relations upon becoming a public firm. If you are looking to be an industry leader, and grow a company hard and fast, you are developing a high-potential venture. All forms of financing will be open to you at different points in the development of your company.

The *foundation company* lies somewhere between these two extremes. The founder has both the technology and the desire to be an industry leader, yet wants to grow the company in a less meteoric fashion. The technology entrepreneur is not attached to having the firm remain small and sees the company developing capabilities in all business functions, as appropriate. The management team is more conservative with respect to its involvement of equity investors and chooses to have the company remain privately held. The desire to remain privately held is a differentiator between high-potential ventures and foundation companies.

Using Table 4-1 as a heuristic, three different visions were presented. It is important to keep in mind that one's vision for the future doesn't have to remain static. An entrepreneur can make a conscious decision to either retain a specific vision or work towards another reality. Keep in mind that often it is an

Table 4-1: A Heuristic: Different visions for your future

	Revenue	# Employee	Purpose	Private/Public
Life-style	Modest (e.g..Less than $5M)	30-40	Support Owners	Private
Foundation	Moderate (e.g..$10M-30M+)	40-400	Start New Industry	Private
High Potential	Large (e.g.. $30M+)	400+	Growth & Value	Go Public

* The numbers are not to be taken as absolutes, but as relative terms

entrepreneur's vision and his or her understanding of what it will take to realize it – that limits the potential of a company. In order to realize a vision of ever increasing growth and value creation, the founder must constantly redefine him or herself. Such an entrepreneur, is dubbed as a *Transformational entrepreneur*, a person who exhibits the ability to constantly redefine not only himself, but also the roles, capabilities, and vision of those that work with her.

A more detailed treatment of the five major categories for financing a business follows. The model that will be elaborated upon in this discussion is represented in Figure 4-2.

Sweat equity

The first type of financing commonly used by any entrepreneur is sweat equity. How the issue of sweat equity is handled depends upon your vision for the future. If your goal is to develop a high-potential venture, be forewarned that equity investors putting cash on the line will not be impressed by your investment of time and passion. As far as equity investors are concerned, if you have little capital invested in your company, you are not heavily committed. As your financial commitment may be represented in the form of collateral, as well as cash, keep good records on the equipment, real estate, and other hard assets that can be counted as collateral applied to this endeavor.

If during periods of poor cash flow, you defer compensation, be sure to keep good records regarding the cash owed to you by the corporation and have formal agreements with the company regarding terms of repayment. Also talk with your accountant about what is involved with converting debt to equity in the event that you wish to change the terms of repayment.[1] Be sure to talk with a tax specialist regarding issues involved with "deferred compensation[2]", as following the accounting scandals with companies such as Enron, there have been many changes in IRS laws that pertain to this arena. [3]

Another important factor to which you should attend when using sweat equity is how to handle intellectual property developed with your own resources prior to forming your company. If you have clear title to such intangible assets and they provide the foundation for your firm, formalize the relationship of those assets with your company. This can be done either by licensing rights to your firm or selling the intellectual property

Figure 4-2: Roadmap of Financial Options

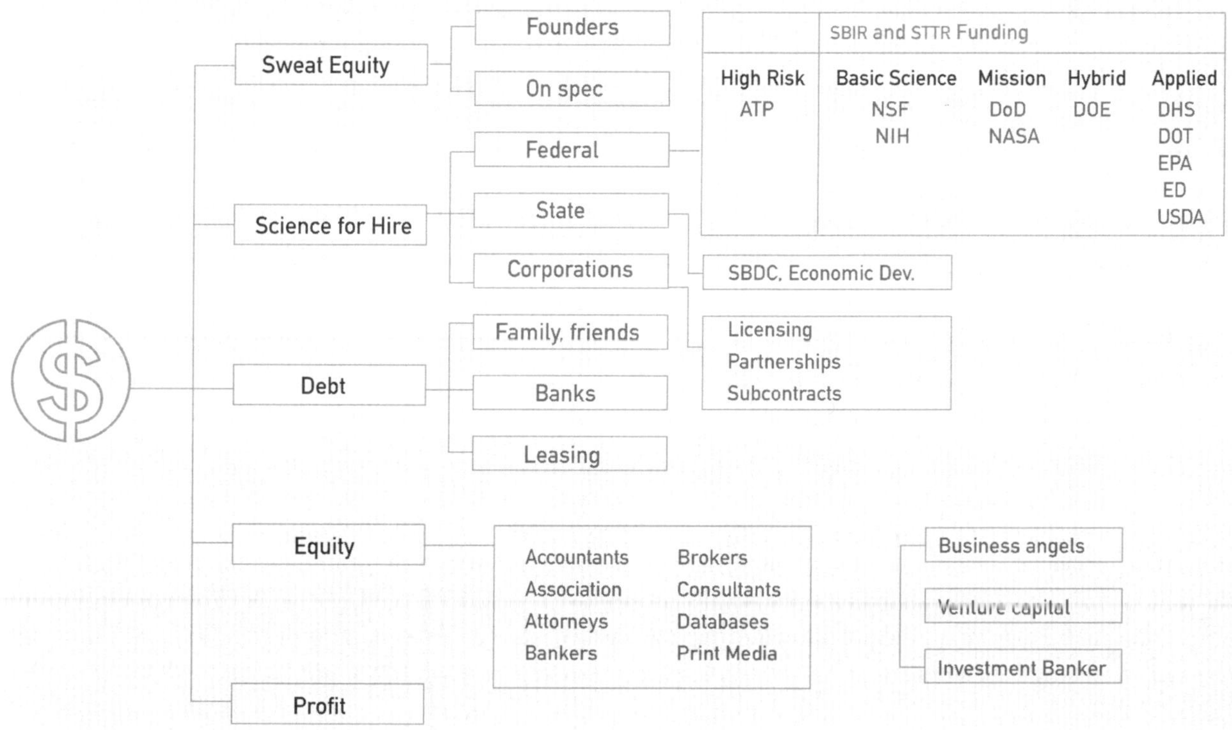

to the firm. A useful resource to consult for ideas is Write Your Own Business Contracts .[4]

Sweat equity is invested not only by founders, but sometimes by service providers. It is not uncommon for founders to seek the assistance of service providers on a speculative basis. When cash is lean, entrepreneurs often seek patent attorneys, market research firms, business consultants, and other recruits to the management team who are willing to become involved on spec (speculation). It is important that you keep in mind that such service providers are taking a high risk and are, therefore, likely to ask for a substantial return. Be sure to have contractual arrangements with every party who becomes involved with your company in this fashion. Be aware that, if you give away a substantial portion of your company at the outset, you will have little to bargain with later on when you need more cash. Be sure to think through the merits of debt and equity arrangements as repayment to professionals who apply their skills and time to your project in this fashion. Consult an accountant and/or an attorney regarding the long term implications of every such arrangement you make.

A young company requires the passion and enthusiasm of the founder, as well as others involved with a company, when it is at the 'possibility' stage. This level of personal commitment and sacrifice results in a special relationship that few in your company will share. However, it is important to keep in mind that the sweat equity which gave birth to the company will not be valued by equity investors. To quote the founder of Micro-Solution "Investor's don't care about your dreams and goals. They love that you have them. They love that they motivate you. Investors care about how they are going to get their money back..." [5] *Most equity investors believe that commitment is assured by the degree that you have committed your financial resources. It is, therefore, important that you document items which have value - such as collateral provided to the company and intangible assets such as intellectual property for which you have clear title and which you have licensed to the company.*

Science-for-Hire

The next financing mechanism sought by many advanced technology firms is "science-for-hire" arrangements. Such arrangements allow the entrepreneur to be compensated for solving R&D problems of significance while providing the wise entrepreneur with an opportunity to develop intellectual property that can be commercialized through his/her company. Federal, state, and private sources all provide 'science-for-hire' opportunities. The Advanced Technology Program (ATP) is unique in funding high risk technology for economic growth. The Small Business Innovation Research (SBIR) and the Small Business Technology Transfer (STTR) programs provide funding to small businesses with innovative technologies which can solve problems of specific interest to the federal government. Some agencies such as that National Aeronautics and Space Administration (NASA), and the Department of Defense (DoD) are mission agencies; whereas the National Science Foundation (NSF) has historically had a focus on basic research. Agencies such as the Department of Energy tend to be more applied in their research focus. Information on each of these programs can be obtained from the referenced site.[6]

Figure 4-3: Science-for-Hire Funding Option

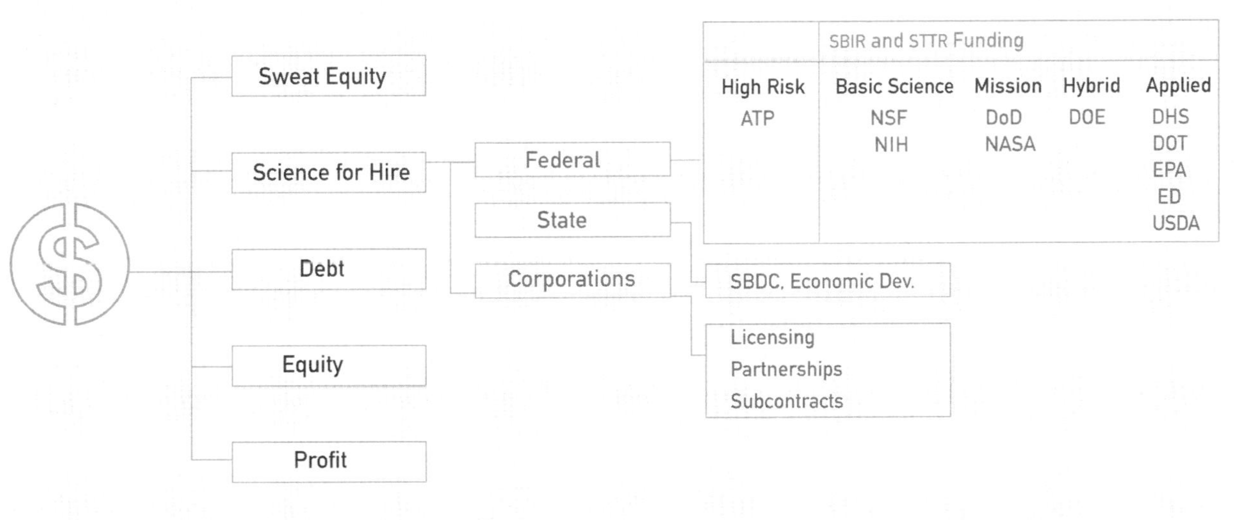

Most federally funded R&D programs allow the entrepreneur to retain rights to the intellectual property created while performing the work. It is the right to retain ownership which provides incentives for the entrepreneur and which provides small businesses with the opportunity to commercialize. The government typically receives a non-exclusive license to the technology for government purposes. On September 24, 2002, the Small Business Administration (SBA) Office of Technology issued the "Small Business Innovation Research (SBIR) Program Final Policy Directive". For companies working with the Department of Defense, it is highly recommended that you read and understand the implications of this directive relative to SBIR data rights. The Directive can be downloaded from the referenced link.[7]

Many states also support federal initiatives through services offered by another SBA initiative, the Small Business Development Center (SBDC).[8] There is a lead organization in each state and a network of 1100 service locations around the country, usually associated with a university or a community college. Fifty percent of the funding for these centers comes from SBA. Their services are usually offered at little or no charge to small businesses. Historically, the SBDCs have been very helpful with orienting advanced technology firms to the benefits of participating in SBIR and STTR programs. Assistance is often provided with proposal writing and review.

Some states also offer matching state funds for SBIR winners, often through State Departments of Economic Development. States that are currently offering such programs include Hawaii, Michigan, and Oklahoma. Companies are encouraged to contact the Department of Economic Development for their state to determine what other initiatives there are in the state that may assist in business development and growth.

Another major source of science-for-hire funding is corporations. As the development and exploitation of a rich technology platform requires considerable resources, federal R&D programs will only take an awardee part way through the R&D process. In most cases, the technology entrepreneur must team with other entities in order to commercialize the technology. Sub-contracting, licensing and participating in research and development partnerships with large corporations provide excellent opportunities for small companies to extend their effectiveness in bringing technology to market. Increasingly, Fortune 500 companies are looking to leverage their internal research and development (IRAD) dollars by teaming with good, small businesses whose technologies can provide them with a leveraging advantage.

Debt Financing

Science-for-hire arrangements can be extremely advantageous to small advanced technology firms, especially if the entrepreneur views this work as an opportunity to develop intellectual property that can be used as the foundation for their business. With science-for-hire arrangements, money does not have to be repaid, nor equity parted with. If performing R&D for the Federal government, it will receive a non-exclusive license for government purposes on intellectual property created. However, you will retain all other rights. It is an ideal arrangement. However, this form of capitalization will only take you so far. At various times in the evolution of your firm, you will need to consider debt financing. As mentioned earlier, debt financing gives its owner (the lender) the right to be repaid the investment with interest irrespective of the success or failure of your business.

When should you consider such financing?

» when you need assistance with cash flow while performing on R&D contracts,

» when you need working capital and you wish to retain as much equity as possible in your firm,

» when making large purchases of equipment, buildings, real estate,

» when planning acquisitions, or

» when you wish to refinance existing debt

There are various debt instruments and various organizations from which you can seek debt financing. Typical debt instruments include:

» promissory notes
» secured & unsecured loans
» lines of credit

Debt financing can be obtained from family and friends, banks, finance companies, leasing companies, brokerage houses, federal government, mutual funds, and state and federal governments. In most instances a short-term loan is considered to be less than one year in duration; whereas a long term loan is one to five years.

Borrowing from Friends and Family

When borrowing from family and friends both you and they take a risk. Important relationships may be damaged if you fail to honor your debt. Also, such lenders may assume that they own

Figure 4-4: Debt Financing Options

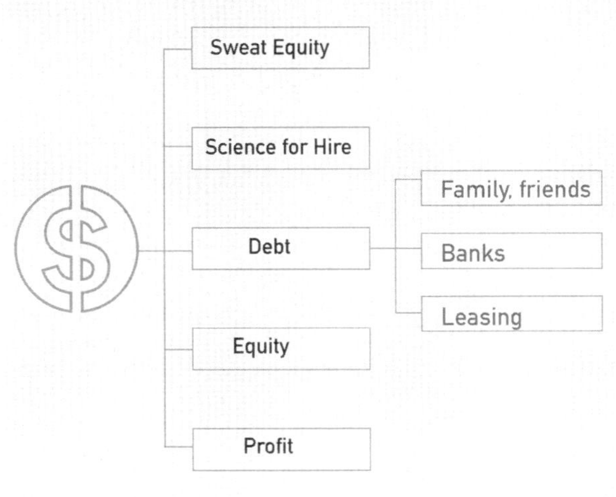

part of your business and try to act as equity investors meddling in the daily activities of your firm. However, such problems can be avoided. In a brief article entitled How to Borrow from Family and Friends [9], one entrepreneur describes how he successfully used this source of financing during the first year of his start-up. First, he formalized the relationship with each lender by drafting Promissory Notes due within a specified time period. An option was added to the Note allowing him to roll the loan over as necessary and an interest rate was agreed to. The entrepreneur's intent was to view these loans as short-term and shift to bank debt within a year. He did this successfully while maintaining good relationships with all involved.

Another important item to note is that the IRS may examine such arrangements to see if they are truly debt or equity financing. Be sure to discuss this matter with your accountant[10]. A good Promissory Note should clearly indicate the name of the person to whom debt is owed, the maturity date, who is obligated to pay the debt, the interest due, the right to enforce payment, and the status of the debt relative to other forms of financing. The note should clearly indicate the name of the person to whom debt is owed, the maturity date, who is obligated to pay the debt, the interest due, the right to enforce payment, and the status of the debt relative to other forms of financing.

Borrowing from Banks

Believe it or not, banks are becoming more interested in attracting and retaining small businesses as clients. Why? Many large businesses are going elsewhere to meet their capitalization needs as it is easier for them to obtain equity capital and funds from institutional debt markets. However, the problem for banks is that there is also much competition for small business from commercial finance and asset-based-lending firms, leasing companies, brokerage houses, mutual funds, and microenterprise lending institutions. In defining a small business, the Small Business Administration utilizes a dual criteria of revenues and number of employees taking into account the North American Industrial Classification System (NAICS).[11]

Once your company has developed sufficient history, you may wish to approach commercial banks for a loan or a line of credit for your business. Talk with your accountant or lawyer and ask which banks they would recommend. You might also talk with your local Chamber of Commerce to determine which banks are involved with the local community and take an active interest in regional economic development. Most resources indicate that in order to make this an option, you should develop a relationship with your banker. You need to educate your banker regarding your business, your business plan, as well as your annual sales projections.[12] Also be prepared to share your personal financials, usually for the past three years.

As mentioned earlier, there are many sources that one can approach for debt financing besides banks. In all cases, before approaching a lender, one should take stock of the assets that they have and try to match these assets with the appropriate type of lender to approach. Most lenders will require collateral for loans that is, something that can be sold to reimburse them for their loan if you default. One form of collateral that is interesting to explore is receivables.

Receivable-Lending Institutions

When a company has a receivable, such as a contract, back order, purchase order, or work in progress, they can consider approaching a Receivable-Lending Institution or a factor for financing. A Receivable-Lending Institution is often a division of a Commercial Bank that uses your receivables as collateral in providing you with a loan. Usually the money is provided as a line of credit for up to 60 days. The amount advanced is a percentage of the receivable and varies with the size of the invoice. Interest rates on such arrangements are typically higher than on traditional secured loans.[13]

A closely related form of debt financing to cover short term needs for working capital is a revolving line of credit. Working capital loans of this nature are usually short term (less than a year) and can be secured or unsecured. If the company is in the start-up mode, the founders may need to pledge the use of personal assets for collateral. Unsecured loans are a possibility for companies with outstanding credit histories.

Leasing

Before making the decision to purchase equipment, land, buildings, or any other tangible asset - consider leasing. This will require that you sit down and talk with your accountant about the pros and cons of such decisions and the impact leasing will have on your balance sheet. Why your balance sheet? In science you use calibration devices all the time - so do investors. All sources of capitalization look at the health of your business by attending to financial ratios that are based on either your Balance Sheet and/or your Income & Expense Statement.

The Balance Sheet is a snapshot of your business at a specific point in time It is the only financial record in which you will see the phrases assets (A), liabilities (L), and shareholder equity (E). A formula is applied to demonstrate the relationships amongst these items

Assets = Liabilities & Shareholder's Equity

Tangible assets include items such as Cash, Accounts Receivable, Loans to Stockholders, Land, Equipment, Real Estate, and Pre-Paid Expenses. Liabilities include items such as Accounts Payable, Loans from Stockholders, Retainers, and Advances. The decision to purchase or lease a tangible item affects whether or not it is considered an asset on your balance sheet and will affect the ratios, or measuring devices that investors examine. Leasing is referred to as "off-balance-sheet" financing as it does not appear as an asset on the balance sheet, and only the payments that become due show as a liability. Therefore, if you know that you are going to need a loan, you will want to make your balance sheet look as good as possible. A good accountant can advise you how the lease/buy decision will affect your balance sheet.

There are, of course, other more obvious reasons to lease: (1) you want to avoid a large cash outlay, or (2) you don't wish to purchase equipment which may become obsolete. In a lease scenario, the entity providing the lease is referred to as the lessor of the property. The entity obtaining the lease is referred to as the lessee. There are two broad categories of leases: Traditional and Modified.

Supplier Credit

You may not consider it debt financing - but companies with a good credit rating benefit from the 15 to 30 day terms their suppliers provide at 0% interest. If you can speed up the rate at which you are paid by your customers, you can minimize the need for other interest bearing loans to pay your suppliers You can speed up the rate at which your receivables are paid, either by billing at the time services are rendered (instead of waiting till a specific time each month) and/or by providing customers with an incentive to pay quickly. Other good money management techniques include requesting progress payments and up-front mobilization fees.

Equity Financing

The phrase equity financing refers to a class of investments that share a number of common features. First, equity financing is speculative. With all forms of equity investments no guarantees exist that investors will be repaid. Realizing a return on such an investment is dependent upon the success of your business. An investor reaps a large financial reward if your company is successful and no reward if your company fails. For this reason, equity investors command hefty compensation commensurate with their risk.

Another feature that equity investors share is ownership in your business. Equity also implies the exchange of stock in return for money - as it is through ownership that the investor will profit from the success of your firm. For this reason, it is important that founders do some serious soul searching and decide if they are willing to share the control, as well as the risks and rewards of their company.

There are a variety of sources that make equity investments including professional venture capitalists (sometimes referred to as traditional or institutional investors and venture funds), business angels (also referred to as the nontraditional or informal investment community), and investment bankers. Common vehicles utilized by this community for raising funds and/or cashing out include Private Placements and Initial Public Offerings (IPO's). Both of these activities are regulated by the Securities Exchange Commission (SEC) as a means of protecting unqualified investors from unscrupulous entrepreneurs. As an aside, the SEC considers qualified or accredited investors to include:

- Company officers and directors,
- Individuals with an annual income of over $200,000 annually,
- Individuals whose net worth is over $1 million,
- Broker/dealers,
- A wide range of financial institutions are also considered accredited or qualified investors.[14]

A modified version of the model we have been developing is depicted below showing the primary sources of equity investments and the wide range of intermediaries that often serve as a buffer between entrepreneurs and equity investors. This community,

Figure 4-5: Equity Financing Options

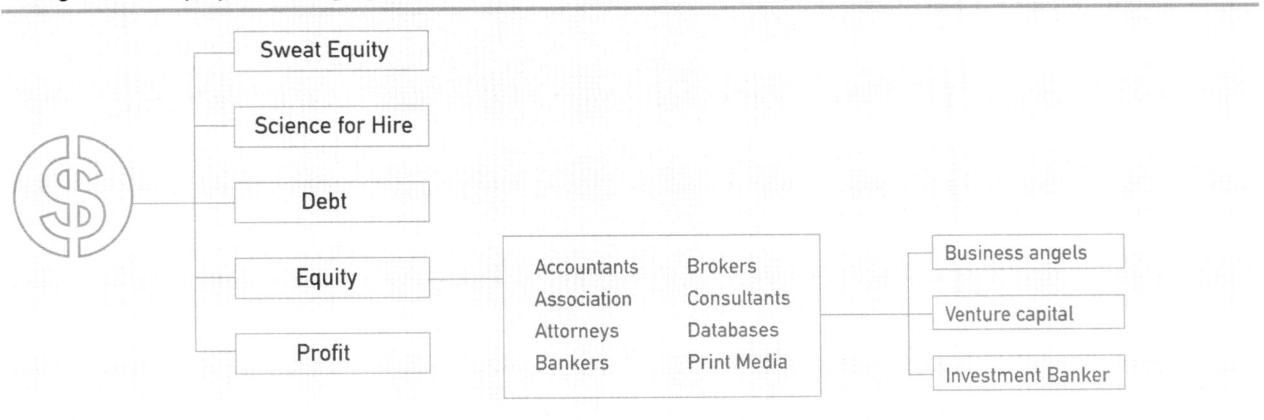

more than any other, relies heavily on the use of intermediaries. Although one can also go directly to equity investors, the recommendation of a trusted intermediary is often beneficial.

The Availability of Equity Financing

The availability of equity financing from business angels, venture capitalists, and investment bankers varies widely. Although one hears frequently about the venture capital (VC) community, the business angel market is considerably larger.

Business Angels

Business angels are typically self-made men with large net worth. This group includes medical professionals, lawyers, accountants, successful entrepreneurs and middle managers looking to move out of large corporations. As the transactions of angels are unregulated, it is hard to determine the actual size of this risk-capital pool. Some have estimated this to be a $50 billion/yr. capital pool and others estimate it to be considerably higher. However, everyone agrees that this is the largest source of financing for start-ups in the country. It is estimated that angels have backed between 50,000 and 100,000 companies and that 29% of angel funding has been provided at the seed stage (William Wetzel, 1989; Frank Hughes, 1989). One benchmark to keep in mind when trying to gauge the actual size of the informal risk-capital market is that in the US alone in 2000 there were over five million households with a net worth of $1,000,000 or more, this was up from 2.82 million in 1992.[15] According to a recent study by the University of New Hampshire's Center for Venture Research, in 2004, 42,000 angels plowed $18.1 billion into early-stage companies.[16]

Institutional Venture Capital

The size and investment interests of the venture capital market vary tremendously from year to year. For example, the total amount of venture capital committed in 1980 was $661 million. In 1996 it reached a high of $11.6 billion. According to Ernst and Young, in 2004 venture capital investments in the US reached $20.4 billion invested in 2,067 deals[17]. Highest investments were in biopharmaceutical companies, health care services, and information technology.

Clear geographic patterns exist in venture capital investments. For example, in 2004 companies in the San Francisco Bay area consummated 31% of all deals, representing 35% of the capital invested or $7.1B received by 638 companies. US venture capital firms are also planning on expanding their overseas investments in 2005. According to a recent survey 20% of US-based VC respondents planned to increase their global activity.[18] Countries of greatest interest included China, India, Canada/Mexico, Continental Europe, Israel, and the United Kingdom.

US companies are also top investment targets for foreign VC's. In a recent survey, it was noted that 48% of Canadian VC respondents were already investing in US firms, with 67% indicating that they planned to invest in US firms during the next five years. Similar responses were found for VC's from Israel, Continental Europe, and Asian Pacific regions.[19]

Historically, the venture capital market is far more conservative than the business angel community. A significant difference between angels and institutional venture capitalists (VCs) is that business angels invest their own money, whereas VCs invest other people's money - primarily from

Table 4-2 Foreign Investor websites

Foreign VC's	Website
British Venture Capital Association	www.bvca.co.uk/
Canada's Venture Capital & Private Equity Association	www.cvca.ca/
China Venture Capital Association	www.cvcri.com/
European Private Equity and Venture Capital Association	www.evca.com/
Japan Venture Association	www.jvca.jp/en/

pension funds. With this level of fiduciary responsibility, VCs have historically been more conservative in their investments than angels. However, in recent years, VC's have gone back to making early stage investments. In fact, in 2004, 33% of all venture capital deals were seed- and first round, compared with 31% in 2003.

IPO market (Initial Public Offerings)

As mentioned earlier, Initial Public Offerings (IPOs) are regulated by the Securities & Exchange Commission (SEC) and involve the sale of stock to both qualified and unqualified investors. The size of this market is also quite volatile, ranging from $6 billion in 1969 to approximately $40 billion in 1993 and plummeting to $2 billion in 2003. The following table provides information on IPOs between 2000 and 2004.

Table 4-3 PO Investments by year[20]

Year	Number IPOs	Total Offer Amount ($M)	Average IPO size ($M)
2000	264	25,499	97
2001	41	3,490	85
2002	24	3,474	103
2003	62.8	2,023	70
2004	84.5	11,015	118

The implication for a small entrepreneurial company looking to get on the fast track is that the potential source of funding for seed- and early-stage investments changes rapidly. However, there are many other factors to consider besides the relative availability of funds when deciding if you will seek equity investment and from what source. To assist in understanding if and when you should go to the equity market, first familiarize yourself with the terminology used to describe the stages when investments are made.

Stages of Equity Financing

Equity investors use various terms to describe the stages at which equity financing is provided. These terms reflect the degree of risk and changes in the types of activities typically accomplished by the firm receiving the investment. Moving down the list from top to bottom one moves from the most to the least risky. Each of these terms is described below. As there is some variation in how investors use these terms, seek clarification of terms to confirm that they are being used in the same way.

The term **Early Stage Financing** includes those stages when no revenues are being generated (**Seed Financing and Start-Up Financing**).

Seed Financing refers to early stage financing of under $1,000,000. Such monies are usually spent on product development, market research, business plan development, and the assembly of the management team.

Start-up Financing refers to early stage financing typically provided to those who are "ready to do business".

First-Stage Financing is funding needed to initiate full scale manufacturing and sales.

Second Stage Financing is capital provided at times of expansion to provide operating capital for a company that is shipping product, although the company may not yet be profitable.

Mezzanine Financing is for companies that are beginning to turn a profit and require funding for expansion of various functional elements.

Bridge Financing is funding provided to a company that plans to go public within six months to a year.

Leveraged Buy-Out refers to the using the assets of the acquired company to help fund its acquisition by an outside party.

What do Equity Investors Look for?

Equity investors look at the management team. Unlike banks and other sources of debt financing that require collateral to assure repayment of their loans, equity investors view the management team as paramount to the success of the business and realizing a return on their investment. A seasoned, well-balanced team serves as a form of human collateral, as it is the management team which makes the opportunity come alive. It is often said of venture capitalists that they prefer a Grade A management team with a Grade B plan, to a Grade A plan with a Grade B team. This statement is not intended to minimize the importance of a good business plan, rather to indicate that, if you are seeking venture capital, you will need to have a strong management team. According to John Preston, a strong management team is one which "Keeps a healthy balance sheet; has a clearly focused strategy; and is realistic about marketing."

The implications of this statement for a technology entrepreneur are that, before approaching an equity investor you should realize that venture capitalists don't deal with sole proprietors. A well balanced management team has at least 3 business functions covered by individuals with expertise in those areas: (1) finance and administration, (2) sales & marketing, (3) and R&D, engineering, manufacturing (as appropriate).

If a venture capitalist is investing large sums of money in your company, it is likely that he or she will require a seat on your Board of Directors and will take strong interest in your company's success. This is advantageous, as the investors will want to maintain their track record of portfolio success and will, therefore, work harder on your behalf if they have invested heavily in your firm.

The venture capitalist becomes an important part of your team. When courting equity investors, ask for references; ask for the names of other entrepreneurs in their portfolio that you can contact; and ask about their contacts in your industry and their experience with your technology. Look for the synergy and the value they can add.

Keep in mind that venture capital firms often invest in conjunction with others. They may invest as part of a syndicate (a cluster of investment firms) or alone. In addition, a number of Fortune 500 companies have venture capital arms affiliated with them or other VC firms with which they often team. If your technology or product would eventually be a good acquisition candidate for a large firm, determine if that firm has a VC arm or a venture capital company with which it teams.

What do equity investors want in return?

Equity investors make money by helping you to grow your firm rapidly and then cashing out, usually at year 5. The phrase "cashing out" implies a number of things:

- Going public via an Initial Public Offering, or
- Selling stock either back to the company or to another company at a premium.

These two techniques for liquifying the initial investment are referred to as **Exit scenarios**. The whole intent of equity investors is to invest money in exchange for equity (ownership of stock); to sell the stock (liquify their investment) in about 5 years; and to realize a substantial return on their investment (ROI). A substantial return is approximately 5 to 10 times their initial investment. That would mean that on an investment of $3 million, they would look to make $15 to $30 million in 5 to 10 years. This is done by substantially increasing the value of your company. If this scenario doesn't interest you or if your business doesn't realistically lend itself to this type of return, equity investments are not for you.

The relationships between stage of investment and expected ROI?

The earlier one seeks an equity investment, the greater the ROI expected by the funding source. In addition, one will give up greater equity in the firm if seeking equity financing early in the development process. According to Garner, et al "It is not uncommon that first- and second-round capital might take 40 to 60 percent of the equity shares, and succeeding rounds of financing, including public offerings, may leave the original owners with as little as 5 to 20 percent of the stock." (1994, p 70). The amount of equity to be taken depends on the amount of money you are seeking and the valuation the potential investor places on the company. For example, if you are seeking a $5M investment, and your funding source values your firm at $15M, you will need to give up 33% equity. If you seek equity investment when risk is very high, valuation will be lower and the % equity you surrender will be higher. It is often best to defer seeking equity investments until risk has been reduced.[21]

As long as you are doing a good job of creating value, most venture capital firms are not interested in running the day-to-day operations of a firm. However, if your ability to manage the enterprise doesn't keep stride with the demands of a fast growing venture, you run the risk of being replaced. Technology entrepreneurs can minimize the likelihood that this will occur if (a) they seek a role in the rapidly growing company which allows them to utilize their strengths or (b) they form a spin-off company to which they license technology developed in a closely held firm and seek a good management team and equity investments in the spin-off.

Business angels, venture capitalists, and investment bankers look for similar things in making equity investments. However, business angels, being an informal, part-time investment source, tend to be more lenient and patient with their money. More detailed information on each group follows.

Business Angels

Who should approach them? In an earlier chapter we introduced a way of classifying entrepreneurial companies: life-style firm, foundation company, and high-potential ventures. Any of these could benefit from approaching a business angel. A life-style company might approach an angel for a loan; whereas a foundation company or high-potential venture might approach them for an early stage equity investment. If one needs a relatively small amount of money (defined as under $500,000), you might be best served by approaching a business angel.

How to find a business angel?

Unlike banks or venture capital firms that publish their addresses and phone numbers, business angels do not. Investing is not the primary activity of business angels, but something they do on the side. Angels will either seek out investment opportunities on their own or work through intermediaries that act as a buffer and filter. According to William Wetzel, the most common source of referrals are friends, business associates, or active personal searches. Other, less used sources include investment bankers, business brokers, commercial bankers, attorneys, and accountants.

So how do you find an angel? Look close to home - within a 50 mile radius. Network with your colleagues. Ask your accountant, lawyer, doctor, or other successful entrepreneurs who in the community invests in start-ups. Visit them, call them, and take your business plan.

Other tactics that you could try include participating in a computer matching service, attend venture capital club meetings, and contacting Investor Magazine.

The Capital Network (TCN)

The Technology Capital Network is a database that acts as an intermediary between entrepreneurs and investors. Both venture capitalists and other funding sources are entered into a database along with entrepreneurs for a subscription period of at least one year. Each time a new subscriber arrives, either capitalist or entrepreneur, a run is made through the entire database to find matches between entrepreneurs seeking funding and investors seeking viable alternatives. Prior matches are screened out to avoid duplicate matchmaking.

Matches are made against a profile of each entrant. A questionnaire is used for both investors and entrepreneurs. Additionally, entrepreneurs must provide a copy of the Executive Summary from their business plan and one page financials.

When a match is found, the unidentified material describing the entrepreneur and the opportunity are mailed to the matching capital sources. When the capital source(s) indicates further interest, the names of each party are supplied to the other, and they are left to arrange meetings and follow up.

This service has been in existence for over 20 years. Funding of this network is accomplished through fees and sponsors. The fees vary between $100 - $250 per year for entrepreneurs depending on the size of their company, $399 per year for private investors. See **thecapitalnetwork.org** for more details.

ACE-NET

A similar resource is the Active Capital Network, which is derived from the original Angel Capital Electronic Network (ACE-net) sponsored by the SBA in 1995. This is a 501-c-3 not-for-profit organization that matches entrepreneurs with potential investors. See **thecapitalnetwork.org** for more details.

Venture Capital Clubs

The business angel community acts in distinct ways in different parts of the country. In New York state, for example, one can find out about meetings of the informal venture capital community by contacting the local Chamber of Commerce. According to a 2005 article by Craig Douglas there are 80 organized angel investor groups nationwide.[6] However, in other states they are not aligned in this fashion and require a different approach. To find out if there are venture capital clubs in your area, contact the Association of Venture Capital. Venture capital clubs tend to meet on a monthly basis and invite 2 - 4 entrepreneurs who are interested in raising money to come and make a 15 minute presentation to a group over breakfast. Many times the audience will contain many service providers, but enough angels are present that you can begin the process of networking locally at such events.

How do angels make money?

The angel market is a less sophisticated market than the professional venture capital market. However, they look for a Return on Investment (ROI) in a similar fashion to the VC community. However, their terms and conditions are usually more lenient. Consult the next section on venture capital to understand their expectations.

Inctitutional Vonturo Capital Community

In the US there are oever 1,200 institutional investment companies. Some of these are partnerships, others are affiliated with large corporations, and still others are affiliated with the government (SBIC- Small Business Investment Corporations and MSBIC- Minority Small Business Investment Corporations). Such funds are staffed by professional money managers who make decisions regarding the investment of other people's money in businesses that have a high promise of return. The funds that they invest typically come from pension funds, corporations, and insurance companies. It is for this reason that most professional venture capital funds prefer to enter at the level of Second Stage Financing, and not before.

How to find out about Venture Capital Community?

As this is a professional, full-time endeavor, venture capitalists make their whereabouts well known. Rather than approaching them cold, it is still best to have a personal introduction. Don't approach them until you have your business plan prepared! The primary source for finding out about venture capitalists is **Pratt's Guide to Venture Capital**. This source is updated annually and is found in the reference section of most libraries. Pratt's lists investors by technology /service areas of interest and also by geographic location. You will find the name, address, fax, and phone number of appropriate contacts plus information regarding the level of investment that they make, the kinds of financials that they wish to see, and if they are making any investments at the time. It is a very useful source.

Processes and documents

Venture Capitalists see hundreds of business plans in any given week. Most of the plans don't make it past a cursory review. According to Pratt's Guide, 60% are rejected after a 20-30 minute scanning, and 25% are discarded after a lengthier review. The remaining 15% are looked at in more detail and of these, 10% are dismissed due to irreconcilable flaws in the management team or the business plan. Only 5 out of 100 are considered to be viable investment opportunities and 3% result in successful financing.

Again, let me stress that if you are seeking institutional venture capital it is imperative that your firm have a management team. Sole proprietorships are NOT of interest. The management team must have an appropriate balance of experience and authority to cover marketing & sales; research & development; operations; and finance and administration. If you get to first base with a venture capital investor, following due diligence, a number of documents would be involved in realizing the opportunity. These include:

- Letters of Intent
- Financing Agreements
- Operating Covenants

Investment Bankers

Private Placement

The Private Placement process is regulated by the Securities and Exchange Commission (SEC). Up until this point in our discussion of financing options, the SEC has not been mentioned. However, both Private Placements and Initial Public Offerings (IPO) do involve this quasi-judicial administrative agency of the U.S. Federal government, as well as counterpart organizations in each state. When a company begins to consider financing methods regulated by the SEC, they are approaching a new level of complexity, one that is best not considered by Life-Style firms. High potential ventures and foundation companies, however, may find private placements a good financing option to consider. For an excellent discussion of this topic, pick up a copy of *The Entrepreneur's Guide to Going Public* by James B. Arkebauer.

In this discussion, Private Placements are mentioned prior to Initial Public Offerings because, for many small companies, they offer a solution to a vexing problem - the expense of IPO's. Nonetheless, to truly understand private placements, one needs to understand some of the legislative background which determines the activities of the SEC.

The Securities and Exchange Commission was formed in 1934 pursuant to the Securities Exchange Act of 1933. The purpose of this Act was to form an entity that would guard against fraudulent sales practices, supervise the registration of securities, and regulate the over-the-counter and securities markets. The New York Stock Exchange (NYSE), American Stock Exchange (AMEX), the National Association of Securities Dealers Automated Quotation System (NASDAQ) and Over-The-Counter (OTC) markets are all regulated by the SEC and its regional offices. The SEC and the Act of '33 require that when securities are sold that information is fairly and fully disclosed to the public. This task is accomplished in many ways including an elaborate and expensive registration process, the preparation of a document referred to as a prospectus, and limitations on other information the company may divulge once an underwriter has been signed. The expenses of an IPO will be discussed in a few moments. At this point, however, it suffices to say that for many companies these expenses are prohibitive.

Due to the inability of many small companies to participate in the IPO process, new legislation was passed in 1980 referred to as the Small Business Investment Incentive Act. One of the results of that legislation was that in 1982 the SEC implemented another exemption referred to as Regulation D or Reg D, for short, This had profound and positive implications for small business. In 1988, other revisions were implemented making it easier still for small businesses to engage in equity fund-raising.

Regulation D clarifies exemptions to the SEC regulations as articulated in the Act of '33 and provides the basis for Private Placements. There are 6 rules which constitute Regulation D:

Rule 501 - definitions and terms

Rule 502 - conditions, limitations, and information requirements

Rule 503 - SEC notification requirements

Rule 504 - raising money through securities sales up to $1 million

Rule 505 - raising money through securities sales of between $1 and $5 million

Rule 506 - raising money through securities sales over $5 million

Rather than providing details on each of these rules, let me encourage interested parties to read Arkebauer's book and to contact a regional SEC office, as well as your state SEC office for information on the registration process for Private Placements (Regulation D), and other SEC exemptions. Also request a copy of a small brochure called Q&A: Small Business and the SEC from a regional SEC office. The phone numbers and addresses for the twelve regional offices are listed below:

Securities & Exchange Commission
Mark Schonfeld, Regional Director
Northeast Regional Office
3 World Financial Center
Room 4-300
New York, NY 10281
(212)336-1100

Securities & Exchange Commission
Boston District Office
Walter G. Ricciardi, District Administrator
73 Tremont Street, Suite 600
Boston, MA 02108-3912
(617) 573-8900

Securities & Exchange Commission
Arthur S. Gabinet, District Admnistrator
Philadelphia District Office
The Mellon Independence Center
701 Market Street
Philadelphia, PA 19106-1532
(215) 597-3100

Securities & Exchange Commission
David Nelson, Regional Director
Southeast Regional Office
801 Brickell Avenue, Suite 1800
Miami, FL 33131
(305) 982-6300

Securities & Exchange Commission
Richard P. Wessel, District Administrator
Atlanta District Office
3475 Lenox Road, N.E. Suite 1000
Atlanta, GA 30326-1232
(404)842-7600

Securities & Exchange Commission
Midwest Regional Office
175 W. Jackson Boulevard, Suite 900
Chicago, IL 60604
(312) 353-7390
e-mail: chicago@sec.gov

Securities & Exchange Commission

Randall J. Fons, Regional Director
Central Regional Office
1801 California Street, Suite 4800
Denver, CO 80202-2656
(303) 844-1000

Securities & Exchange Commission
Harold F. Degenhardt, District Administrator
Fort Worth District Office
801 Cherry Street, Suite 1900
Fort Worth, TX 76102
(817) 978-3821

Securities & Exchange Commission
Kenneth D. Israel, Jr., District Administrator
Salt Lake District Office
15 W. South Temple Street
Suite 1800
Salt Lake City, UT 84101
(801) 524-5796

Securities & Exchange Commission
Randall R. Lee, Regional Director
Pacific Regional Office
5670 Wilshire Boulevard, Suite 1100
Los Angeles, CA 90036-3648
(213) 965-3998

Securities & Exchange Commission
Helane L. Morrison, District Administrator
San Francisco District Office
44 Montgomery Street, Suite 1100
San Francisco, CA 94104
(415) 705-2500

In addition, be sure to contact the appropriate state organization to determine filing fees and regulations that the state has for Private Placements. A source that you can consult for such information is The National Directory of Addresses and Telephone Numbers. You will find this in most libraries, by consulting a librarian. Often this is held at the reserve desk and lists the telephone numbers for many state agencies. To get you started, following is a list of state agencies to contact for selected states.

California

Department of Corporation
320 West 4th Street, Suite 750
Los Angeles, CA 90013-2344
(213) 576-7500

Massachusetts

Massachusetts Securities Division
One Ashburton Place, 17th Floor
Boston, MA 02108
(617)248-0177

Ohio

Ohio Division of Securities
77 S. High St. - 22nd Floor
Columbus, OH 43215-6131
(614) 644-7381

Initial Public Offerings

When one conducts an Initial Public Offering (IPO) or "Goes Public", the life of that firm will never be the same. From that day forward the company will have many owners, all of whom need information about every aspect of your business and all of whom will have a say in the future of the company. Management teams that are unwilling to share control of their business, as well as the risks and rewards, are not good candidates for an IPO. On the other hand, the rewards of going public are many. It is a means to recapitalize a firm, and appreciate stock value. Going public brings prestige and glamour to a company. It is a good strategy to use if positioning for an acquisition or a merger. It is also the primary vehicle used by the venture capital community for "cashing out". The downside as mentioned previously includes loss of control, the requirements regarding disclosure; and the expenses associated with the IPO and of operating as a public company afterwards.

Well, how much money are we talking about? What are the expenses associated with conducting an IPO? The costs fall into 4 categories:

Underwriter costs
Professional costs
Up-front costs and
Hidden and future costs

An underwriter is an investment banker of a broker/dealer who serves as an intermediary between the company offering securities for sale and the investing public which purchases them. The underwriter's fee, sometimes referred to as a commission or underwriter's discount,, is a percentage of the stock sold. For smaller offerings, the current standard is approximately 10%. In addition, the underwriter receives an expense allowance ranging from 1 to 4% of the monies raised in the IPO. Thus, if your IPO was for $10,000,000, the underwriter's discount at 10% would be $1,000,000 plus an expense allowance, say of 2% of the IPO, would be an additional $200,000. Thus, in conducting an IPO to raise $10,000,000 - the underwriter's cost in this scenario would be $1,200,000. Issues regarding best efforts or firm commitment terms need to be carefully attended to.

Professional fees include the cost of attorneys and accountants and can vary widely on an issue of this size between $20,000 and $200,000. In large part, what determines professional expenses are the amount of corporate cleanup resulting from previous arrangements, poor record keeping, and related complexities.

Upfront fees include costs for printing the Registration statement, another document referred to as a red herring and the definitive prospectus. The total printing costs can vary between $10,000 and $40,000. There are also filing fees with the SEC, the state, the National Association of Securities Dealers, and other entities. Many of these fees are expressed as a percentage of the total amount of the offering.

After the IPO, the company will have the continued obligation to prepare and print a variety of disclosure documents including a Form SR: Application of Proceeds; Form 8-K: Current Reports; Form 10-K: Annual Report; Form 10-Q: Quarterly Report. Thus, a publicly-traded company needs to add staff or contract with financial public relations firms to continually produce such documentation throughout the life of the public company. The role of management also shifts to assure that good relationships are maintained with the shareholders.

You can see how Arkebauer would conclude that for smaller offerings, total costs and expenses can reach 24% to 39% of the offering. Again, let me direct the reader back to the section on private placements and indicate that many of the expenses, restrictions, and reporting requirements associated with the IPO are obviated by the private placement mechanism.

Summary: Equity investors

The risk-capital community is made up of three distinct types of equity investors: business angels, venture capital, investment bankers. The business angel community is the largest and is responsible for much seed financing. Such investors are investing their own funds and make a couple of deals a year. The venture capital community is considerably smaller, and makes fewer investments in early stage companies. VC's invest other people's money - primarily from pension funds. They tend to be more risk averse and wait to enter a deal when technology and market risks have been somewhat decreased. The IPO market has been booming and is appropriate for high-potential ventures to consider. It is an expensive process and one which totally changes the future operating procedures of the company. In all cases, equity investors take equity or ownership of company stock and are looking to make a significant return on their investment.

Summary and Conclusions

The purpose of this chapter is to introduce the five broad areas of financing which are available to technology entrepreneurs to capitalize the growth of their firm: sweat equity, science-for-hire, debt, equity, and profit. Not all forms of financing are available to companies at the same time. Debt financing becomes available when the company has sufficient collateral. Equity investments becomes increasingly available as technology and market risks are decreased. From a financing perspective, the most difficult time for technology entrepreneurs is during the early R&D phase when the private sector is loathe to make investments. Sweat equity and science-for-hire programs enable such companies to develop new technology and to involve private sector capital markets when R&D risk has been decreased.

Chapter 4 Endnotes

[1] Blechman, Bruce and Levinson, Jay Conrad. Guerrilla Financing: Alternative Techniques to Finance any Small Business. Boston: Houghton Mifflin Company, 1991.

[2] Lamaute, Daniel. Protecting the tax advantage of your deferred compensation. http://ezinearticles.com/?Protecting-the-Tax-Advantage-of-Your-Deferred-Compensation&id=11545

[3] Dinell, David. Big changes underway for deferred compensation plans. http://www.bizjournals.com/wichita/stories/2005/01/24/focus1.html

[4] Barrett, E. Thorpe. Write your Own Business contracts: What Your Attorney Won't Tell You. Grants press: The Oasis Press, 1994.

[5] Rules of Success #1: Sweat equity is the best equity! http://www.blogmarverick.com/entry/4732831173095828

[6] http://www.sbirworld.com

[7] http://www.zyn.com/sbir/sbres/sba-pd/

[8] http://www.sba.gov/sbdc/aboutus.html

[9] Andresky Fraser, Jill. Raising Capital: How to Borrow from Family and Friends. Inc. Magazine, July 1995.

[10] Hess, Robert. P. Desk Book for Setting Up a Closely Held Corporation. Englewood Cliffs: Institute for Business Planning, 1985.

[11] http://www.sba.gov/size/sizetable2002.html

[12] Choosing a bank for your small business. Gaebler Ventures, March, 2005

[13] Garner, Daniel; Owen, Robert, and Conway, Robert. The Ernst and Young Guide to Financing for Growth. New York: John Wiley & Sons, 1994

[14] Arkebauer, James. The Entrepreneur's Guide to Going Public. Dover, New Hampshire: Upstart Publishing Company, 1991.

[15] Cannon Financial Institution. http://www.cannonfinancial.com/cgi-bin/newsDetail.cfm?ID=94

[16] Venture and Angel Capital Reporter, Feb 2005. http://www.evancarmichael.com/journal_archives/2005_02_01_archive.html

Chapter 4 Endnotes (cont)

[17] U.S. Venture-Capital Investment Increases to $20.4 Billion in 2004 in First Year-Over-Year Increase Since 2000.
Ernst & Young/VentureOne Quarterly Venture Capital Reports, Jan 21, 2005

[18] US VC's to Expand Global Investments, June 22, 2005

[19] Ibid

[20] Total Venture-Backed M&A Valuations Nearly Doubled in 2004. National Venture Capital Association, February 8, 2005

[21] Division of equity. How equity gets divided initially and at harvest. www.venturecoach.com

[22] Douglas, Craig. Angel investors add capital, sophistication to model. Boston Business Journal, June 24, 2005

Commercialization Strategies

" You read a book from the beginning to end. You run a business in the opposite way. You start at the end, and then do everything you must to reach it."

- Harold Geneen

Chapter 05

The phrase Commercialization Strategy refers to the series of financing options that a company entertains to move its technology/product from concept to the market place.

What is a Commercialization Strategy?

The phrase *commercialization strategy* is used frequently in the literature associated with the Small Business Innovation Research (SBIR) program. In the DoD solicitations it is referenced as *your company's strategy for converting the proposed research into a product or a non-R&D service with widespread commercial use – including private sector and/or military markets.* – but what does that mean? How can the phrase be operationalized in a way that is useful?

In reflecting upon the stage-gate work of Robert Cooper as applied to new product development within large organizations, it seemed both useful and instructive to define commercialization strategy for small advanced technology firms in terms of the financing options that a company entertains to move its technology/product from concept to the marketplace. Small businesses must turn outwards when seeking funding for growth, as opposed to the strategy used within large corporations and in government bureaucracies turn inwards for financing.

It was also beneficial to tie the need for funding to critical milestones, as opposed to utilizing the concept of stages as defined by Cooper. Some milestones may be technology specific, such as seeking FDA approval for therapeutics; while others may be product generic such as intellectual property protection, or company specific such as "start-up" phase. When looked at in this fashion, the concept of "commercialization strategy" becomes a powerful heuristic that can assist small businesses in understanding the multi-faceted activities associated with turning a concept into a product with widespread commercial use and the funding required to achieve this.

The phrase *commercialization strategy* refers to the series of financing options that a company entertains to move its technology/product from concept to the market place. As discussed in the previous chapter, an increasing number of financing options become available to a company as the technology/product reaches completion, as collateral is developed, and as market risk decreases. But you have to get to that point first!

The financing options available to your firm also depend on your *vision for the future*. Do you wish to remain a contract R&D firm and license your technology to others, or do you wish to perform most business functions within your firm? Are you willing to share control of your enterprise with equity investors or is your goal to develop a closely held firm? These are some of the important considerations which will affect the preliminary shape of your commercialization strategy. Your vision acts as an anchor point. Any strategy must therefore begin with a recognition of this and then map out a series of financing options to commercialize the technology or product.

A commercialization strategy will also be affected by *personal philosophies* about business. Some founders start with the belief that "I want to grow this company without giving up any equity." Others may decide "I don't care who else gets rich off my business, as long as I retain the right to do what I enjoy most and make good money in the process." Still others may assume that "I am going to pay for the best help available. I don't believe in getting something for nothing." Such philosophies usually go unexpressed, but certainly affect the choices that you as an entrepreneur will make in developing your commercialization strategy.

A commercialization strategy is affected by:

» Your vision
» Your business philosophy
» The stage of technology development
» Market risk
» Competitive activities
» Window of opportunity

Companies that are developing a technology platform which has the ability to affect multiple industries must also include an assessment of which applications they think will develop first. This should be discussed in their commercialization strategy and potential markets rank ordered in terms of their readiness. A company should position itself to hit market *windows of opportunity* on time.

Vision, business philosophies, and a logical assessment of market opportunities are all important considerations to make in developing your commercialization strategy. However, if positioning your firm to be a high-potential venture, the ultimate strategic choices made will be decisions that are required to stay ahead of the competition and to hit the market window of opportunity. Estimate when you will be able to market a commercial product, when your principal competitors will be ready to market and when your target customers will become responsive to your technology/product. Work backwards from this target date, setting your firm's marketing, research, and financing milestones on the timeline necessary for you to hit the projected date of market entry. Seizing your market advantage will increase the likelihood of realizing the objective of becoming a fast-growth firm which will create value for you, your commercial partners, and your investors.

When to Develop a Commercialization Strategy

Most people don't aimlessly wander through life without a sense of direction. As a child, one's vision for the future is often shaped by significant others, but as a teenager equipped with reason and skills in self-reflection, one begins to entertain multiple career paths. Upon reaching maturity, career paths come into greater focus, although they always remain dynamic and must be in tune with the realities of changing times. A commercialization strategy is similar in its evolution.

It is good to have a commercialization strategy in mind from the outset. It not only provides direction, but also acts as a cohesive force. However, it is dynamic and will change. You should expect that your commercialization strategy will be revised frequently as your understanding of the market, industry, and competitors grows. At all times, a clear company vision and an articulation of your business philosophy will serve as anchor points. A working familiarity with the pros and cons of various financing options will enable you to position yourself appropriately and revise your strategy as dynamic forces in the marketplace require that you revisit your strategy.

Prototypical Commercialization Strategies

The purpose of this chapter is to introduce you to a variety of strategies that we have seen advanced technology firms use successfully. In our short-hand form we refer to these strategies as:

1) Licensing with developmental funds
2) Strategic alliances
3) Equity investment in the parent company
4) Equity investment in a spin-off
5) Initial Public Offering

These descriptors use the name of the ultimate or last step in the financing strategy as the name of the overall approach. This is a protocol that we have found to be useful. However, many other financing vehicles are used, leading up to that last financing step. In the tables which accompany the description of each prototypical strategy, an indication of complementary financing steps is included, accompanied by an expression of a hypothetical vision and philosophy statement which also affected the choices made.

Strategy #1: Licensing with developmental funds

Many life-style firms use licensing as the commercialization strategy of choice. In this manner, the advanced technology firm specializes in technology development and limits its marketing and sales activities to the overtures it makes to potential licensees. The licensees, in turn, perform all of the other tasks associated with commercialization - marketing, sales and distribution, engineering, manufacturing, and the like. In this day of shrinking R&D budgets in large corporations, licensing-in is increasingly a strategy of choice if the technology enables the licensee to enter new markets, or retain market position without having to make costly investments in the original R&D, skilled personnel, and/or equipment.

Table 5-1 provides a thumbnail sketch of the commercialization strategy used by a small, advanced technology firm using a licensing strategy. This table is followed by an excerpt from interviews with representatives from two companies describing why they use this strategy and how they make it work for them.

Under the Federal Acquisition Regulations (FAR), a small business such as ours, retains the rights to the technology they develop for the government outside the government arena. As a result, we have quite a few undeveloped, patented technologies 'on the shelf'. We generate 4-5 patented technologies each year.

Large corporations become familiar with both our expertise and our technologies through our technical literature and conference presentations. Later, they approach us to solve a

Table 5 - 1: Sample Strategy - Licensing

Vision: *Lifestyle company*
Business Philosophy: *Do what I enjoy*

Milestone	Financing Method
Start- Up	Sweat Equity
Concept Development	SBIR
Intellectual Property	Retained Earnings
Application Development	Licensee
Production	Licensee

problem in one of our demonstrated areas of expertise. This usually involves developing one of our undeveloped technologies to solve a specific problem of interest to them. Many of the technologies, though patented by us, are still at quite an early stage of development. A great deal of inventing must still take place during the development process to adapt our technology to our client's specific application needs.

With our private clients, we have written many of our R&D agreements as 'best effort' because of the typically high risk nature of the projects. A bad relationship would be a fixed price and set deliverable for something that is essentially a research project. If you can't deliver, you can wind up working for free until you get it right. Since we're dealing with science and the unknown, it may not be possible to solve the problem as originally configured. Also, in our contractual relationships involving licensing of our products, we will not indemnify the large company for our technology. It is just not feasible for a small company."

Listed below are additional comments from another company that is actively shifting its R&D contracts from the Federal arena to the private sector.

"Most of our private contracts have been 3 - 5 years in duration. The companies for which we work know that there are no quick fixes in this R&D field. Projects of long duration require the active involvement of a champion to assure continued financial support and a good relationship. However, problems inevitably arise due to the long duration of the projects.

Our champions are typically very enthusiastic but, if they retire or move away, the chemistry of the new relationship is often different. Technology decisions are very subjective and personality specific.

From our perspective, all of our relationships have been satisfactory, even though the character of these relationships has changed over the past 10 years. At first we retained no rights to technology that we developed; now we negotiate to retain more rights for ourselves.

ABCTech typically works under conditions of Cost-Plus-Fixed-Fee and always presents the potential clients with a clearly defined scope of work. Historically the firm has met or exceeded their goals.

Invariably, hiring us is a hell of a lot cheaper than doing the work inside. A large company may have an internal interest in examining an area for only 2-3 years. They wouldn't want to spend $1 million for machines and/or make a commitment to long term staff for a project of limited duration. Because of our expertise and our equipment, we're up and running within a week. When a company hires us there is no learning curve, whereas there is with new internal projects undertaken by large corporations."

Summary

The two parties interviewed clearly leveraged the R&D developed under science-for-hire arrangements. They paid careful attention to intellectual property; were mindful of the importance of developing and maintaining relationships with champions; and entered contractual arrangements with corporations on a realistic basis.

Strategy #2: Strategic alliance

Continued soul searching often leads company founders to decide that they don't wish to assume certain business functions. This is often the case when one makes a component or an enhancement to a system. After weighing the pros and cons of manufacturing and marketing the component to a limited number of system integrators, it may seem more appropriate to form a strategic alliance with an entity in the supplier chain. Your immediate customer could become a site for testing your technology/product, a potential licensee, or an investor in your firm. When you make a decision to mutually align yourself with a customer, you have developed a strategic ally or teaming partner. Many forms of strategic alliances can be formed for purposes of marketing, R&D, manufacture, equity, joint ventures, and/or licensing.

Table 5 - 2: Strategy - Strategic Alliance

Vision: *Foundation Company (R&D / Manufacturing)*
Business Philosophy: *Conservative*

Milestone	Financing Method
Start- Up	Sweat Equity
Concept Development	SBIR
Intellectual Property	Retained Earnings
Prototype Development	SBIR
Production Scale Up	Equity investor, converted to debt
Marketing / Sales	Strategic Alliance

Zentech received its first SBIR grant in 1986. Their decision to respond to RFPs has traditionally been driven by the company's marketing and financial strategies. Routinely, Zentech examines the market looking for "market-pull" opportunities for their technologies and products. If they see opportunities to commercialize a particular application, they then examine RFPs from the various federal agencies to determine if there is a good strategic fit. Zentech will not bid on RFPs for which they have not independently assessed a market need that fits with their company's mission.

Zentech manufactures a widget that is sold to manufacturers of a high tech system. In 1986, Zentech employed 42 people. Today, they employ 135. Their growth has been primarily dependent upon a philosophy that can only be characterized as "getting close to the customer." This trial and error approach has been of great value.

Zentech initially spent a lot of time knocking on doors, presenting their idea of what the customer wanted, and then receiving corrections from the customer. Through the process of "getting close to the customer" they have developed a strategic alliance. When initially assessing the market, Zentech realized that the opportunity for a return on its investment would only come if the widget was successfully integrated into their customer's high tech system. Therefore, in mapping out their R & D and marketing strategies, they anticipated the final goal not as production of the widget, but as utilization of the widget as a critical component of the customer's high tech system. That last phase of their plan has been financed by the customer. The customer's motivation in this process was sparked by the fact that the use of the widget in a new high tech system would open up new markets.

Funding has always been a challenge to Zentech. They initially received equity financing from an overseas firm. The foreign investor provided the cash and Zentech provided the technology. This initial funding enabled them to conduct their preliminary work with customers. However, funding problems on the part of the investor, coupled with their early success, led Zentech to buy back its equity.

For Zentech, the hardest part of the commercialization process has been obtaining good data on performance in actual field locations. They had to expend a lot of effort to gain permission from potential customers to install the equipment, obtain good field data, and convince them to continue running the tests.

At one point, when reviewing their strategies for growth, Zentech considered getting into the manufacturing of the high tech instrument. However, when they assessed this market they learned that 20-24% of the gross sales of the instrument market were spent on sales promotion and service. Upon reflection Zentech decided that they did not wish to develop a large sales force or customer service department or pay for the costs involved with developing the high tech item themselves. They made a strategic decision to continue manufacturing the widget and not get into the high tech instrument business. They only spend 5% of their gross dollars on sales and services, have a smaller staff, and need only one location.

Zentech presently has 14 on-going programs, including one SBIR program. They must ramp staff up and down quickly and plan shifts for their staff between programs, sometimes anticipated over a year in advance. Staff members are shifted to support funded programs. Zentech has commercialized one model of widget, obtained a "design win" on another, and applied for three patents. Its management feels that the strategies being followed are allowing company growth while staying within the constraints of prudent financial management.

Summary

Strategic relationships such as this are on the increase, intertwining the future of companies in a sequence of customer-supplier relationships (Hanan,1992). A good alliance is like a good marriage and requires that respect and fair play characterize the relationships. Ohmae (1989) recommends that in order to develop successful collaborations, participants need to:

- make a personal commitment to the alliance,
- have mutual respect and trust,
- take time to develop and maintain the relationship,
- clarify the relationship in a contractual form and then quickly put the contract away,
- clarify mutual expectations and timeframes,
- maintain an awareness of the partner's problems,
- learn to interpret particular responses in a culturally appropriate way,
- recognize a partner's independence, and
- celebrate success together.

Some ideas about how to maintain good relationships are expressed in the interview excerpt below:

"We put a lot of effort into establishing and maintaining relationships, keeping each other informed of travel plans to conferences - so that opportunities to interact remain constant. You have to work the relationships up and down the ladder. Management needs to dialog with management, and technical people in both firms need to interact with one another.

Networking is important. Our people attend approximately 20 conferences a year. It is a major investment of time and resources, but enables us to develop and maintain relationships, and to keep interested parties aware of our new research efforts through the conference presentations that we make."

Strategy #3: Equity investment in the parent company

Often times the founder knows at the outset what type of firm he or she wishes to develop. If the founder has the vision to become a high-potential venture she will make decisions from day 1 which position the company for rapid growth. An example of such planning follows:

Table 5 - 3: Equity Investment in Parent Company

Vision: *High potential venture*
Business Philosophy: *Rich is good*

Milestone	Financing Option
Concept Development	Sweat Equity
Prototype Development	Science for Hire
Product Introduction	Private Placement
Market penetration	Debt Financing from equity investors

FastTrack had its eyes on becoming a fast-growth company from the get-go. The founder had both a business and a technical background and was very familiar with Federally-funded science-for-hire programs. After investing sweat equity to get the company started, the founder applied for SBIR funding. After winning both a Phase I and Phase II award, he quickly assembled a multi-disciplinary team Vested in the vision of becoming a high-potential venture, the team worked diligently on issues related to business planing, flexing their time to complete this task by utilizing assistance from a local university.

To accelerate the rate of market entry and to allow the company to gear up for manufacturing, the founders decided to conduct a private placement. Equity investors were courted for a couple of years, but only became involved once market risk had decreased and sales were doing well. The team negotiated a loan from an institutional investment firm.

Summary

The vision a founder has for the future of the company directs and focuses its activities. In the example provided, FastTrack, knowing that it wanted to position itself to be a high potential venture, made certain activities a priority and utilized a wide variety of financing options.

Strategy #4: Equity investment in a spin-off

A complex strategy, but one which can be exercised successfully, is a hybrid of approaches already discussed. The founder of the technology firm decides that he or she wishes to keep the company fairly small, focused on R&D, and privately-held. However, the technology entrepreneur entertains spinning off a related company in which equity investments could be made. The intent is to grow the spin-off as a high-potential

Figure 5 - 1:

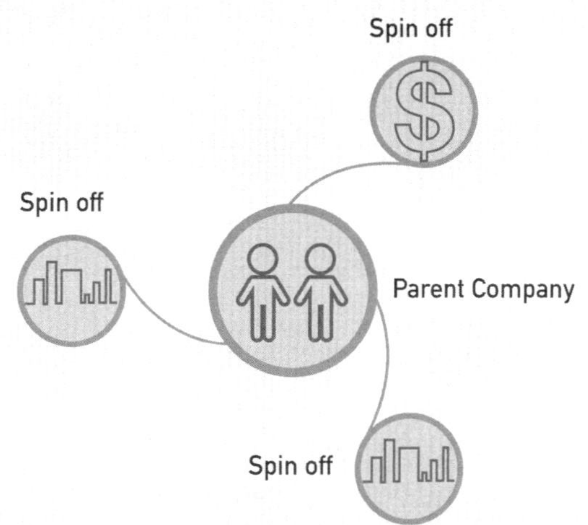

venture. In order to make this strategy succeed issues related to human resources, intellectual property, and non-compete arrangements need to be artfully addressed.

With respect to human resources, any entity seeking equity investment must have an excellent management team in place. The dilemma should be apparent. The founder of the parent company can't be in both the parent firm and the spin-off because of split loyalties. An equity investor wants to be assured that the management team is fully committed to making the venture a success - thus, such an arrangement is unacceptable. The technology entrepreneur, therefore, tends to stay with the parent firm. This requires that another management team is assembled to drive the growth of the spin-off. Most companies contemplating this strategy do not have the resources available to hire a management team for another firm prior to receiving an equity investment. Therefore, they have to grapple with how to address this requirement.

Human resources, intellectual property, and non-compete arrangements need to be artfully addressed.

One strategy is to have a phantom management team in the wings that could step in once equity financing is obtained. This is obviously not an optimal alternative to an equity investor, but one which is understood. A second strategy is to groom a vice president from the parent company to become the president of the spin-off. This has benefits to the spin-off, but creates a hole in the management team of the parent company. Some technology firms, strapped for resources utilize a third strategy and offer the position of president to a retiring executive from a large firm. This is done because the executive may have a golden parachute that he is willing to invest in the spin-off or because it is believed that his contacts should attract capital. This strategy is risky, however, as executives from a corporate environment do not have experience growing a high-potential venture. There is a big difference between building a car (entrepreneurial environment) and driving a car (large corporations).

You will be best served by aiming to involve a management team that has had experience in growing a company, which has contacts in the market of interest, and which has a pedigree that will satisfy the needs of equity investors. The bottom line is - if you want to form a spin-off you must grapple with how to best proceed to put a capable, dedicated team in place to drive the growth of the venture.

The intellectual property issues must also be adequately addressed. Formal arrangements which license or sell the intellectual property to the spin-off must be drafted. The terms need to be appropriate to allow an incentive for the management team and the equity investors, while still providing a return to the parent company. If there are restrictions on market applications to which the technology may be applied, this must be discussed and clarified.

Table 5 - 4: IPO Strategy

Vision: *High potential venture*
Business Philosophy: *I want to try it all*

Milestone	Financing Option
Concept Development	Federal Funding
Prototype Development	Seed financing from business angels
Market test	Retained Earnings
Market introduction	Equity Financing-Fortune 500
Scale-Up	Second Round Financing from VC
New Facility	Private Placement
Expansion	Line of Credit.profits
Market Penetration	IPO

A related issue is non-compete arrangements. You must decide if any R&D will be conducted in the spin-off or if it will take place only in the parent company. You must clarify if the spin-off will have the right to obtain intellectual property from other sources in order to expand its intellectual property estate, or must all intellectual property have to come from the parent.

Summary

A spin-off strategy can work well. However, issues related to human resources, intellectual property, and non-compete issues need to be addressed thoroughly. An equity investor will have no interest in the spin-off, if it is unduly fettered or if it is a sham.

Strategy #5: Initial Public Offering

Perhaps the most glamorous commercialization strategy is an Initial Public Offering (IPO). Going public is the penultimate sign that you have arrived. It is a means to recapitalize your firm, to appreciate the value of stock, and the most common means for equity investors to cash out. It brings lots of attention to your company and is a good strategy to use if positioning to be acquired or merge with another firm. It is also by far the most expensive commercialization strategy, requiring large amounts of money to be paid to underwriters, attorneys, accountants, public relations firms, printers, state and federal organizations. A company that goes this route will never be the same. In exchange for the glamour and the rapid capitalization of the company, one acquires a public of owners who have the right to full disclosure from that time forward.

As can be seen from the list of financing methods used, a company positioning itself for this future will spend considerable time in financial planning. This technology entrepreneur has to be mindful from the start that every time they give equity away - they must anticipate the return for subsequent investors and the founders. As cited at the beginning of this chapter *"You read a book from the beginning to the end. You run a business in the opposite way. You start with the end, and then do everything you must to reach it."*

The Challenge of a Rich Technology Platform

Reaching the goals you set requires planning - business planning made in light of your vision for the future. We leave this section and turn now to the actual process of business planning.

To grow and flourish, a company must have a sustainable competitive advantage—that is, an advantage that will give the company staying power over the long haul. The types of things which provide a company with such an advantage include:

Figure 5 - 2: Technology Platform

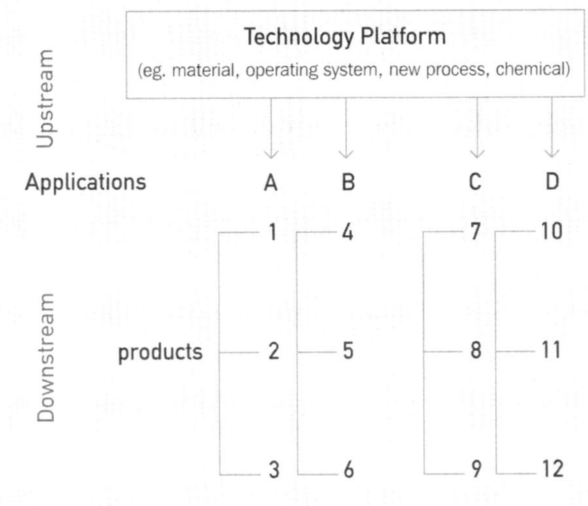

- Intellectual property: patents, trade secrets, copyrights, trademarks
- The uniqueness of the technology and the limited number of people who have expertise in this area (hopefully, many of them are employed by the company)
- Cost of entry
- Strategic allies and champions
- Marketing and sales capabilities, access to distribution networks, and the quality of the work done
- The company's record with respect to selecting successful new products or technologies, as well as its ability to keep to development timelines

This chapter focuses on how to assess the possible applications of a rich technology platform and on how to combine this assessment with decisions and actions which will assure that your company is appropriately developing those aspects of sustainable competitive advantage associated with its particular technology.

Figure 5-1 depicts the possibilities presented by a rich technology platform, such as a new composite material. The properties of the material make it ideal for use in a wide variety of applications as diverse as leisure (golf clubs) and spacecraft (shielding). The dilemma for the small firm is how to effectively exploit all these possibilities. The answer is that a small com-

Figure 5 - 3: Financing options as a function of applications and resources required

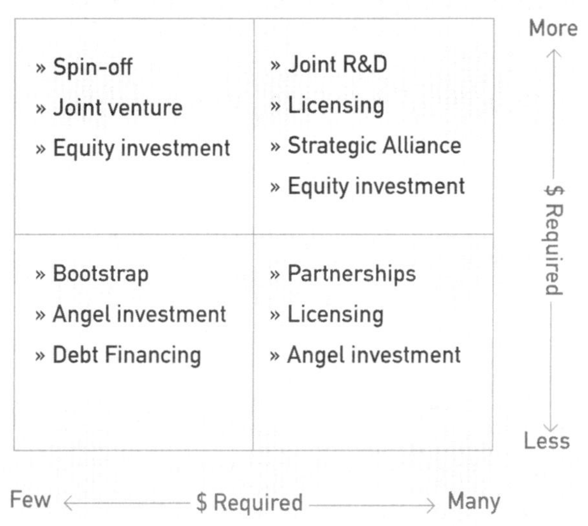

pany can't—on its own. Limitations of time, money, and resources make it infeasible for most companies, large or small, to fully exploit all the possibilities presented by a revolutionary technology. In such situations, a company must consider implementing a constellation of strategies, and decide which application it will pursue on its own and which it will pursue in combination with others. Figure 5-2 is a shorthand way of representing which strategies to consider. Such considerations are made as a function of the number of possible applications to be pursued and the amount of financial resources required to exploit them.

Figure 5-2 represents financing options to consider as a function of the number of applications for the technology, as well as the perceived financial resources required. For example, if a technology has few applications and requires limited resources for successful commercialization, the firm should be able to realize this opportunity on its own, by bootstrapping. However, even with limited applications, if significant funding is required, one should consider seeking direct investment in the company, a joint venture, or a spin-off. If the technology has many possible applications, then one should consider a wider range of strategies, involving a larger universe of potential partners. Most new technology entrepreneurs don't have a good basis for knowing how much money its takes to bring a product to market, so it is important that this figure be examined. For example, "The R&D costs to generate and maintain the technology required for each new chemical entity is now greater than $100 million and increasing. ...To maintain the 10% pace of investment, each new chemical entity would have to generate, on the average, $1 billion in sales over its lifetime, assuming no inflation." This is obviously not a task a small company can tackle on its own.

The implications are very clear. A company should assess whether it or other entities can best exploit various options. For example, if it truly won't take a lot of money to complete production and bring the product to market, the small company may be the best candidate to do it. However, as the amount of money required and the number of possible applications increase, the universe of commercialization strategies to consider also expands.

When trying to determine the constellation of strategies to pursue, you should simultaneously consider three issues:

1) How can the basic and application R&D be expeditiously completed?

2) Which firms/investors will make the best partners to fully exploit the technology?

3) How can you assure that your company maintains an essential role in the commercialization of the technology it originated?

Completing Research and Development

To maintain a substantial lead, firms developing pioneer technologies must assess not only what research and development needs to be accomplished, but also which partners may be good to involve in "upstream" activities. The greatest flexibility comes from strategic alliances, including consortia and joint ventures that are structured to preserve organizational autonomy and individual incentives. Before deciding which firms/investors to approach regarding the downstream applications of your specific opportunities, you should assess the structure of the industries and the extent to which the opportunities can be partitioned.

Partitioning of multifaceted opportunities is usually the result of intellectual property protection and economic barriers. In the example represented in Figure 5-3, the company has developed a portfolio of intellectual property that protects the process for creating the material as well as the devices used to produce the composite. These both fall within the category of upstream applications. The company has also developed downstream, application-specific intellectual property it can license separately.

Figure 5 - 4: Strategic Mind Map for a Rich Technology Platform

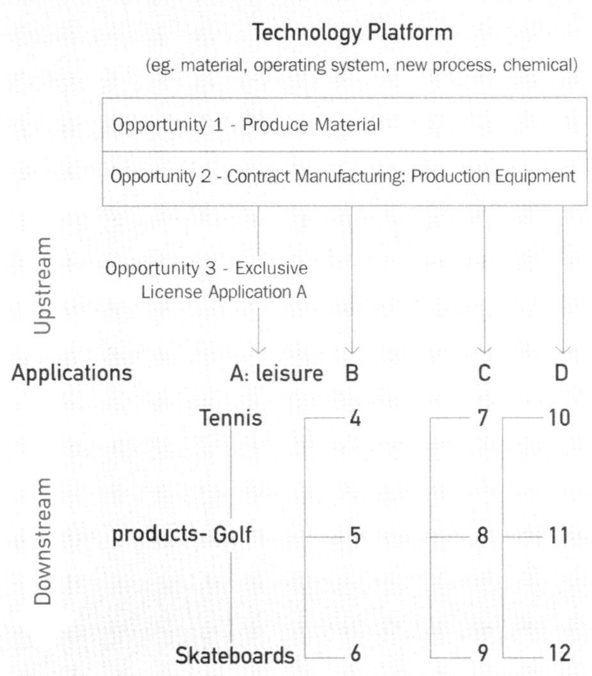

A company interested in application-specific licenses would have to purchase the composite material from the Licensee that holds the exclusive patent on the production of the composite—or, if economically feasible, should consider trying to obtain an application-specific license or sublicense for its own production needs.

Economic Barriers in Technology Partitioning

The economic barriers that can be used in partitioning an opportunity are not actually created by the licensee, but rather are leveraged by him or her. With economic barriers, one is really taking advantage of the downstream infrastructure and the position of the dominant players within it. In other words, the goal is to prevent others from entering that market by making use of the existing infrastructure and relative positions of the key players.

When looking at the dynamics of various industries, one consideration should be to examine each industry relative to the presence of a dominant design . This is essential, according to Teece, since clever market entry strategies will keep innovation imitators at bay. Building on the work of Abernathy , Teece maintains, "In the early stages of development of many industries and product families, designs are fluid, manufacturing processes are loosely and adaptively organized. ... Competition among firms manifests itself in competition among designs."[1] This is evident in products and protocols such as Apple vs. IBM computers, Netscape vs. AOL, VHS vs. beta, and the like.

Prior to the emergence of a dominant design, a company can position its product to become an industry standard and/or should "hang loose" and resist becoming too tied to a design which may ultimately "lose." Teece recommends that if a company has the ability to promote a dominant design, it should do so. However, if it lacks this capability, the firm should wait for the dominant design to emerge. Once a dominant design has emerged, the emphasis shifts to more evolutionary innovations capable of driving down costs. At such times, it is often advantageous for a company (large or small) to team with other players with complementary assets and products. If a company has bet on the wrong horse, it is still possible to participate in the new design regime by forming strategic alliances through technology swaps, joint R&D, co-development, or sharing of complementary assets. Teece clarifies what he means by complementary assets by drawing the distinction between what a customer perceives as a product and simply a device. An item that fully meets a customer's defined need will tend to be viewed as a product. For example, an optical scanner sold with a range of software, cabling, and customer support is likely to be viewed as a product—whereas a scanner sold without software is likely to be viewed as a device. A company which provides only part of a solution to a customer need should look to producers or providers of complimentary products, components, and services as potential strategic allies.

Other industry characteristics that are important to consider when deciding upon the commercialization strategies to be pursued include:

- Cohesiveness of the industry
- Premarket testing, certification, and regulatory requirements
- Product liability issues
- Channels of distribution

When an industry is fragmented, the formation of a strategic alliance is often an advantageous commercialization strategy to pursue. When significant capitalization is required for premarket testing or to address product liability issues, significant investment will be required by a potential licensee, strategic ally, or equity investor. An understanding of the dynamics within the various industries to which a rich technology platform can be applied is important before beginning the process of mapping out the commercialization strategies to be pursued. Finally, the company needs to consider how to structure relationships so that the originating company will maximize its participation in the financial benefits that result from commercialization of the technology.

Maximizing Financial Return

Before determining how to maximize financial return from the commercialization of the technology platform, you must begin by generating a list of possible applications for the technology. Once this has been accomplished and you have examined the structure of each related industry, the company must decide where in this panorama it wishes to "hang its hat"—the place Heuss and Jolly refer to as the center of gravity.[2] It is impossible to determine how best to maximize your return from other relationships before deciding where in this panorama you wish to play. Determining your center of gravity is a function of your interests, your vision, and other considerations which allow you to maintain a degree of control over the evolution of the technology.

The progenitor's relationship to a newly created technology is unique. The inventor brings a heightened desire and commitment to see his or her technology utilized. Therefore, if you have a strong vision for your technology, you should carefully consider how far down the commercialization path you wish to proceed. As the progenitor, you are more likely to pursue a given path longer than others will. (According to Heuss and Jolly, licensees may drop a line of pursuit earlier than a progenitor.) Thus, if there are areas of technological risk which you feel would be difficult for others to navigate or to which they would be less committed, you should consider staying with the technology development course longer, before handing it off to another entity for the final stages of commercialization. The progenitor's commitment is a double-edged sword, however. Although persistence has its value, an inventor also needs to know when to let go. Nevertheless, in all cases, the more technology risk is decreased, the greater the return you can negotiate.To remain attractive to potential partners, the technology entrepreneur should keep his or her technology in the spotlight, even going so far as to develop trademarks to help accrue goodwill. As Heuss and Jolly point out, developing trademarks"offer the potential to prolong market acceptance even after the underlying technology rights expired."

Licensing

Never enter licensing negotiations unprepared!

Chapter 06

When searching for a potential licensee, it is important that what you have to offer fits with the partner's strategic direction; also, that it falls into an area where the potential licensee cannot do better on its own.

Many small firms select licensing as their commercialization strategy of choice, after concluding that they don't wish to act as a manufacturer, marketer, or distributor. Although it is important to recognize and understand your interests, your firm's approach to licensing will be more comprehensive and successful if you view licensing as the conscious choice to provide one or more entities with the right to exploit your technology for mutual gain. When viewed in this fashion, you will become more concerned about the selection of an appropriate licensee, as well as the best method of structuring a mutually beneficial relationship. The word "selection" is not meant to imply that potential licensees line up to court a technology entrepreneur. In fact, the reverse is often true. Nonetheless, the word "selection" appropriately conveys the care and considerations that you should make in looking for potential licensee(s). Remember: licensing doesn't just happen. It requires considerable planning and resources.

Why Companies License-In

Licensing-in is a unique form of sales in which the inventor/technology entrepreneur provides the potential licensee with a compelling reason to license his or her technology. To effectively make your case, it is important to understand why a potential licensee would be interested in licensing-in. Companies are interested in increasing their assets. Intellectual property (patents, copyright, trademark, trade secret, know-how) are considered assets—but intangible and risky ones with poor, if any, liquidity. The dilemma, however, is that such assets are essential for future corporate growth.[1] Larger firms invest as much as 10% of sales on R&D. "The cost of original research is high and therefore requires maximum market penetration to pay for it." [2] If a company can decrease the costs associated with strategic R&D and at the same time minimize risk, licensing-in becomes an appealing option.

Licensing-in describes the process of obtaining rights to use the intellectual property of others, external to a company.

Strategic Fit

Technology will be licensed-in or acquired by a firm if it meets a strategic interest that the company is not capable of addressing on its own. In all cases, if a potential licensee can do the development work better itself, it has no desire to look outside. Pioneer technologies present a novel opportunity, however. In such cases, there is an increasing trend toward financing options that share risk. According to Teece[3], these include the following:

- R&D joint venture with Option to License
- R&D joint venture with Option to Purchase
- Strategic alliances

When licensing is the option of choice, the intellectual property being considered must offer the licensee one or more of the following advantages. The intellectual property should (1) present a new business opportunity to the licensee which builds on its core competencies; (2) provide better access to markets that the licensee wishes to penetrate; (3) offer additional products to sell through existing distribution channels; (4) preclude other organizations from having access to the technology; and/or (5) decrease production costs. When presenting your opportunity to a potential licensee, you must therefore make your case in consideration of the potential licensee's strategic intent. You must examine the licensee's priorities and demonstrate how your technology would meet the licensee's strategic goals. Such information about publicly traded companies is readily available.

Outsourcing R&D

A company actively looking to license-in technology has many choices. Representatives of a firm can look for technology from universities, other manufacturers, and agents. They can find out about opportunities through an examination of patent and scientific literature, attendance at trade shows, and/or participation in meetings of the Licensing Executive Society. It is important that technology entrepreneurs recognize that large firms dedicate limited resources to such search activity; that their searches are strategic in nature; and that there are many sources to which they can turn. The bottom line is that in order to make your case, you need to be well prepared.

From the licensee's perspective, the Technology Acquisition Process[4] features a number of steps, including:

» Identification of need
» Technology sourcing
» Technology assessment
» License negotiation
» Financing
» Transfer of technology
» Implementation
» Termination of license

Synergy with Strengths

From the preceding list, three general categories of concerns are recommended for the licensee to consider relative to technology assessment: technology concerns, market concerns, and overall concerns. The licensee should assess the new product or processes and its relationship to the licensee's technology strength. The firm must also assess issues pertaining to potential implementation, including the numbers and types of employees involved, the feasibility and costs associated with manufacturing, and how much additional funding is still required. On the market side, the company must assess potential sales, profits, use of marketing, sales and distribution channels, and competitive advantage. Overall, the fit with the company's strategic direction and risks must be examined. Because the Technology Acquisition Team has to sell its management on the merits of the technology of interest, it is important that a potential licensor make it as easy as possible for the potential licensee to buy, by addressing its needs. Also, to assure that a win-win situation is achieved, it is important that you have a means of assessing the value of what you are presenting—and that you understand the various aspects of licensing negotiation to which you will be exposed.

The balance of this chapter assumes that you have already determined that licensing is one of the best ways to exploit the market potential of your technology. As such, it is assumed that your objective in reading this chapter is to understand more about what is involved and how to prepare for successfully locating a licensee.

What is a License?

Formally speaking, a license is "permission granted by an owner or inventor, generally for a consideration, to a person, firm, or corporation to use the owner's proprietary information, invention or material."[5] All forms of intellectual property can be licensed, including patent, copyright, trademark, trade secret, and know-how. The nature of the "use" granted in the license varies and can include manufacture, use, lease, sale, distribution, or any combination thereof. When the owner of intellectual property grants a license to another entity, it retains ownership or title to the intellectual property. An initial word of caution: the definitions of all terms used in a licensing agreement need to be carefully considered— especially those associated with the licensed property, the licensor, and the licensee.

Definition of Licensed Property

The licensed property should be defined with great specificity. Registered items (trademarks, copyrights, and patents) should include the registration number.[6] There are a number of situations where exceptional care should be taken in drafting the definitions. Biotech is a most noticeable example. Fordis and Griffen note that difficulties arise because: (1) many biotech products are not the subject of issued or pending patents; and (2) there are a number of ways to define the biotech products. Special care should also be taken in licensing computer software: it should be made explicit as to whether or not the license applies to both the object and source code. A single license may be drafted to cover one or multiple products/technologies and various forms of intellectual property. "The more restrictive the definition of licensed products, the smaller the potential royalty base."[7] You should expect there to be a natural tension in licensing negotiations, as each party is motivated to obtain what is best for the organization it represents.

Licensor Title

The licensor must have clear title to the rights it is conveying. This may seem straightforward and self-evident. However, when dealing with biological materials, especially those derived from humans, the issue of ownership is complex and often disputed.[8] Sometimes, to avoid any infringement issues, a potential licensee may conduct a right-to-use study in order to assure clear title.[9]

Ownership issues are not always straightforward.

Of equal importance is the consideration given to the definition "licensee." The licensor must be certain that he or she understands whether or not the term licensee is extended to subsidiaries, related companies, and affiliates, or strictly to the entity named. When specifying whether the license is exclusive or non-exclusive, the licensor should carefully attend to the implications that this statement has for his or her own work. Most licensors don't intentionally wish to exclude themselves from being able to make use of the intellectual property. However, this could inadvertently be the result of carelessness when granting an exclusive license. The rights of the licensor should be clearly stated in an exclusive license. Often a licensor may grant an exclusive license, but one that reverts to non-exclusive status if certain conditions are not met.

Territory

Territory deals with the specific geographic area to which the license applies. It should be noted that a license could vary from narrow use—one that is restricted to one site or plant at a specific location—to one that is global in scope. Within a licensing agreement, many other issues are important to address. These include Indemnification, Arbitration, Best Efforts, Technical Information, Assignability, Sublicensing, Rights & Remedies, Termination, Approvals, Changes, Technical Assistance, and Improvements, among others. Such issues require careful attention by both parties.[10] Always be sure that you understand the full implication of everything in the agreement and seek appropriate counsel.

ISSUES:

Indemnification	Arbitration
Best efforts	Technical Information
Assignability	Sublicensing
Rights and Remedies	Termination
Approvals	Technical Assistance
Improvements	

How does one make money from licensing?

The most common form of remuneration is a royalty. Royalties may take many different forms, including running base, lump sum, or prepayment-of-running royalties. Royalties can be calculated at a constant rate, change over time, and/or specify mandatory minimum and/or maximum payments. Other sources of revenue can be built into a license including consulting, and upfront development fees (usually booked against future royalties.)

Unless substantial benefits (profits) can be made, there is no point in making a deal.

Size of the Opportunity

The manner in which the royalty rate is derived depends upon many factors, including industry standards, the degree of development, the magnitude of the licensed property, and market potential.[11] Many technology entrepreneurs approach licensing with the mistaken belief that they don't need to understand the market, assuming that that's the licensee's job. As a result, the importance of "sizing the profitability pie" must be stressed.[12] With the exception of the progenitor of the technology, you should expect that everyone else who becomes involved with the technology is interested in its potential to generate wealth. According to Epstein and Politano, "Unless substantial benefits (profits) can be made, there is no point in making a deal." Estimating the size of the pie is a way of determining whether the deal is worth pursuing. Epstein and Politano name six items that should be considered when sizing an opportunity. These include: market size, stage of market development, special status of technology in question (e.g., a pioneer patent), economic health, benefits from association with licensor, and synergy with licensee's marketing, sales, and distribution strengths. Prior to making his initial approach to the licensee, the licensor should have addressed these issues and should be prepared to make the case that there is an opportunity that can be exploited for mutual benefit. Don't expect the potential licensee to do this for you. In order to structure a "win-win" deal, both parties need to be prepared.

Another element of preparation is understanding the relative contributions both parties will make. There is often the tendency for technology entrepreneurs to overestimate their technology's contribution. This assumption often reflects a lack of understanding of what the licensee must add to the mix in order to commercialize the technology. Factors that strengthen the licensor's bargaining position include the following:

- A positive track record as an experienced and valued licensor
- R&D-generating capability (a good facility with a rigorous R&D program)
- Items that contribute to goodwill, such as trademarks
- Related patents, trade secrets, and know-how
- A reputation for enforcing patents against infringers

The licensee's bargaining position is augmented by the amount of risk it assumes, as well as its established manufacturing, marketing, and distribution capabilities.

Consulting

Another way for the licensor to accrue more value from the licensing relationship is to limit the technical, sales, and service support provided as part of the licensing agreement,[13] and to instead offer these services—when provided above a certain level—as consulting services, through an annual retainer or per diem.[14] If the licensor has marketing strengths, it could also seek to retain marketing rights on excess production of the licensee in areas that it does not serve.

Royalty Rates

It is debatable as to what is the best approach to calculating royalties. The base to which royalty rates are applied can include: (1) net or gross profit; (2) net or gross sales price; (3) the gross production of the licensee. The method of calculating the royalty rates also varies. Regardless of its shortcomings, one of the most commonly used methods is comparison with industry standards. It is important to recognize that these standards vary widely. Table 6-1 provides a summary of a number of different types of standards:

Table 6-1: Sample Industry Standards in Selective Fields

Chemicals: (Epstein and Politano, 1995)
1-3% of net sales for low margin items

Computers: (Epstein and Politano, 1995)
3-5% of net sales

Pharmaceuticals: (Fordis and Griffen, 1991)
Research reagents (expression vector, cell culture) 1-5% of net sales

Diagnostic products (monoclonal antibodies, DNA probes) 5-8% of net sales

Theraputic Products: (monoclonal antibodies, expressed proteins)
5-10% of net sales
Vaccines (5-10% of sales)
Animal health products (3-6% of net sales)
Plant/agricultural products (3-5% of net sales)

Semiconductors: (Epstein and Politano, 1995)
1.75-3% of net sales

Types of Licenses

There are many types of licenses. They reflect differences in both the "use" and the "type" of licensed material. A sampler of licensing agreements—product, hybrid, multimedia, and software—follows, with brief definitions of each.

Product License

A product license is appropriate in the prototypical situation in which a licensor grants to the licensee the right to make, use, or sell a defined "Product." In such an agreement, items typically specified are the application of the product, any territorial restrictions, the time frame, and whether or not the license is exclusive or nonexclusive. Villeneuve et al.[15] point out a number of areas of caution in negotiating such licenses. These include: (1) the royalty base; (2) the inclusion of technology, rather than only products; (3) the importance of marketing obligations of the licensee in exclusive licensing arrangements; (4) sub-licensing; and (5) grant-backs.

As indicated earlier, the base to which royalties are applied may vary. It is therefore very important that you are clear regarding the definition of the base, and that you also probe to assure that the base fits all intended applications by the licensee. For example, assume that you have negotiated a royalty based on the sale of the licensed product. This does not entitle you (unless specified) to benefit from revenue made by the licensee in providing a service in which he utilizes the licensed product. This is because the royalty base was defined in terms of sales of the product and did not specify revenue generated from services in which the product was used.

A licensee tries to obtain as much value for its organization as it can from an agreement. Therefore, it is common for the licensee to push to expand the domain of licensed property. The licensor must carefully consider the implications of what is being asked for. Assume, for example, that the licensee wishes to add to the product license and gain access to know-how, trade secrets, and patents owned or controlled by the licensor presently and in the future. The implications are profound. First, with respect to your future technology developments, you would be providing these to the licensee in this one agreement and would thereby limit your future business options. Second, such statements have implications for any licensed-in technology you have. By virtue of having "control" over patents you are licensing from others, you may be obligated to sub-license these as well.[16]

The third area of negotiation requiring caution is with respect to exclusive licenses. The licensor will not benefit from an exclusive license if the licensee does not make significant marketing and sales. Therefore, the licensor should carefully attend to the licensee's marketing obligations—going so far as to specify the nature of the actions to be taken by the licensee. This is better than settling for the "best efforts" obligation. Another way to assure that the licensee makes significant efforts is to require a significant upfront payment as well as minimum royalty payments. The licensee will only recoup these expenses if it makes sales. When there is a financial penalty for failure to attend to marketing and sales obligations, it is less likely that marketing and sales will be given short shrift.

Another item meriting careful consideration is sublicensing. Sublicensing refers to granting to a licensee the right to license to a third party. This provides the licensee with the right to have things made, used, or distributed by others. However, this may not be beneficial to a licensor. A license can therefore indicate that no sublicensing is permitted without prior written approval of licensor, or that the licensee may sublicense subject to meeting specific conditions.[17]

The final situation to be considered is the area of improvements and grantbacks. When you are dealing with dynamic forms of intellectual property (e.g., trade secrets and know-how), it is reasonable to assume that this body of knowledge will grow. The question becomes who receives the benefits of this growth. If the licensee is given the rights to use the technology, it is very likely that the licensee will discover new knowledge. It is, therefore, common for a licensor to seek a "grantback" of any improvements in the initial field of use. The terms and conditions associated with this are subject to negotiation.[18]

Hybrid Licensing Agreement

A hybrid licensing agreement is one which includes "a license for an issued or pending patent, together with some other form of intellectual property rights that is not coextensive with the patent[19]." Such licenses present a new issue: what do you do if a pending patent that was part of an agreement does not issue? In such a situation, it is suggested that the royalty rate be decreased.

Multimedia Licenses

Multimedia licenses are complex because of the variety and sheer number of intellectual property items included. Multimedia products typically include text, movie images, still images, music, audio, and computer software—all of which are subject to copyright and other forms of protection. Epstein and Politano point out that a multimedia developer may need to negotiate over a hundred separate agreements in order to obtain all of the rights needed for one multimedia product. The other factor that makes multimedia licenses difficult to negotiate is that many content developers ask unreasonable and prohibitive fees, making such projects untenable. (See Smedinghoff [20] for a detailed treatment of the legal issues involved with licensing multimedia products.)

Software License

Given the dynamic nature of the software industry, software licenses present many special considerations. These include: (1) rights to updates and new releases of the software; (2) testing and development support; (3) whether or not source code is included; and (4) royalty payments. If, for example, a software developer is trying to promote a new industry standard, it is not uncommon for it to provide a non-exclusive license [21] and accept a flat fee, rather than an ongoing royalty. (See Villeneuve et al. for a more detailed discussion of this topic.) Most mass-market software is distributed with shrink-wrap licenses. These licenses indicate that, by virtue of opening a certain package, users accept the terms of the licensing agreement. This is done because it is not feasible to obtain a signed license agreement from every user.[22] Another type of license referred to as a run-time license is used with "authoring tools." These are used in the development of multimedia products, and are required for use of the final multimedia product.

Preparation for Licensing

The intricacies of licensing are important to understand if you don't want to walk into negotiations blindly. Any company interested in licensing-in has developed a method for examining opportunities which may meet its strategic needs, as well as a method for assessing its opportunity potential.[23] You should do no less, especially if licensing is going to be the primary commercialization strategy used by your firm. Specifically, you should pursue the following steps:

» Identify a potential licensee
» Assess the ability of the licensing opportunity to generate value
» Put together your negotiation team
» Estimate the costs of the effort
» Make your case
» Negotiate a license
» Determine financing
» Implement the license
» Terminate the license

Don't walk into negotiations unprepared!

Identifying a Potential Licensee

When searching for a potential licensee, it is important that what you have to offer fits with the partner's strategic direction; also, that it falls into an area where the potential licensee cannot do it better on its own. Furthermore, the potential licensee must have financial resources available, have a good sales and distribution network, and not an excessive dose of the Not Invented Here syndrome. These are the same factors Manfroy et al. suggest the licensee consider about its organization before starting down a path. In this "lock and key" situation, each of you has part of the solution and each is looking for an entity to fill the complementary role. The Workbook in this Guide addresses in great detail the methods and resources for collecting information on potential licensees. You have limited time and resources available for your endeavor, and you need to expend your resources on appropriate prospects. Identification of Potential Licensees is the first element of the Licensing Package™.

Assessing the Ability to Generate Value

The inventor of a technology wants to see it utilized, and often perceives licensing out as a means of doing this and completing a cycle. However, if the inventor intends to become involved with licensing as a strategy of choice that he will use frequently, he must attempt to develop some objectivity concerning the technology. Does this opportunity have the potential to create significant value? Not all inventions do, and those which don't are often not good candidates for licensing. Methods for assessing the size of the opportunity are presented in the Workbook. If an opportunity exists, we recommend putting together a Business Opportunity Preview™ to share in total or in part with a potential licensee, once appropriate Non-Disclosure Agreements have been signed. A Business Opportunity Preview is the second element of the Licensing Package™.

Putting Your Team Together

You need a negotiation team that you can draw upon at the appropriate times. You will most likely need the services of an attorney, a negotiator, and someone who can assist with valuation—and you should anticipate the costs associated with their efforts.

Estimating Costs and Pay-Back

As was mentioned at the outset, licensing is a unique form of sales. As such, it has associated expenses. It is recommended that you develop a marketing and sales plan specifically for licensing the technology in question, to assure that you anticipate both the time and the expenses associated with the effort. Out-of-pocket expenses will include travel to the potential licensee's site, the development of presentation materials, and the costs associated with putting together your licensing team. In addition, you should factor in the time that you will need to devote to this endeavor.

When in the midst of negotiations, carefully consider the implications of all the items that have a price tag associated with them. Such items include indemnification, maintenance of patents and responsibilities relative to infringers, technical assistance, and travel. Carefully consider how to create the best revenue stream for your company and a win-win situation for both you and the licensee.

Making Your Case

Once you have selected the appropriate domain of potential licensees and developed the materials to be used in making your case, you should determine the best approach to a potential licensee. Common choices include introductions by a colleague or consultant, participation in national events that focus on licensing and/or professional meetings and trade shows, and submission of unsolicited inquiries. Although some people recommend making inquiries sequentially, it is often best to start interacting with a number of relevant prospects simultaneously. This goal is not to play one potential licensee off of the other, but simply to make the most of what is usually a limited market window of opportunity. Once a potential licensee shows interest—and perhaps requests a "stand-still" agreement—then you can focus your efforts on that one party. The importance of making a compelling case to potential licensees cannot be underestimated. You don't have to divulge a lot of information about what you have, but in your initial approach you should demonstrate an understanding of their strategies, their needs, and the manner in which what you have can further their aims.

This is important, because most large companies erect a large initial hurdle to potential licensees. They routinely request that interested parties sign a disclosure document indicating that everything that is shared with them they are free to use. Some companies will only interact with outside sources after a patent has been issued for the invention in question. The reason for this behavior is that the first priority of any large company is to protect its assets. Large firms with a strong emphasis on R&D have hundreds of research projects on-going at any given point in time. No single point of contact could possibly have the knowledge of the breadth and diversity of projects in-house. For this reason, when first contacted, any large firm will routinely provide an inventor with a disclosure document indicating that whatever the inventor shares with the company, the firm is free to use. This is done to protect the company from possible lawsuits that could arise if someone submits an idea to the company which is rejected, and on which the company is already working. The inventor could incorrectly conclude that his or her idea was stolen because of the timing of the product release subsequent to his or her inquiry. For large firms, safety comes from adopting a set of procedures and protocols that minimize the likelihood that these types of situations will arise. That is why you have to work hard to create initial interest.

You need to decide at the outset what information you will disclose readily and what information you need to hold back until the potential licensee has signed a confidentiality agreement.

License Negotiation

Much was said earlier in the chapter about issues to be addressed during negotiations. Before getting to that point, however, the company will conduct due diligence on the technology and the market. During this period it is important that you provide the potential licensee with information that they can use to sell up-line. It is vital to the success of the project that many champions are formed along the way. A well-developed Business Opportunity Preview can serve that need. The following account from an executive experienced with high-tech licensing matters highlights many aspects of the attitude you want to bring to the table during licensing negotiations.

Attitude is Everything

In the following excerpt from an interview with Mike Weiner, Chairman and Founder of Manning and Napier Information Services—and previously the Founder and CEO of Microlytics, a Xerox spin-off—it becomes clear that success depends more on your attitude and attention to detail than on what you think you can do than on what you are told the rules are. There are always exceptions to the rule!

I began to use personal computers at Xerox, and then moved into the software marketing business. I found that the company wasn't taking advantage of its software assets, and I wanted the opportunity to take some of its assets outside. I kept looking for people in the company who were supportive of my idea and ignoring those who were opposed. Most were opposed.

Unlike the employees who left to form companies such as Adobe, 3COM, and others, I was able to form a unique relationship with Xerox where Microlytics would have an arms-length relationship with Xerox and license software that was under utilized and not of strategic interest. I have a no-fee consulting arrangement with the company that allows me access while assuring confidentiality. Having an outlet such as Microlytics is useful to a large firm. Technology assets are like milk. If you don't do something with them on a timely basis, they spoil.

We have had several licensing arrangements with Xerox. Our initial license provided Microlytics with broad sub-licensing rights that were pivotal to our early success. We went from $3 to $14 million in three years. During the past 10 years, we have dealt with the same corporate staff and the same R&D staff and maintained excellent relationships. In looking at what makes licensing successful, there are many factors. On many occasions employees who leave a large company become very arrogant in their dealings with the firm. That is counter-productive. Xerox is like family, and there is a tremendous amount of informal networking that takes place.

What we tend to do in our negotiations is to be sure that we understand the issues of concern to the company with whom we are negotiating and address those issues. During licensing negotiations with any firm, if you agree to something in your verbal conversations, it is your obligation to address any omissions that you see in the written document—omissions which not only favor you, but also omissions which favor your negotiating partner. There must be reciprocity. You must be straight. Issues regarding "know-how" are addressed up front. We also negotiate "flowback" rights and specify which divisions get the rights in "licensing-back" arrangements. Many times what we will do is select a company which we think will be the best possible partner and offer the company a "no-cost, stand-still agreement" (30-60 days). This allows the internal champion the time and incentive to try and gain a corporate commitment. However, this offer has to be genuine on your part, and not a ploy. In negotiations, it helps to be high-minded. Be consistent and over time many of your partners will become that way also. However, it is imperative to review carefully any licensing agreement that you sign. You can never have too many eyes looking at a document.

We have also walked away from deals because we have assessed the guys we are dealing with to be disreputable. I would recommend to anyone entering a licensing arrangement that he should start by thinking about and defining the nature of the relationship that he wishes with a licensee. Begin to act as if you have that type of relationship—model it in your actions. Then articulate to the potential licensee what relationship you want. Attitude, more than anything else, determines outcome. Also, above all, for an inventor or an entrepreneur, consistency, credibility, and integrity are your greatest assets. Don't forget what you have agreed to.

When licensing arrangements go bad, it is usually because the licensee finds or develops an alternative technology, and then devalues yours; or management changes and doesn't know about the relationship—or devalues it. Or it's due to buyer's remorse or greed and avarice. However, you should keep in mind that it is hard to unseat the status quo and, if you are, work hard to maintain those relationships and your position.

Scientists and engineers want to see their ideas and inventions validated and come to fruition. Corporations which don't provide this run the risk of frustrating their best and brightest. Yet most companies cannot hope to market all the productive output of a bright and creative workforce. This is where an employee intrapreneurship and a licensing-out policy can pay substantial dividends, including reduction of employee turnover.

Implementation

During the implementation of a license, you should continue to monitor the extent to which the terms of the agreement are being met. As the summaries below reveal, failure to raise issues early can lead to unforeseen difficulties.

Relevant legal cases

Introduction

In this section, we present a sample case in which contractual licensing arrangements deteriorated and resulted in litigation. In this case, intellectual property protection was granted at the Federal level.

CASE 1: Coleman v. Corning Glass Works

(U.S. District Court, Western District of New York, 1985)

Dr. Coleman, the owner of a U.S. patent, entered into a licensing agreement with Corning Glass Works, granting Corning an exclusive license for the commercial development of a commercial integrated blood serum separator under his patent. Corning terminated the agreement three years later, alleging that a commercial, functioning blood separation machine could not be made in accordance with Dr. Coleman's patent. Allegedly, independent research by Corning had also resulted in the development of a superior approach to designing a serum machine.

Corning continued development of its serum machine, the "Corvac Serum Machine," and began production in 1975. Corning then sold the entire product line to Sherwood Medical Industries three years later. Dr. Coleman alleges that the blood separation device manufactured and sold by Corning (the Corvac Serum Machine) was within the scope of his original patent. Corning moved for summary judgment on the grounds that the plaintiff was too late in bringing this suit (16 years after the initial licensing agreement was signed).

The court agreed with Corning, and Dr. Coleman lost the suit on the grounds that he was too late bringing suit.

Some Lessons to be Learned by Independent Inventors

- *Plan for what each party can or cannot do with shared information if a signed agreement is terminated.*
- *Act sooner, rather than later.*
- *Be sure of which statutes of limitations may be applicable.*

Some Lessons to be Learned by Corporations

- *Good documentation is required of independent creation.*
- *Act in good faith and try to structure "win-win" situations.*

Elements of a Licensing Package™

A Licensing Package is a means of compiling pertinent information that you will need during the licensing process. It should contain the following three components:

(1) Business Opportunity Preview™
(2) Analysis of Potential Licensees
(3) Negotiation Issues

Activities designed to surface the information needed to develop each section of this package can be found in the Workbook in this Guide. Each of these elements will be used in a different way. The Business Opportunity Preview™ is the document used to make your business case. It clarifies the nature of the opportunity at hand. The Executive Summary should not contain any proprietary information, and should be used in your initial interaction with a potential licensee when your discussions are not covered by a Confidentiality Agreement. The balance of the document can be used in part or in its entirety, once you have clearly established the interest of the potential licensee. Much of the information should only be shared with a potential licensee once a Confidentiality Agreement has been signed. However, you may find it necessary to share elements of this document with a potential licensee prior to signing a Confidentiality Agreement, in order to enable him or her to sell up-line. Information that demonstrates that you understand customer specifications and that demonstrates customer receptivity to the product is often appropriate to share. A suggested outline for a Business Opportunity Preview™ follows.

Part 1
Business Opportunity Preview™

1.0 Executive summary

1.1 Description of industry
» *Overview*
» *Industry drivers & issues*
» *Opportunity & threats*
1.2 Technology available for Licensing
» *Brief description*
1.3 Licensing arrangement
» *Types of partners sought*
» *Types of arrangements*
1.4 Brief Company Introduction

2.0 Company & technology
2.1 Brief company introduction
» *Mission*
» *Location, size, history*
» *Overview of company capabilities*
» *Management Team*
2.2 Technology/product description
» *Detailed description*
» *Present state of development*
» *Intellectual property*
2.3 Related technology (only if appropriate)

3.0 Customers
3.1 How need is currently filled
3.2. Important product specs and features
3.3. Degree of customer interest
3.4. Decision-makers and influencers
3.5. Basis for purchase decision
» *Frequency*
» *Timing of purchase decision*

4.0 Market
4.1 Market definition
» *Market segmentation*
Across applications (if appropriate)
Within applications
4.2 Market Size
» *Served available market*
» *Rate of market growth*

5.0 Competitors
5.1 Indirect & Direct competitors
5.2 Competitive advantages
» *Features, Advantages, Benefits*

Part 2
Assessment of Potential Licensees

The second element of the Licensing Package is referred to as the Assessment of Potential Licensees. This document is for your internal use only, and is intended to prompt the capture of all relevant intelligence needed in determining the domain of potential licensees to approach. You should plan on selectively using information from this document in your discussions with potential licensees, or use an Executive Summary to reflect your understanding of the potential licensee's direction. Consult the Workbook for guidance on how to gather appropriate information. The key thing to remember in completing these activities is that you are not looking for static information about the company, but are gathering information that will confirm to the licensee the importance and relevance of what you have to offer. You are looking to confirm synergies and availability of funds.

A suggested outline for this document follows:

Assessment of Potential Licensees

(A) Domain of potential licensees
» *Candidate 1*
» *Candidate 2*
» *Etc.*

(B) Candidate 1
1. Core competencies (R&D, manufacturing, marketing, sales, distribution)
2. Strategic Direction
3. New business trends: Outsourcing R&D, Acquisitions & Mergers, Divestitures
4. Issues facing the potential licensee
5. Strategic advantages of your technology to the licensee

(C) Candidate 2
1. Core competencies (R&D, manufacturing, marketing, sales, distribution)
2. Strategic Direction
3. New business trends: Outsourcing R&D, Acquisitions & Mergers, Divestitures
4. Issues facing the potential licensee
5. Strategic advantages of your technology to the licensee

Part 3
Negotiation Issues
This third element of the Licensing Package is also a proprietary document and is directly related to your Strategic Plan. After reviewing your Strategic Plan, complete the following.

(1) Relevant Intellectual Property
1.1. Patents (issued and pending)
1.2. Trade-secrets
1.3. Copyrights
1.4. Trade secrets
1.5. Know-How
1.6 Licenses you hold from others

(2) Partitioning of the Opportunity
2.1 Upstream/downstream
2.2 Industry
2.3 Geographic location

(3) Rights You Wish to Retain
» *Itemize applications*

(4) Consulting and/or Development Role
» *As part of license*
» *In addition to license*(5) Grant-backs & Improvements

(6) What You Are Willing to Provide
» *Itemize*

(7) What Licensee Would Need to Provide
» *Degree of technology risk*
» *Royalty*
» *Other fees*

(8) Financial Projections
» Income to licensee
» Income to licensor

Conclusion
Licensing is one of a variety of strategies that can be used to successfully commercialize a technology. Success in this arena requires that the potential licensor becomes skilled in locating the best potential licensee, developing a compelling case, and nurturing the relationship through the stages of due diligence, negotiation, and implementation. A company that is serious about licensing should develop a Licensing Package as a means of pulling together all pertinent information that will be needed during the licensing process.

Chapter 6 Endnotes

[1] Parr, Russell L. Insights Into Royalty Rate Economics. Les Nouvelles, Vol 25. No 2.

[2] Andonian, Joseph. Environment Changing in Pharmaceuticals. Les Nouvelles, Vol 24, No 2.

[3] Teece, David. Capturing value from Innovation . Les Nouvelles. Vol 26, No 1.

[4] Manfroy, Willy, Patterson, William and Staackmann, Joachim. Technology Acquisition Process. Les Nouvelles. Vol 24 No 4.

[5] Goldscheider, Robret. Companion to Licensing Negotiations: Licensing Law Handbook 1993-94. Deerfield, Il: Clark, Boardman, Callaghan, 1993.

[6] Epstein, Michael A and Politano, Frank L. Drafting Licensing Agreements.Englewood Cliffs, NJ: Aspen Publishers, 1995.

[7] Greeley, Paul D. Effective License Negotiating Techniques. Les Nouvelles. Vol 25 No 1.

[8] Fordis, Jean Burke and Griffen, Susan Heberman. Avioding Traps in Licensing Biotechnology. Les Nouvelles. Vol.26, No 2.

[9] Greeley, Paul D. Effective License Negotiating Techniques. Les Nouvelles. Vol 25 No 1.

[10] Goldscheider, Robret. Companion to Licensing Negotiations: Licensing Law Handbook 1993-94. Deerfield, Il: Clark, Boardman, Callaghan, 1993.

[11] Parr, Russell L. Insights Into Royalty Rate Economics. Les Nouvelles, Vol 25.No 2.

[12] Epstein, Michael A and Politano, Frank L. Drafting Licensing Agreements. Englewood Cliffs, NJ: Aspen Publishers, 1995.

[13] Greeley, Paul D. Effective License Negotiating Techniques. Les Nouvelles. Vol 25 No 1.

[14] Epstein, Michael A and Politano, Frank L. Drafting Licensing Agreements. Englewood Cliffs, NJ: Aspen Publishers, 1995.

[15] Villeneuve, Thomas F, Gunderson Jr., Robert V., and Kaufman, Daniel M. Corporate Partnering: Structuring and Negotiating Domestic and International Strategic Alliances. Aspen Law & Business, 1995.

[16] Villeneuve, Thomas F, Gunderson Jr., Robert V., and Kaufman, Daniel M. Corporate Partnering: Structuring and Ne gotiating Domestic and International Strategic Alliances. Aspen Law & Business, 1995.

[17] Goldscheider, Robret. Companion to Licensing Negotiations: Licensing Law Handbook 1993-94. Deerfield, Il: Clark, Boardman, Callaghan, 1993.

[18] Goldscheider, Robret. Companion to Licensing Negotiations: Licensing Law Handbook 1993-94. Deerfield, Il: Clark, Boardman, Callaghan, 1993.

[19] Goldscheider, Robret. Companion to Licensing Negotiations: Licensing Law Handbook 1993-94. Deerfield, Il: Clark, Boardman, Callaghan, 1993.

[20] Smedinghoff, Thomas J. Multimedia Legal Handbook: A Guide from the Software Publishers Association. New York, NY: Aspen Law and Business, 1998.

[21] Villeneuve, Thomas F, Gunderson Jr., Robert V., and Kaufman, Daniel M. Corporate Partnering: Structuring and Ne gotiating Domestic and International Strategic Alliances. Aspen Law & Business, 1995.

[22] Epstein, Michael A and Politano, Frank L. Drafting Licensing Agreements. Englewood Cliffs, NJ: Aspen Publishers, 1995.

[23] Manfroy, Willy, Patterson, William and Staackmann, Joachim. Technology Acquisition Process . Les Nouvelles. Vol 24 No 4.

Section 2 | Workbook

The Dawnbreaker® Business Planning Process

"If you don't know where you are going, you will probably end up somewhere else."

- Laurence J. Peter

Chapter 07

Plans are nothing. Planning is everything. Dwight D. Eisenhower

Introduction

The purpose of the first section of this book was to provide the reader with a perspective on business planning and to clarify why it is useful to have a book specifically designed for scientists and engineers. If you have just opened this book to Section II, we encourage you to go back and read Section I to learn about commercialization strategies, alternative methods of financing, commercialization teams, and the unique focus of this book. The second section is intended for use by entrepreneurs who are either developing a business plan for the first time or who wish to improve an existing plan.

Dawnbreaker® Business Planning Approach

» Emphasis on Research
» Team approach led by founder or management team
» Profound Simplicity

What makes this approach unique? Most books on business planning emphasize the format of a business plan. In other words, the emphasis is on the stylized format for representing a business opportunity. However, such books give little attention to the process of business planning. What makes our approach unique is the emphasis on planning – on the process of conducting the business research prior to writing the business plan. We utilize a metaphor familiar to scientists and best described as theory construction. Hypotheses are generated and then tested in a systematic fashion. Through this research process predications are made about the probability of outcomes resulting from the implementation of various strategies.

Another unique feature of the Dawnbreaker process is the emphasis on team involvement. By being intimately involved with the business planning process, you and your team will learn new market analysis skills, will learn more about your customers, competitors, and potential strategic allies, and will be in a far better position to negotiate financial arrangements of benefit to your company. Just as a technology/product is dynamic and evolves, so will you and your team, if you assume the responsibility for your firm's business planning. If you by contrast, you turn this whole process over to a consultant, you in essence are paying for them to learn about your business. This statement is not meant to imply that you shouldn't involve others in the planning process. You must involve others in order to leverage your time, to prevent group think, and to learn new skills. However, the entrepreneur must drive the process and be involved with key aspects of business planning.

Once the business research process has been completed, your task then becomes to package the business opportunity in ways that reflect profound simplicity. You will first draft a business plan paying tremendous attention to detail, but little attention to page limits. This will be your first draft and, like drafts of other technical papers that you write, it will need revision. Paying attention to details first assures that all aspects of your business plan will have substantiation. Next, you will refine the document and produce a 3-35 page business plan that clearly builds a case for investment – investment by you or others. Not all opportunities are equally as appealing and you should examine them as objectively as possible. Next, you will revise the Executive Summary so that it is a 2-3 page stand-alone document which presents the highlights of your opportunity in a brief, no-proprietary firm. Finally, you will put together a series of 25-30 view graphs, with no more than 25 words on each, that can be used in making presentations to potential allies, licensees, and investors.

So why use the phrase profound simplicity? The first presentations that you make to potential investors will utilize the briefest materials developed – a slide presentation or an Executive Summary. Using these tools you will have only a few moments to express the opportunity simply and to engage their interest. However, once interested they will want details. This is the type of information represented by your business plan and mastered by you in the process of business planning. The phrase profound simplicity then reflects the fact that there is much depth behind your simple presentation. Anyone can make a good presentation, but not one that can readily be supported by increasing levels of depth. We have seen numerous entrepreneurs lose the interest of potential investors whose attention they first engaged with flashy presentation, but which they couldn't maintain, due to lack of diligence and depth in planning.

The documents that you will produce in this process include a:

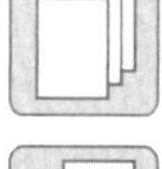
First draft of a business plan (no page limit)

Revised business plan (30 – 35 pages)

Stand-Alone Executive Summary (2-3 pages)

Slide presentation (Set of 25-30)

Getting Started

This business planning process is designed to be completed within a 16-20 week period, concurrent with your other responsibilities. You should plan on the process requiring approximately 200 person hours from the team. Your first task will be to determine how to leverage your time to accomplish the various tasks involved with business planning. To help you determine how to best leverage your time, the skills involved with the various stages of business planning are highlighted, with ideas presented as to where you can turn for assistance.

In looking at Table 7-1, you will notice that your active involvement is required with all tasks to varying degrees. We are frequently asked how much time is required to complete each task. That is hard to estimate because it depends on the efficiencies of the people involved. However, we have attempted to indicate relative times in the 3rd column. It is recommended that you rely heavily on others during the following stages:

» Data gathering
» Number crunching
» Editing

These three tasks take approximately 40% of the estimated time. If you are participating in a Dawnbreaker program, much of the data gathering associated with potential markets and competitors will be gathered by our team for you to then synthesize.

If you are a company of 5-10 people, don't be intimidated by the prospects of this process. We have worked with over 1800 small advanced technology firms utilizing this process. Our general ex-

Table 7-1: Relative time spent on various business planning activities

SKILLS	SOURCES OF ASSISTANCE	PER CENT TIME
Hypothesizing	You, management team	5%
Data gathering	State programs, RTTC, students, consultant	25%
Review & synthesis	You, management team, board	10%
Decision making	You, management team	5%
Strategizing	You, management team, board	5%
Number crunching	You, management team, accountant, state program, consultant, SCORE	15%
Re-evaluation	You, management team, board	5%
Writing	You, management, board	10%
Editing	You, editor	20%

perience has been that smaller companies (under 30 employees) often are more dedicated to business planning than larger firms as the founder is more readily involved in the planning process. In larger firms, the task of business planning is often assigned to individuals further down the management structure.

When you are ready to start the business planning process, begin by deciding who within your firm will be involved with this process and what roles they will play. If additional resources are needed, it is recommended that you consider utilizing the services of a Small Business Development Center (SBDC) or a neighboring university. However, as cautioned earlier utilize these services appropriately for assistance with data gathering or accounting. Do not relinquish roles that involve synthesis, decision making, or re-evaluation to others – as these are the responsibilities of management.

Before starting the business planning process, we begin with an important benchmark, referred to as a Mind Map.

What is a Mind Map?

If you ask any entrepreneur:

» Who their customers are?

» How large is the market?

» How much money they will need to bring their product to market?

» Who their competitors are? and similar questions

- they will give you an answer.

This unwritten plan which directs the day-to-day activities of the entrepreneur we call a mind map. It contains untested hypotheses and assumptions which guide the behavior of the entrepreneur. A mind map differs from a business plan by virtue of the fact that the former is not based on rigorous research. A mind map therefore, contains considerable conjecture and little certitude. As you begin the process of developing a business plan, it is important to start by articulating your mind map as this contains the untested hypotheses and assumptions which will serve as the starting point for your business research. In other words, during the business planning process you will try to refute or verify the hypotheses that are guiding your current

Figure 7-1

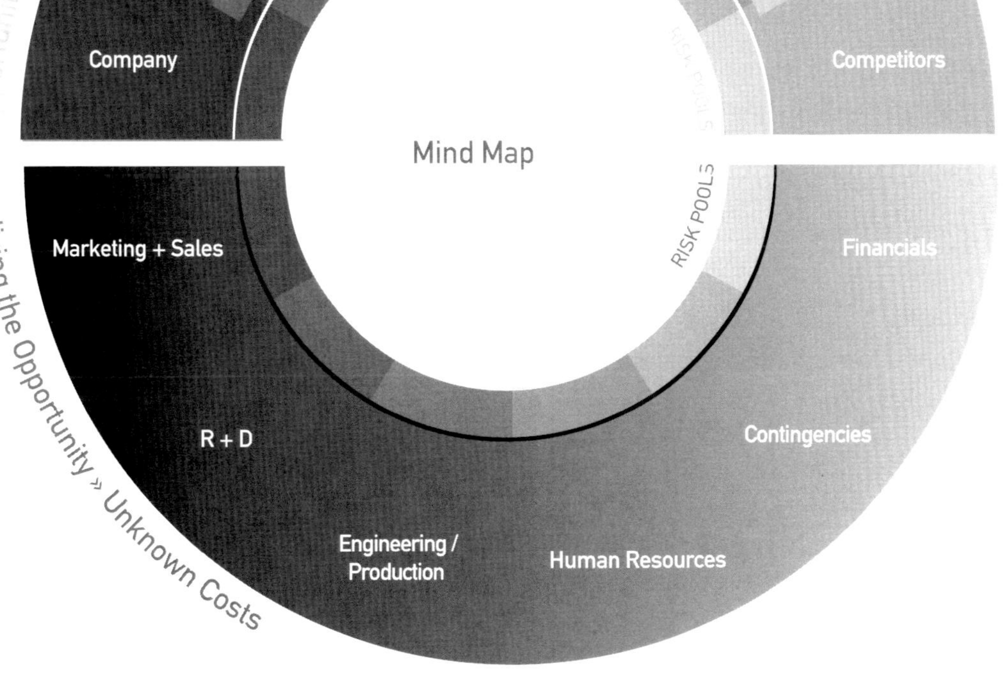

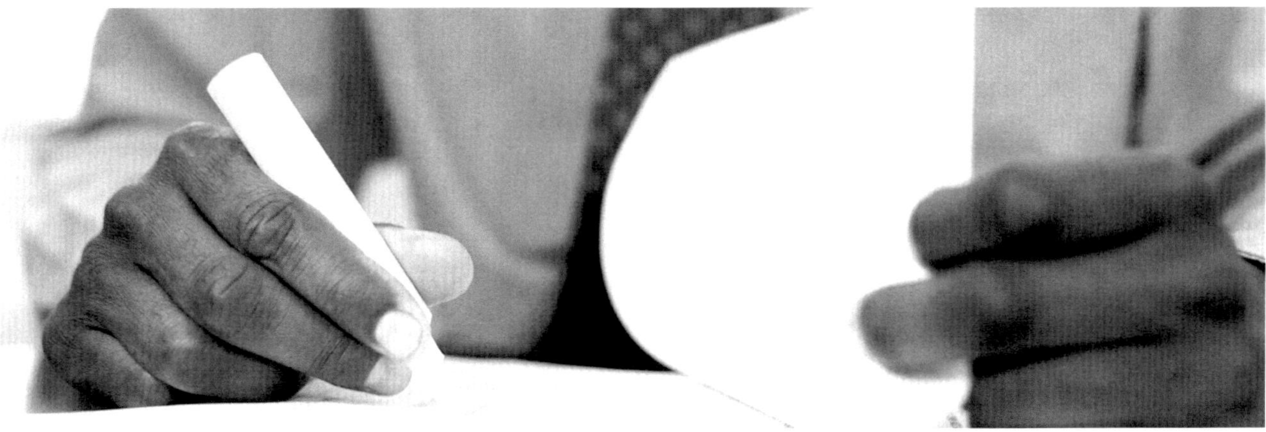

activities by systematically conducting primary and secondary research and by considering alternative strategies.

The key components of a mind map are answers to questions related to your technology, market size, customer needs, competitive landscape, and money required.

How to complete the Mind Map

The Mind Map activity is unlike all others - in that it does not require any research in its preparation. The objective of the mind map is simply to document the implicit assumptions that you make about your business opportunity and which guide your day-to-day operations.

The reason we have included worksheets for the mind map activity is to prompt spontaneity in your response. Jot down your thoughts when you're on the plane; or when you have a quiet moment in the office early in the morning or on the week-ends. If you will be working through this business planning process with an experienced advisor - be sure to type up your responses to the mind map in complete sentences before sharing it. Otherwise, your answers may be too cryptic for him or her to follow and will have little value for others who are assisting you in this process.

What if I Already have a Business Plan?

If you already have a business plan, you have probably picked up this text because you wish to improve or update an old document. In all likelihood, you are hoping that you don't have to change the old document very much. You're probably busy and looking for shortcuts. However, clinging to an old business plan can restrict your thinking, especially if too much of the document is outdated, if it reflects an old strategy, or if it was truthfully never a good document in the first place. On the other hand, your business plan may serve as a fairly good starting point and only require slight modification.

If you are starting this process with an old business plan in hand, we recommend that instead of completing the mind map, you substitute the Self-Evaluation of your business plan. In using these criteria you will notice that the accompanying "notes" force you to select or restrict certain ratings. We have done this in an effort to remove some of the subjectivity inherent in scoring one's own business plan.

If you find when doing the self-evaluation that the overall rating of your existing business plan is poor - consider setting the document aside in its entirety and starting the business planning process from the start - as if you had no document. In that case, after completing the Self - Evaluation, you would complete all of the Chapters as they appear in this workbook.

To summarize - if you are starting the Dawnbreaker® business planning process with a business plan in hand, start by completing the self- evaluation of your old business plan. You and the business coach assigned to work with you, will then jointly determine how to customize the program to meet your needs.

Mind Map

The following worksheets collectively constitute the mind map. Complete all of the activities without conducting any research. The intent of The Mind Map is merely to capture your internal guide. If you are starting this process with a business plan - proceed directly to the evaluation criteria and skip the Mind Map. Please note that throughout the Mind Map, as well as the remainder of the workbook we refer to your product. However, as appropriate substitute service or process, if those are more appropriate descriptors of what you are offering.

Mind Map

General instructions: The following set of 12 questions constitutes the Mind Map. This activity not only serves to benchmark your starting point, but also gives rise to the hypotheses to be tested during the business planning process.

Technology

(7-1) What technology/product/service/or process are you looking to commercialize?

(7-2) What performance criteria are important to your targeted customers? End-users?

(7-3) What is the estimated selling price for this product and on what is your answer based?

Customers

(7-4) What is the need which your product fulfills? How widespread is this need?

(7-5) Who are the customers for this product? Who are the end-users?

Competitors

(7-6) What other companies are addressing this same need?

(7-7) What other approaches are there (high and low tech) for addressing the same need from the customer's perspective?

Market size

(7-8) What is the current size of your market niche?

(7-9) What is the rate of market growth for this niche market during the next 5 years?

(7-10) What are the market drivers?

Financial Resources

(7-11) What commercialization strategy will you use to bring this product to market?

(7-12) How much funding do you anticipate will be required to bring this product to market?

Business Plan Evaluation Criteria

As mentioned earlier in this chapter, if you are starting the Dawnbreaker® business planning process with a business plan in hand, we recommend that you substitute the Self-Evaluation for the Mind Map activity. This self-evaluation will help you determine areas of strength and weakness in your existing business plan and will, in turn, help pinpoint the content of your subsequent Planning Reports.

When you evaluate a business plan, one can assume many different vantage points. In developing the following criteria, we assumed the perspective of an external investor and developed the criteria to assess the extent to which the document addresses an investor's needs. As the term "external investor" can include many subgroups: strategic partners, equity investors, debt financing sources, and the like, one might wish to further refine these criteria to meet the specific needs for other applications.

Our objective for including these criteria in this document is to help a company which already has a draft plan to look at it through another set of eyes. This self-evaluation is important because, if you are convinced that your plan is perfectly satisfactory - you will not be willing to part with it. If someone else points out its flaws you may also reject their guidance. In your heart of hearts you may wish to believe the plan is good, as truly you may not wish to spend the time associated with revising the plan and developing a sound business case. However, growth requires letting go as necessary. Therefore, these criteria are offered for your use in evaluating your existing plan. When used correctly they also set the stage for determining how to modify the business planning process to address the weaknesses of your current business case.

Instructions: The questions included in the Self-Evaluation criteria are organized around 5 themes:

Part 1: Sensitivity to strategic ally/investor needs
Part 2: The Opportunity
Part 3: Strategies for realizing the opportunity
Part 4: Management team
Part 5: Presentation of plan

In our own use of the evaluation criteria, we give weight to clusters of questions, viewing them as factors. However, for the reader's use with starting the business research process, this is unnecessary. Start by re-reading your old business plan. Then, carefully read each of the following questions and provide a rating to each. Pay careful attention to the notes associated with many of the questions. These are intended to remove some of the subjectivity associated with this evaluation process. Circle your responses directly in the text. Be sure to give yourself a "0" rating to a question if the section referenced is missing in its entirety from the business plan. There are 16 questions in all, 5 is always the highest score one can give, while 1 is the lowest for areas that are addressed in the plan. 0 is given as a score when relevant information is absent. Please be sure to rate all questions.

Business Plan Self-evaluation Criteria

Part 1: Sensitivity to Investor Needs

1) The extent to which the business plan indicates a sensitivity to the investor's needs. In other words, does the plan show evidence of a knowledge of the investor's needs and does it address them?

0 Not Addressed   1 Poor   2   3 Average   4   5 Excellent

Note: Score as "1" if the company addresses only its need for capital and resources and does not acknowledge or address the investor's needs. If the plan is for internal use only, look at the extent to which a good case is made to sell upline or the extent to which the company justifies that it is a good opportunity for them.

Rationale for Score:

2) The degree to which the Executive Summary tells a compelling story for the investor.

0 Not Addressed 1 Poor 2 3 Average 4 5 Excellent

Note: A compelling story clarifies the mission of the company, the size of the market, the sustainable competitive advantage, the amount of funds required, and how the funds will be used. If the company is self-funding, does it tell a compelling, believable story for the firm.

Rationale for Score:

3) The extent to which a logical case is presented which provides a sound rationale for the business opportunity, i.e., evidence of real customers, sizable markets, the detailed plans to realize the opportunity provided.

0 1 2 3 4 5

Note: If there is only evidence of real customers, don't score higher than "1"

Rationale for Score:

Part 2: Opportunity

4) The Mission Statement is the cornerstone of any Business Plan and needs to answer the questions: What business are you in? What products and/or technologies are involved? What markets do you serve? How do you segment the market? What is your sustainable competitive advantage? Rate the goodness of the mission statement.

0 1 2 3 4 5

Rationale for Score:

5) The extent to which the business plan reveals intimate knowledge of the customers and end-user needs based on discussions with potential customers.

0 Not Addressed 1 Poor 2 3 Average 4 5 Excellent

Note: Score as "1" if it appears that the needs of the customers are inferred, rather than the result of direct interaction.

Rationale for score:

6) The extent to which the market is sized appropriately and is substantial in size and/or growth potential.

0 1 2 3 4 5

Note: Score as "1" if the company presents no data to substantiate claims regarding market size. Also, score as "1" if the plan simply states that it is a multi-million dollar market without providing any data to substantiate this claim.

Rationale for score:

7) The strength of the intellectual property strategy and position.

0 1 2 3 4 5

Note: Use "1" if no evidence of a strategy is present or if the technology is said to be "patentable."

Rationale for score:

8) The extent to which the plan addresses market and competitive risks.

0 Not Addressed 1 Poor 2 3 Average 4 5 Excellent

Note: Do not give a score greater than 3 if the plan doesn't include comparative information on direct and indirect competitors. Also, score as "1" if the business plan indicates that there are NO competitive risks.

Rationale for Score:

9) The extent to which the plan shows evidence of understanding the pricing of competitive products and competitive ways of solving the customer's needs.

0 1 2 3 4 5

Note: If only competitive ways of solving customer's needs are addressed and information on pricing sensitivities is lacking, don't score higher than "3".

Rationale for Score:

10) The extent to which (a) the sustainable competitive advantage of this product/ technology is compared with (b) the feature, advantage, and benefits of competitive products/technologies.

0 1 2 3 4 5

Note: Score as "1" if both a and b are absent from the plan. If only sustainable competitive advantage is addressed, score no higher than "2".

Rationale for score:

Part 3: Strategies

11) Please rate the strength of the commercialization strategy.

0 Not Addressed 1 Poor 2 3 Average 4 5 Excellent

Rationale for score:

12) The extent to which well-conceived objectives exist for each relevant functional area as appropriate (R&D, Engineering, Manufacturing, Marketing/Sales, Human Resources) with timelines, staffing levels, and budgets identified.

0 1 2 3 4 5

Rationale for score:

13) The extent to which there is evidence of adequately assessing the total functional costs associated with implementing each strategy.

0 1 2 3 4 5

Note: Score as "1" if assumptions do not accompany the financials for each functional area either in the corresponding plan section or the integrated financials.

Rationale for score:

14) The extent to which the plan contains appropriate contingency plans, clarifying alternative paths to be taken if different types of problems arise.

0 Not Addressed 1 Poor 2 3 Average 4 5 Excellent

Note: Score as "0" if no contingency plan is present.

Rationale for score:

Part 4: Opportunity

15) The extent to which the management team has mapped out a sound staffing plan in all functional areas to execute the commercialization strategy reflected in the business plan.

0 1 2 3 4 5

Note: Staffing plan has to be for 5 years. If only a description of current HR plan is included, do not score higher than "1".

Rationale for score:

16) Your confidence in the management team's ability to successfully realize the opportunity based on your assessment of available information.

0 1 2 3 4 5

Note: Do not give a score greater than "3" if (a) the management team of Board of Directors or Advisors does not contain people with a variety of business skills (i.e., marketing/sales; finance and administration R&D/Engineering,) (b) the business plan is for a spin-off company and the principal in the parent company will be driving both entities once spun-off, or (c) one person is wearing all functional hats after year 1.

Rationale for score:

Part 5: Presentation of plan

16) To what degree is the plan very accessible to a busy investor. In your evaluation consider if the plan contains all of the following: Table of Contents, page numbers, subheadings, easily readable font, adequate spacing and margins for notes, and good graphics. Also consider how compelling is the writing style and the clarity and strength of the business case.

0 1 2 3 4 5

Rationale for Score:

Using the Results of the Business Plan Self-Evaluation

The objective of the self-evaluation is to pinpoint areas of weakness in your existing business plan. With this information in hand, it will be possible to selectively proceed with the business planning process as opposed to completing all of the activities included in subsequent sections of this workbook. Let me again reiterate however, the importance of conducting the business research prior to revising your business plan. The task at hand is not simply a writing task. The objective of the business planning process is to expand your understanding of the business environment and your opportunity, so that you may cogently present a sound business case when you rewrite the business plan. The research must however, be conducted first and be done thoughtfully.

The End Point

Whereas the mind map benchmarks your starting point, the following outline represents the end point or the manner in which you will represent your business opportunity once you have completed the business research process. Keep in mind that a business plan is only as good as the research which precedes it, and avoid the temptation to rush and put together a document without having completed the planning process.

Also important to keep in mind is that the format of a business plan will vary depending upon the nature of the business. For example, the outline which follows is for a manufacturing firm. If, by contrast the business case is for a software company, one might remove the production plan and add a customer service section.

Business Plan Outline (Detailed)

Cover Page
Table of Contents

1. Executive Summary

2. Company & Technology

2.1 Brief company introduction
- *Mission*
- *Location, size, history*
- *Overview of company capabilities*
- *Customers & past performance*

2.2 Technology
- *Brief description*
- *Applications*

2.3 Product/Service
- *Brief description*

  2.3.1. Intellectual property status

2.4 Commercialization strategy - brief overview

3. Industry Overview

3.1. Industry definition and description
- *New products and developments within the industry*
- *Major players within the industry, factors driving dynamics*

3.2. Legislation and policies driving the industry
- *Future and historical trends*

4. Customers

4.1 Customers & end-user
- *Need addressed by the technology/product/service*
- *How the need is currently filled?*
- *Features, Advantages, and Benefits; Price point*
- *Who has the need? - Differentiate between end-users and customer needs*
- *Distribution channels used by customers and end-users*

4.2 Buying behavior
- Decision makers
  - *Who makes the decision to buy*
  - *Who influences the purchase decision*
  - *Characterization of decision makers*
- Basis for purchase decisions
  - *Frequency of purchase decisions*
  - *Basis for purchase decisions*

5. Market

5.1. Market definition

  5.1.1. Primary market

  5.1.2. Secondary markets

5.2. Market size and trends - Primary market
- *Current total and served-available markets*
- *Predicted annual growth rate*

6. Competitors

6.1. Indirect competitors

6.2. Direct competitors
- *Who are they?*
- *Strengths and weaknesses*
- *Market share of competitors*

6.3. SWOT analysis

7. Marketing / Sales Plan

7.1. Opportunity statement

7.2. Marketing & sales objectives

7.3. Current customers (if appropriate)

7.4. Potential customers
- *Customers targeted for intensive selling efforts*
- *How other customers will be identified and qualified*
- *Product features emphasized and contrasted with competitors*

7.5. Pricing
- *Basis for targeted price point*
- *Margins & levels of profitability at various levels of production & sales*

7.6. Sales Plan
- *Sales force analysis (reps, distributors, direct)*
- *Sales expectations for each salesperson & each distribution channel*
- *Margins given to intermediaries*
- *Service and warranties*
- *Organizational chart for sales/marketing staff, indicating planned growth for 3 - 5 years*

7.7. Advertising
- *Year 1- Detailed Marketing Communications plan*
- *Years 2-5 (general)*

7.8. Sales/Marketing Budget
- *Assumptions*

8. R&D Plan

8.1. R&D Objectives

8.2. Milestones and current status
- *What remains to be done to make the product marketable?*

8.3. Difficulties and risks

8.4. Staffing

8.5. R&D Budget
- *Assumptions*

9. Manufacturing/Engineering Plan

9.1. Objectives

9.2. Use of Subcontractors

9.3. Quality control

9.4. Staffing

9.5. Manufacturing/Engineering budget
- *Assumptions*

10. Human Resource Plan

10.1. Staffing Objectives

10.2. Organizational structure - phased over 3-5 years

- *Introduction of management team*
- *Key individuals to be recruited and plans for doing so*
- *Board of Directors, Advisory Board*
- *Incentives for commitment*

10.3. Human Resource Budget

- *Assumptions*

11. Contingencies

11.1. Potential Risks

- *Impact and responses*

12. Financials

12.1. Financial Objectives

- *Commercialization strategy (elaborated)*
- *Use of funds*
- *Terms and conditions of any previous financing arrangements*

12.2. Plans for obtaining investors or strategic alliance

- *Profile of investor or partner sought*
- *Leveraging advantage for investor/partner*
- *Detailed plans for obtaining investor/partner*
- *Costs and time associated with securing investor/partner*

12.3. Pro Forma Profit & Loss statements

12.4. Pro Forma Cash Flow projections

12.5. Pro Forma Balance Sheet

12.6. Alternative return scenarios

- *Exit scenarios*

This detailed outline is included as a preview of the end product. It is organized in a way that builds a logical business case, both for internal and external use.

Getting from here to there- the business planning process

As mentioned in Section 1, we recognize that it is difficult for busy entrepreneurs to add business planning to their already hectic schedules. In order to do this successfully, we have found that the process needs to proceed at a speed that is rapid enough to keep the project on the front burner, but not so rapid that it gets tossed off. It is therefore, our recommendation that the process be broken down into segments that can be tackled in 2 to 3 week periods. The research always precedes the writing of the plan. However, the manner in which this is done can vary. Most people may prefer to conduct all the research first, as each new thing that you uncover will change some of the preliminary conclusions that you drew earlier. Others prefer to write sections of the plan as they complete relevant research, knowing that they will have to revise it as more data is collected.

Proceed in whatever fashion works best for you, but plan to complete a deliverable at the end of every 2 to 3 week period and share it with members of the team you have assembled to be involved with the planning process. We refer to these deliverables as Planning Reports. The balance of the book is organized around Planning Reports which provide the opportunity to consolidate information gathered during the previous 2 to 3 week period. The information gathered is sequenced in the fashion which will make business planning easier to complete. A general overview of the primary topics covered in the planning reports is listed below.

Table 7 - 2: General content of planning reports

Planning Report #1	Mind Map
Planning Report #2	Strategic planning
Planning Report #3	Customers and End-Users
Planning Report #4	Markets and Competitors
Planning Report #5	Operational plans
Planning Report #6	Financials

For those having already conducted preliminary research who are starting with a draft of a plan, please note that the content of the planning reports will be customized.

* from now on the word product only will be used. However, you should assume that you could substitute the word technology, process, or service as appropriate.

Figure 7-2: Overview of schedule for Interim Reports

	Planning 1	Planning 2	Planning 3	Planning 4	Planning 5	Planning 6
Week 1	Mind Map					
Week 2						
Week 3		Strategic Planning				
Week 4						
Week 5			Customers End-Users			
Week 6						
Week 7						
Week 8						
Week 9				Markets Competitors		
Week 10						
Week 11						
Week 12					Operational Plans	
Week 13						Financials
Week 14						

Strategic Planning

"Columbus didn't just sail. He sailed west."

- Golightly

Chapter 08

Above all else, starting, growing, and maturing a business requires energy and commitment.

Above all else, starting, growing, and maturing a business requires energy and commitment. The energy is yours and the commitment is nothing less than that which you would dedicate to your offspring. Because a business demands so much from its founder, as well as from others who grow and steer the enterprise, we recommend starting the business planning process with strategic planning. Strategic planning involves clarification of the company's identity; determining its future direction; and charting a general course to arrive at the future envisioned. Figure 8-1 visually represents the various topics addressed in this chapter. The strategic planning topics relate not only to the section of the plan referred to as "Company", but also to the overall evaluation of the opportunity.

Business choices are limited or facilitated by a founder's vision.

Hypothetically, a business opportunity could be realized in various ways. For example, if the opportunity is large enough one could take the company public. Other commercialization strategies available for opportunities of most sizes include teaming with a strategic ally, licensing the opportunity to another, or retaining most/all of the equity and seeking debt financing to fuel corporate growth. In part, the choice made depends upon the founder and his or her vision for the future. The vision must be sufficiently engaging that the founder will commit the time and energy required for its realization. Particularly with revolutionary technologies, the path to ultimate market acceptance is tortuous and requires considerable time, dedication, and persistence. Therefore, if the opportunity is to be realized, its initial champion - the technology entrepreneur - must be sufficiently motivated by the vision and strategies chosen to keep pushing forward.

Individuals are motivated by different things. For the scientist or inventor, the motivation is most often seeing the technology utilized. Others are motivated by the desire to control their own destiny, by the adventure associated with doing new things, or by profit motive. Depending on the motivation, the vision, as well as the commercialization strategy chosen will vary.

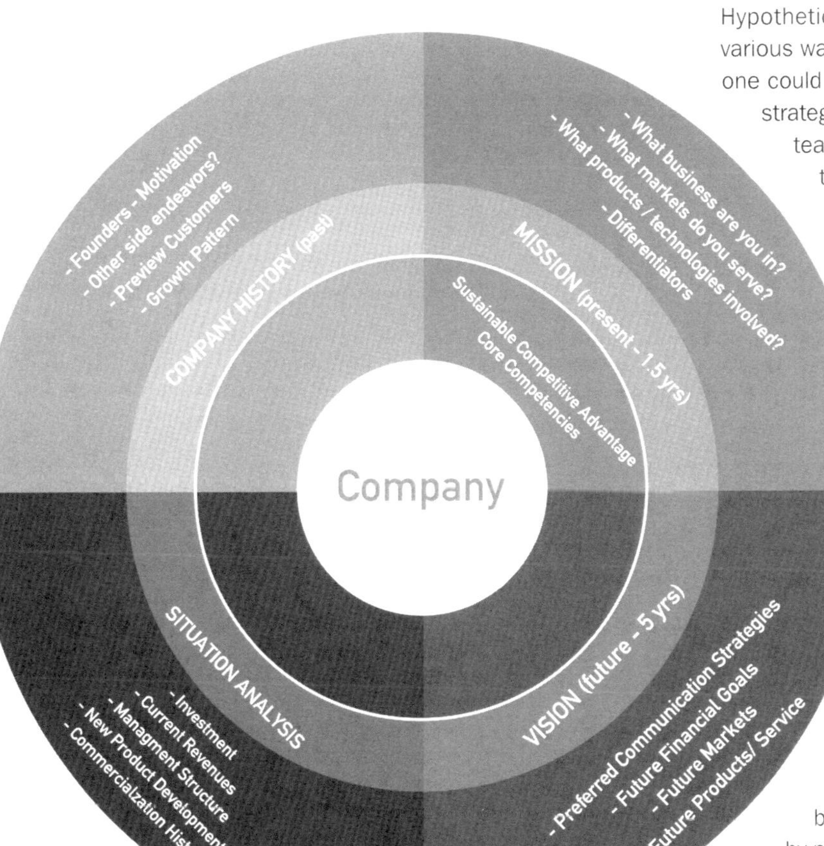

Figure 8-1: Overview of Topics covered in Chapter 8

It is for this reason that the management team of a company may need to be changed in order for a different vision and commercialization strategy to be realized. If an entrepreneur is attached to having a small firm and motivated primarily by the challenges posed by the work itself - it is unlikely that he or she would wish to pursue an Initial Public Offering (IPO). More importantly, from an investor's perspective such a firm would be of little interest, as it would not be positioned for creating value (financial growth). By contrast, the same opportunity - guided by an entrepreneur who wishes to confront the challenges of a multi-functional enterprise, who is willing to give up equity, and who can envision him - or herself guiding a large enterprise - might be a very good candidate for an IPO.

Clearly, more than personality and motivation determine strategy selection. The actions of your competitors; advances in competitive and/or enabling technologies; the urgency of being profitable; and other external factors play a key role in strategy selection. However, the ultimate course embodied in a business plan reflects the motivation and vision of the management team. For that reason, we start our journey together with strategic planning.

Perspective

Plans are nothing. Planning is everything! Our spin on this statement is that a business plan is only as good as the research that precedes it. To assure that you conduct the business research well, we use a Planning Report Process. Each Planning Report contains the results of the research and planning that you and your team conduct in response to the questions posed in chapters 8 - 11. Finding the answer to each question in this chapter constitutes the planning task to be completed during the next 2 week period. Each set of responses becomes an Planning Report.

A business plan is only as good as the research that precedes it.

As you start the Planning Report process, you will notice that each question (task) includes the following subsections:

- Relevant section of business plan
- Why this is important and how it relates to risk mitigation
- Background
- Activities
- Reality check

The notation of relevant section indicates the part of the business plan to which the research and planning activities relate.

Relevant Section of the Plan: This section identifies the relationship between the activity and the section of the business plan that you will draft later. When you are ready to start preparing the plan, it will be useful to "chunk" refined information into the plan that resulted from completing these activities. Once you have brought relevant information forward, you can then manipulate the information to develop a compelling business case.

Why is this important and how does this relate to risk mitigation? The purpose of this section is to clarify the importance of this type of information to the business case and to identify potential sources of perceived risk that can be addressed by this information.

Background. Relevant concepts are identified and discussed in this section.

Planning Activities. The planning activities take the form of open ended questions or tables that need to be completed in response to this question.

Reality Check: When a question is posed, it is so tempting to just put down any answer. Most of us are good at making up something plausible, especially if it is with respect to an endeavor about which we may not be objective. However, self-delusion doesn't serve anyone well. Therefore, the section labeled reality checks, provides assistance in determining if you have answered the questions adequately. However, it is highly recommended that you have a skilled mentor with relevant experience provide you with feedback and guidance on your answers. Once feedback has been provided and you have considered the comments, it is recommended that you modify your answers to reflect your ultimate decisions regarding the information at hand. In this fashion, when you begin to draft your plan, you will be able to pull forward well-thought through and well-developed nuggets of information into the draft plan itself.

Business Plan Preparation

The activities covered in this chapter relate to the information that you will use in completing the section of the business plan referred to as a "Brief Company Introduction." It is suggested that after completing the planning activities in this chapter, and having received feedback from your mentor, that you transfer relevant information resulting from this process to the business plan outline. In this fashion, when you are ready to start drafting the business plan itself, the key information that you will need will be readily available. Please keep in mind however, that the information that you transfer will need to be "fleshed out" further, so that it represents a compelling business case. The bits of information that you originally transfer, will not by itself result in a compelling business case.

The materials covered in this chapter relate to this section of the business plan.

2. Company and Technology

2.1. Brief company introduction

- ***Mission***
- ***Location, size, history***
- ***Overview of company capabilities***
- ***Customers and past performance***

Leveraging your time

It has been our experience that the best way to conduct strategic planning is to set aside a block of time off-site where you and your trusted advisors (in the case of a sole proprietor) or you and other members of your management team or Board of Directors (in the case of a larger company) can focus on these issues. In order to be efficient in your planning, it is best to do this in a setting where interruptions can be minimized. You need the time to reflect, to consider alternatives, and to dispute direction. If possible, plan this session for a week-end. Other alternatives, might be early morning hours before the phone starts to ring or a couple of evenings dedicated to this task. It is recommended that the company founder prepare the information associated with Questions 8-3 and 8-5 prior to holding the strategic planning session. Then, when you assemble, you can begin the session by reviewing the Situation Analysis and new product description. With this as background, you can work collectively on the other tasks in this Planning Report. In preparation for this session, everyone should read Chapters 4 and 5.

Issues

The following issues are often encountered by individuals working on a business plan. Some suggestions are made for addressing these stumbling blocks.

I'm the Principal Investigator (PI), but not part of management team. I have no insight into strategic planning issues. I've just been told to develop a plan. What should I do?

This is a difficult situation and one that we encounter frequently. Strategic planning issues must be addressed by a company's management. Therefore, it is recommended that before you begin this process that your mentor talks with your management to enlist their involvement in this preliminary phase. If you are not working with a mentor, and if you have been tasked to draft a business plan, you will need to bring to the attention of your management that there are some activities with which they will need to be involved in order for the resulting product to be of value to them.

An alternative approach is to conduct a market assessment first to determine if an opportunity truly exists for the technology. Then, you could bring the results of your findings to management and ask if they wish you to proceed with drafting a business plan. In other words, change the sequence of activities – confirm the market opportunity exists first and then engage management in strategic planning before developing the business plan.

We do about 30 research projects per year. This is a fairly atypical project. Why do I need to bother with the company mission, vision, etc. when I'm not sure if this direction has a future with our firm?

On occasion, I have heard companies say "We don't have any strategic focus, our direction depends on what research awards we win." Hopefully, that's not the situation with your firm. On the other hand, testing the waters and exploring the wisdom of applying one's core competencies in a different way, before investing more company resources in a new direction is a good way to explore high risk opportunities. In this case, it is highly likely that this R&D strategy is consistent with the mission and vision of the company, although it may appear to be disparate. If you are developing a business plan the mission and vision of the company are still relevant to the future of the experimental technology.

We have multiple core competencies in the company and this project fits into one of those areas. Do I deal with the mission for the company as a whole or just for this project?

Both. If you are responsible for a technology area, you will have much more say over the mission of your area, than you will over the mission of the company. However, the mission for your strategic business unit (SBU), needs to be consistent with the mission of the company as a whole. Concentrate your efforts on those areas where you have greatest influence and control.

We've just gone through a strategic planning session and have developed a mission statement, but its not like the one you have described here. Can I just use the one that we developed at our off-site?

No. Unfortunately, the word "mission" does have different connotations. Many organizational development consultants focus on the internal audience when developing a company mission statement. This is fine for that intended purpose. However, the mission statement that is developed within the context of this program has an external audience in mind consisting of potential and existing customers, partners, and investors.

We used this method last year and developed a good plan. Do I need to re-do everything?

No, that would be a waste of time. Just take a quick look at what you did before and confirm whether or not the situation has changed in any way.

Why can't I just write the plan? It seems redundant to do these exercises and then write the plan.

Would you write a research report, before conducting the research? Would your research be redundant? Are your hypotheses and assumptions always positively confirmed? The answer, of course is "no" The same is true of business research. Most entrepreneurs start with hypotheses regarding customer needs, market size, competition, and the resources required. However, these hypotheses need to be tested via a process of gathering independent information that may refute or confirm the hypotheses. The truth of the matter is that considerable change occurs during the process of gathering such information – change in product definition, change in your understanding of the customers interest, change in your understanding of the resources required. Such changes should help increase the likelihood of successful commercialization. No, you can't simply assume that the untested hypotheses are true and write a plan. There are no shortcuts to good planning. However, we have tried to provide various internet-based aides which will help make the process of building the plan easier, once the research is complete.

Estimated time commitment

To complete this activity thoughtfully will require between 8 - 10 hours from the individuals involved with this process. If you are able to hold an independent planning session as suggested, be sure to designate someone during that session to record both the conclusions drawn, as well as key issues which came up during the session. An alternative way to approach this task is to have individuals add their comments into the collaborative learning environment that is provided for this purpose.

If you are working with a trusted advisor, carefully record the conclusions of your strategic planning as responses to the following tasks and share the responses to the following activities for his or her independent feedback.

PROJECT PLANNING: Planning Report 1

Date due for Planning Report 1______________________________

Date strategic planning meeting scheduled________________________

Invited attendees to strategic planning meeting______________________

Question 8-1: What is the history of your company?

Relevant Section of Plan

Business plan – Section 2.1

Why this is important and how does this relate to risk mitigation?

The best predictor of your future actions is your past. Indeed, when you share information about your company's history, you are also revealing much about yourself and how you behave in situations of uncertainty and stress. This will be of great interest to a potential partner and/or investor, as the management team of any company constitutes a major source of risk. Reflecting on the start-up period should also be of interest to you, as it will assist you in becoming more aware of your tendencies.

The types of things that a potential investor or partner will want to know about your firm include:

- Have there been any previous investments in the firm? If so, who made them and what equity positions do they have?
- How is the company managed? Is there a multi-functional management team? How long has the management team been together? Is management financially vested in the company?
- How stable is the employment situation in the firm?
- Has the company been profitable? What is the growth pattern in revenues? Does the company have debt? Collateral?
- Who are the company's existing customers? How much repeat business do they provide? How happy are they with the company's products and services?

Background

A potential investor, using a process referred to, as "due diligence" will evaluate various aspects of an opportunity and of a company to assess potential risk. As a coach, however, looking at what a founder has done and the lessons learned, can surface patterns that may be maladaptive and inhibit the growth potential of your company. It can also surface patterns and tendencies that have worked well.

According to Edward Rogoff[1] your personal reasons for starting your business will be of little interest to a potential funding source and with that I concur. However, your motivation for starting your business and your patterns of behavior in growing your business to date will provide great insight to your coach, whose role it is to increase the likelihood that you are successful in obtaining private sector financing and/or a strategic ally. The activities that follow are aimed at providing you and your coach with insight into the strategies for growth that you have followed to date.

Activities – Question 8-1

If you are the company founder or one of the founders, please address the questions as asked. If you are not the company founder, but are familiar with the history of the company, please answer the questions based on your understanding. If you are unable to answer these questions, it is recommended that the founders be involved in this activity.

Activities – Question 8-1

1) What is your role in the company? Who are the company founders? Are they currently actively involved (all or some)? What was their motivation(s) for founding the company? How many full and part-time employees do you currently have? How has the employment pattern changed over time and why?

2) What is the legal structure of the company? C-Corp, S-Corp, LLC, partnership, dba. Does the company have external investors? Who are they and how much has been invested to date?

3) Has your company sold any product(s) to date? If so, what products have you sold? Who were your customers (can be described in terms of types of customers or specific customers) and what volume did they purchase?

4) If your firm is primarily an R&D firm, what are your primary sources of R&D funding? If the primary sources are SBIR and STTR funding, please indicate those agencies with which you most commonly work and your success in converting your awards from Phase I to Phase II and from Phase II to Phase III.

5) Have there been fluctuations in annual revenue? If so, what has your strategy been to weather such fluctuations?

6) What collateral has the company developed to date (tangible and intangible) and what has your strategy been for doing so? Be sure to describe those assets which enable you to provide marketable services and products. Description should be illustrative, but not thorough.

7) In reflecting upon the history of your company's growth to date, what do you perceive as strengths in the way that you have addressed periodic business uncertainty? What do you perceive as weaknesses? What do you believe will be necessary in order to change the growth pattern of your company? Are you interested in changing the growth pattern? Why or why not?

Reality check? Have I answered this question adequately?

Deliverable: The deliverable is a thoughtful response to the ten questions posed. Although the information generated will not go directly into your business plan, thoughtful consideration will assist you in determining what some of the potential impediments to growth have been and provide insight into future directions.

Question 8-2: What are your core competencies and sustainable competitive advantage?

Relevant section of business plan?

Business Plan – Section 2.1

Why is this important and how does it relate to risk mitigation?

Core competencies and sustainable competitive advantage are related, yet distinct concepts. Both reflect self-awareness, provide business focus and serve as a guide to management in making strategic decisions regarding new opportunities. Core competencies can be defined as fundamental knowledge, ability or expertise in a specific subject area. For advanced technology firms, this readily translates into a listing of areas of technical competence. However, core competencies can also be in other areas of business such as marketing and sales, service, negotiations, and the like.

When considering if one should outsource a particular activity, one should always consider if it is a core competency and be appropriately reluctant to outsource it, if the answer is "yes". When considering venturing into a new direction – one should also ask if this is consistent with one's core competencies. Companies often waste considerable time and money by being distracted, and by migrating into areas where they have little knowledge. One can of course, always strategically decide to expand their core competencies by acquiring/growing new aspects of their business.

Background

The phrase "sustainable competitive advantage" (SCA) was first used by Michael Porter, a Harvard management professor. Simply put - *SCA is an advantage that can be sustained over a long period of time that allows for the improvement of your company's competitive position in the marketplace.* By definition, this advantage differentiates your company from the competition and is not readily reproducible by others.

A related concept is "core competency" defined as "areas of specialized expertise that are the result of harmonizing complex streams of technology and work activity." According to CK Prahalad and Gary Hamel (1990), core competencies should:

- Provide potential access to a wide variety of markets
- Increase perceived customer benefits
- Be hard for competitors to imitate

The relationship between the two concepts can be expressed in the following way: When a core competency is distinctive, can provide a long term advantage, and is difficult to reproduce, it becomes a sustainable competitive advantage. A company can have a number of core competencies, but limited sustainable competitive advantage.

The challenge for a firm is to look at itself and determine what its' distinctive advantages are. Often times an extra and external pair of eyes can be helpful in this regard. It is also important to keep in mind that as SCA is developed over time, start-ups typically lack sustainable competitive advantage and must actively strive to develop it. If upon reflection, you conclude that your competitive advantage is weak or lacking - we will work with you to develop or refine a strategy to enhance it. In so doing, we will help you examine what you can offer, what the market wants and what is the competition's weakness.

Capabilities that are distinctive and more difficult to reproduce are the basis for your sustainable competitive advantage. These include: (1) intellectual property - your own and exclusive licenses that you may also have obtained, (2) strong brand identity, (3) partnerships, (4) in-depth knowledge of your customers, (5) government protected monopolies; certifications and approvals, and (5) unique equipment and sunk costs, and (6) the culture of your company - especially those factors which add to internal cohesion and allow you to respond quickly to changing needs. Items that cannot be readily reproduced by your competitors are the basis for your competitive advantage. "A competitive advantage enables a firm to create superior value for its customers and superior profits for itself."

By contrast, capabilities that CAN be readily reproduced or purchased by your competitors DO NOT contribute to your sustainable competitive advantage, even though they are still core competencies that your firm may possess. Such capabilities often include technical, financial, and marketing capabilities, as well as non-exclusive licenses and general knowledge. Such capabilities are considered, non-distinctive, as they may be more readily purchased.

Sustainable competitive advantage is at the core or your company's ability to grow. Without it - a company has limited economic reason to exist and will eventually wither away. A company should strive to have synergy between distinctive capabilities, as well as those that are reproducible. The task is then to convey this advantage through "branding" which can be defined as "delivering all the promises and perceptions that the organization wants its constituents to hold." What is important to convey, once you have identified your sustainable competitive advantage is your operational excellence, your product leadership, and your customer intimacy.

The activities in this section are designed to provide you with the occasion to systematically reflect upon these at the company or division level.

Activities - Question 8-2

1) What are your company's core competencies?

2) After reflecting upon those items that provide a company with sustainable competitive advantage, please identify those factors which provide your firm with SCA. Be sure to provide a justification for your answer.

3) On a scale of 1 (low) to high (5) how would you currently rate your sustainable competitive advantage. Please clarify the reason for this rating.

1	2	3	4	5
low		moderate		high

4) If you conclude that your sustainable competitive advantage is weak, describe below what actions will you need to take over time to strengthen it? If you conclude that your sustainable competitive advantage is strong – describe below, what you will do to maintain or strengthen this advantage.

Reality check? Have I answered this question adequately?

Deliverable: The result of this activity should be a detailed list of those items which you believe provide your company and this technology/product/service with an advantage in the targeted market. Be as specific as possible - don't merely reiterate selected items from the preceding list. For example, if you indicate that an advantage is unique equipment - describe what type of equipment you have and what makes it unique. If you mention your reputation - clarify what it is and what you must do to maintain it, and so forth.

This deliverable will play a role in the expression of your mission statement and should be considered on an on-going basis, as you look to expand your market share. The greater your sustainable competitive advantage, the less risk a potential partner/investor will perceive in doing business with your firm.

Question 8-3:What is your Mission?

Relevant section

Business Plan - Section 2.1

Why is this important?

A mission statement is an expression of corporate identity. Such an expression possesses both internal and external value. From an external perspective a good mission statement clarifies to potential customers the broad groupings of products or services they can expect from your firm. If you examine the myriad of corporate websites, you will find that most contain a mission statement, a succinct description of their firm's capabilities expressed as a powerful selling tool.

Mission statements are also important to prospective partners and investors as they describe not only the business functions which a company performs, but state what is unique about the organization (elements of sustainable competitive advantage).

Mission statements also have great internal value, serving as a guide for everyone within the organization. For the front line staff (receptionists and secretaries) a mission statement provides an answer to the often-asked question "What does your firm do?" There is nothing worse than having someone answer the phone who is incapable of describing what your firm does. For management at every level a good mission statement serves as a useful guide in decision making, helping those in charge to discern if certain activities are in keeping with or at odds with the mission statement. The discipline which a mission statement provides will help focus the use of scarce resources.

It is important to point out that corporate identities change and correspondingly so do mission statements. However, such changes should be deliberate, rather than whimsical. We recommend that you re-evaluate your corporate mission annually.

Background

You may currently have a mission statement and indeed may have spent considerable time crafting it. It is important to point out that the phrase "mission statement" has various connotations. For many, it is an expression of the company's values. However, we prefer to call that a Value Statement. [2] The purpose of the mission statement that you will create here is to lend clarity to existing and potential customers, partners, and investors on a number of factors.

A good mission statement should answer the following questions.

- What business are you in? This question is answered by indicating the types of work your company performs such as R & D, Engineering, Manufacturing, Marketing, Custom Design, Distribution, and the like.
- What products and technologies are involved?
- What markets do you serve?
- What is unique about your company? What differentiates it from others? (sustainable competitive advantage)

Depending on your situation, the entity for which you are developing the mission statement may vary. For example, if you are a small firm and do not yet have a mission statement, your task will be to develop one for your firm. If you work for a larger firm with an existing mission statement, your task will be to develop a mission statement for the strategic business unit (SBU) or division in which you work or for a planned spin-off.

When writing, always focus on content first and then worry about how to best express it later. In developing a mission statement, it is recommended that you begin by addressing each of the questions listed above. Sometimes, it is also useful to reflect upon the reciprocal to each of these questions as well. In other words, after stating the business functions you do perform, articulate those which you do not. This process helps sharpen the focus on each of the four elements of your mission statement: **business functions, products, markets, and sustainable competitive advantage.**

Once you have generated the information necessary to write a good mission statement, then begin drafting an expression which combines some or most of the elements in an interesting way. You should expect your first attempt to invariably be too long. However, once you have it down on paper, you can refine it - substituting macro words for those which are too detailed, removing irrelevant terms, and the like. Whittle away at the statement until you arrive at an expression of corporate identity which allows latitude, yet provides direction and sounds clear and compelling. If the result is a mission statement which could apply equally well to your nearest competitor - go back and refine it further.

Mission statements tend to vary with respect to the degree of specificity, with some companies opting to provide greater latitude so that they have room to maneuver. My recommendation is that small businesses initially be more specific and focused in the expression of their mission and that over time, the mission is expanded as it matures and seeks more latitude.

Results: The following is an example of a useful mission statement:

"Soarrell Medical Systems develops, produces, markets, and supports proprietary patient-oriented software, biometric smart cards and readers which interface with computerized patient record (CPR) systems. We offer outstanding customer support; share the financial risk with medical practitioners; and facilitate the shift to a new patient-doctor relationship based on patient education. We are dedicated to making it easier for physicians in private practice to spend more time providing quality care."

Activities - Question 8-3

1) Before you take a stab at drafting your own mission statement, read the following and indicate what is missing from these mission statements relative to the four criteria identified above. Also articulate what assumptions would you make about the company, if you saw this mission statement. These are actually mission statements that I've seen.

» "Our mission is to engage in research and development activities that we enjoy, until we retire."

» "We conduct innovative, cost-effective research in areas in which we have expertise."

» "We will become the world's most valued company to patients, customers, colleagues, investors, business partners, and the communities where we work and live."[3]

» You can gather other ideas bout mission statements by looking at how the various members of the MEMS Industry Group, describe their businesses.
See **www.memsindustrygroup.org/memberslist.**

2) Consider your answer regarding sustainable competitive advantage, the criteria identified in the proceeding question, and the missions of your closest competitors. Then, draft a 50-75 word mission statement to represent your company or strategic business unit (SBU).

Reality check? Have I answered this question adequately?

Deliverable: You will have answered this question adequately when you have generated a mission statement which is no longer than 75 words in length, that references the items listed on the previous page. The mission statement should be written in a manner which sounds compelling. Once developed, the mission statement should be in a form that could be posted on your website, appear in printed publicity materials, included in your business plan, and placed in your human resource manual.

Question 8-4: What is your vision?

Relevant section:

Business plan - Section 2.3. In addition sections 7 through 12 are effected by this.

Why is this important?

Earlier in this chapter "mission" was defined as an identity statement. The concept of vision is related and implies change and growth. It is an expression of what you would like to become. A good vision affects not only the selection of commercialization strategies, but also drives the development of your company's operational plans.

Background

Please note that during the planning stage it would be best not to apply these terms (i.e. life-style firm, high potential venture, or foundation company) to yourself when talking with investors, suppliers, or customers - as they may create the wrong impression. In particular, the phrase "life-style firm" may be taken as pejorative when applied externally. However, for planning purposes it may be very useful to use this shorthand internally.

Often, the natural tendency is to confine the vision of a company to its present situation. However, the objective of this activity is to remove this constraint and to "blue-sky" it - looking forward five years. Later, we will add constraints. However, what is important at this time is to bring to the forefront a vision which captures your imagination and energy.

Activities - Question 8-4

In your strategic planning meeting, spend time crafting a vision with your management team, Board of Directors, and/or Board of Advisors. Come to some consensus. If you are a sole proprietor, it would be advisable to find a trusted party with whom you can brainstorm, so as to interject some other thoughts and enrich your thinking process.

1) **Financial Goals**

Complete the following table to contrast current and future revenue by source. Following completion of the table, please be sure to explain the projected changes in sources and quantity of income.

SOURCE	CURRENT YEAR Dollars	%	+ FIVE YEARS Dollars	%
SBIR				
Contract R&D				
Consulting				
Services				
Product A (specify)				
Revenue from sales				
Revenue from Licensing				
Product B (specify)				
Revenue from sales				
Revenue from Licensing				
TOTAL				

2) **Products and Services**

What products and services will your company be providing 5 years from now. What additions will you have made to strengthen your sustainable competitive advantage?

3) **Market Goals**

How will the markets that you serve in the future differ from those that you serve now? Please be sure to clarify changes in market share goals, geographic regions served, and customer type.

4) **Positioning**

How will your company be positioned in the mind of your customers? What will differentiate you from your competitors?

Reality check: Have I answered this question adequately?

Deliverable: Unlike the mission statement that resulted in a succinct 75 word paragraph, the vision activity will result in a number of discrete paragraphs that address questions grouped under the preceding four sub-headngs: (1) Financial Goals, (2) Products and Services, (3) Market Goals, and (4) Positioning. It is important to keep in mind that at this time, you are "blue sky-ing it" and posing the vision that excites you and that you think will be possible. Reality testing of this vision will take place as we complete subsequent activities.

Question 8-5: Situation Analysis

Relevant section:

Your situation analysis effects your commercialization strategy - Section 2.3

Why is this important and how does this relate to conflict mitigation?

Your current situation affects your ability to realize the vision you have charted. In other words, the milestones between your present situation and the future will vary as a function of your starting point. A company that is encumbered with debt; that has intellectual property problems; poor employee morale; or inadequate staff will have a different path to follow than one which starts without these encumbrances. These issues need to be addressed before you can effectively build a new future.

When taking stock of your current situation, be sure to also note positive elements of your situation as these should make it easier for you to pursue certain commercialization strategies on the way to realizing your vision.

Background

"Commercialization strategy" refers to the funding options that a company takes to move a product or service from concept development to market introduction. The types of funding that may be available is effected by many factors including your previous investment history and current financial health.

Activities – Question 8-5

In taking stock of your current situation it is important to assess various aspects of your company's health. The following questions are intended to elicit an honest assessment of your current situation.

1) To date, what products has your company/division actively been involved with commercializing?

2) What revenues resulted from this effort?

3) Who are the current investors, strategic allies, owners and/or partners which support your firm/division?

4) To what degree are they satisfied with the performance of your company/division?

5) If you have licensed-in the technology being commercialized, what constraints are imposed by the terms and conditions of the license? Is it an exclusive or non-exclusive license?

6) Assuming that the technology is developed in-house, do you have clear title to the intellectual property or are there estranged co-inventors.

7) Have you publicly disclosed information about the technology and failed to protect it on a timely basis?

8) Does your firm/division currently have commercial customers? If so, for what product? How is your firm/division perceived by these customers?

9. How would you classify the financial health of your company/division?

10. What % of the company's revenue comes from sale of R&D services?

11. What % of the company's revenue is associated with each product or service which you offer?

12. Do you have a multi-functional management team or in essence do you function as a sole proprietorship?

13. Do you have an active Board of Directors and/or Board of Advisors?

14. How would you rate the overall performance of your existing staff by functional area?

15. Do you have another business on the side?

16. How effective are you at transitioning from R&D to manufacturing, production, or a licensee?

17. Do you have an effective new product development process for screening new R&D initiatives?

18. As appropriate indicate the length of time your firm has had a differentiated department for each of the following: manufacturing, marketing and sales, customer service, research and development.

Reality check: Have I answered this question adequately?

Deliverable: To complete the situation analysis, answer each of the preceding questions as honestly as you can. If you are holding a strategic planning meeting in order to complete some of the activities associated with Planning Report 2 - it is recommended that the situation analysis be prepared ahead of time. Share highlights from the situation analysis at the start of the strategic planning meeting in a form that you deem appropriate.

Summary and Conclusions

The objective of the Strategic Planning activities was to lay a solid foundation for business planning. In the course of completing these activities you have assessed your current situation, described your sustainable competitive advantage, developed or reaffirmed a mission statement, and prepared a vision for the future.

After you have completed the activities and discussed the issues with a trusted advisor, it is recommended that you draft section 2.1, the Company section of the business plan. When drafting this, keep in mind that your goal is to enhance the face validity of your firm by presenting information that demonstrates clear direction, dedication, and results. Depending on the nature and maturity of your company, it may be useful to include photos that show your facility.

Within the company section, the sequence in which you present information is irrelevant. However, it is important that the presentation addresses perceived risks of your target audience (equity investor, strategic ally, or debt financing institution). Be sure that when you discuss the history of your firm that it clearly indicates the motivation and drive which gives the company life, but without being written as "stream of consciousness". Also, it is recommended that within the first two pages that you clearly identify the mission statement of your company or strategic business unit.

Chapter 8 Endnotes

[1] Rogoff, Edward. Bankable Business Plans. Penguin Group, 2004

[2] Tiffany, Paul and Peterson, Steven. Business Plans for Dummies. Wiley Publishing, 1997.

[3] http://www.pfizer.com/are/mn_about_mission.html

Strategies and Differentiators

"Don't tell me why we can't do it, tell me why we can."

- R. Craig

Chapter 09

"Doing projects right" starts with listening to the customer.

Introduction

Robert Cooper[1] maintains that there are two ways to win with new products: (1) doing projects right, and (2) picking the right projects. Doing projects right is the result of listening to the customer, modifying your product design to meet customer expressed needs, and engaging a multi-functional team from the outset. Doing the right project implies having acuity in selecting the winners – Would that we all had such acuity!

This chapter deals primarily with product definition and "doing projects right". Activities are included to help assure that the "voice of the customer" is readily brought into product definition, as features, advantages, and benefits (FABs) or value propositions. Then attention is given to building barriers to entry for potential competitors by enhancing your intellectual property arsenal. Finally, methods for funding product development are considered, taking into account your vision for the future and our business philosophy.

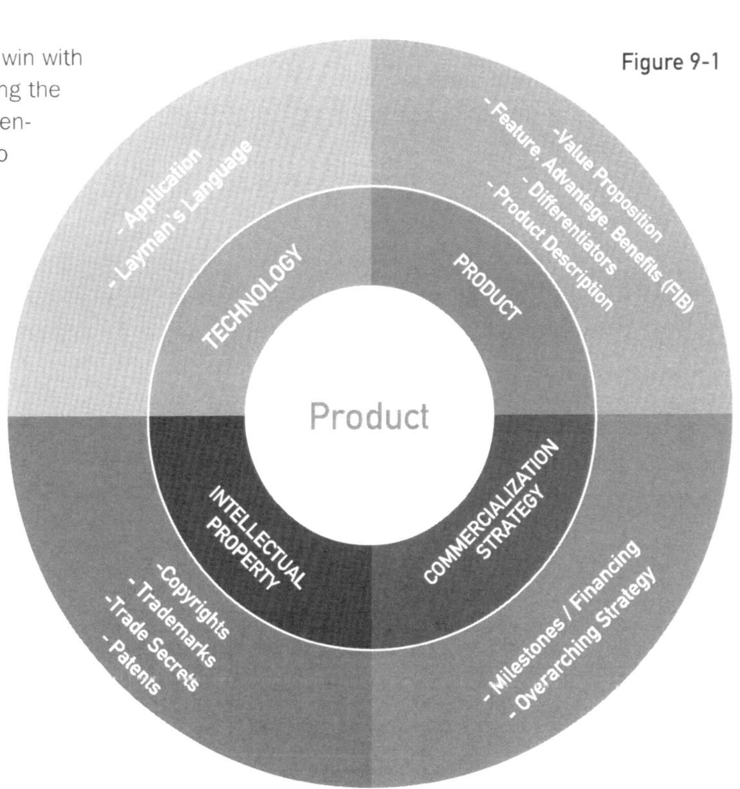

Figure 9-1

Business Plan Outline

The activities addressed in this chapter are designed to accelerate drafting the following sections of the business plan. After working with your business coach to refine the discussion of these topics, information can be readily inserted into the evolving business plan outline.

2.2. Technology
- » ***Brief description***
- » ***Applications***

2.3. Product/Service
- » ***Brief description***
- » **2.3.1. Intellectual property**

2.4 Commercialization strategy

Question 9-1: Describe the technology in layman's language

Relevant Section of Plan

Business plan – Section 2.2

Why is this important and how does this relate to risk mitigation?

Potential investment decisions are usually made by a team after completing a process referred to as *due diligence* which is a multi-faceted evaluation and assessment conducted by potential investors and others they may retain. Aspects of a business that are typically included in such an evaluation extend to a company's management, intellectual property, technology, financial health, and market. Not every member of the evaluation team will be an expert in your field. Therefore, in describing the technology within your business plan, it is recommended that you be instructive to a varied audience and begin with a general discussion which clearly shows the context for your technology. It is always helpful to include photographs or figures that visually represent the technology. Other protocols that are often useful include placing key words in italics or emboldening them, so that they can be readily found on a fast read of your materials. In those instances where the technology is highly complex sometimes people include a brief glossary in an appendix.

Background

In the suggested business plan outline a differentiation is made between technology and product(s). The reason for this is that oftentimes advanced technology firms develop a rich technology platform that gives rise to or spawn multiple, potential products. Therefore, it is instructive to differentiate between the foundation technology and the specific products that will be the focus of the business plan.

Activities - Question 9-1

In this activity, is recommended that you draft the discussion of your technology keeping in mind the intended audience. Carefully select photos or graphics that you can include with the discussion that will enhance the reader's understanding of the technology, and also show its degree of readiness. After having introduced the technology, briefly introduce the possible applications that could be addressed by this technology. Once you have drafted this section and received feedback, it will be ready to transfer into the draft business plan.

1) Describe the technology in layman's language.

Reality Check: Have I answered this question adequately

You will have developed this section well, if upon completion, the reader walks away with an understanding of your technology and possible applications. This section should then lead into the discussion of the specific product(s) that will be the focus of this plan. Avoid the tendency of making this section too long. As this is your area of expertise, this is often a temptation. The length of this section depends upon the complexity of the technology, but should usually be about 1-2 pages. If, after reading this section, someone who is not skilled in your art, still is confused by what you do, the treatment of the subject matter has been inadequate.

Business Plan

Question 9-2: Describe the initial product embodiment and how it will be positioned?

Relevant Section of Plan

Business plan – Section 2.3

Why is this important and how does this relate to risk mitigation ?

When one is developing a capability, focus is often problematic. For example, if one develops a sensor or an algorithm that could be used in a myriad of situations, the possibilities themselves may become overwhelming. One may also be uncertain where in the value chain they should play. In the case of algorithms for example, would one license the algorithm to a software developer; or would they develop the software themselves, or would they embed both the algorithm and the software in a hardware system. What is the company's product? Sometimes the initial product embodiment is not clear-cut. However, one cannot pursue all possibilities concurrently. Failure to decide becomes a definite source of risk as one has limited resources to utilize.

Background

The phrase "positioning" refers to how your product will be perceived by your customers[2]. In other words, the only way that you will ultimately know if your have achieved the desired positioning is to ask them. Is your product positioned by specific and superior attributes, by price, by applications[3]? It is instructive to begin thinking about positioning during the product development process. In fact, research clearly indicates that products are more likely to be successful if there is early and frequent interaction with potential customers. The product development process should assure that *"the voice of the customer"* is reflected in product design.

Activities - Question 9-2

There are three activities in this section that are intended to help with product refinement, and also result in material that can be used in your business plan, and future marketing materials. These activities are referred to as (1) Product differentiation and positioning, (2) Features, Advantages, Benefits (FABs), and (3) Value Proposition.

1) **Product Description:** Please describe the product(s) you will be focusing on in your business-plan. Be sure to include a graphic or a photograph to visually represent the product. As market opportunities relate to particular embodiments of a product, the goal of this section is to describe what you have, what it does, and how it is differentiated from other products. The emphasis in the product description should not be upon the intricacies of how the product works, although a general foundation for understanding those principles was addressed in the technology section.

   In describing your product, think about how you will position it and interject words in your description that clarify if your emphasis is upon a product feature, a product price, and/or a targeted customer group.

2) **Feature, Advantage, Benefits (FABs) :** A useful way to describe a product is by its *features* (product specs), the *technical advantages* that these afford, and the *benefits* that accrue to customers. As a product becomes more refined, it becomes easier to provide a FAB table where F stands for feature, A for advantage, and B for customer benefits. FAB tables often begin as a collection of qualitative statements. However, the goal should be to replace these with quantified statements of benefit. In the following FAB table you will find some examples of good expressions of features, advantages, and benefits. Whenever possible, it is desirable to utilize quantified, rather than qualified terms, especially when comparing a technology with a baseline or standard performance.

Table 9-1 A Sample FAB Table

Feature	Advantage	Benefit
Seat Weight- 10 lbs.	Can be integrated into aircraft	Less pontential damage to pilot if seat is ejected
System Bus: 400 MHz	Can use other, fast components that can communiate with one another	Improves system speed Enables use of 1.6 GHz processrs
Coffee Maker: Removable brew basket	Separates from electronic components	Can pour coffee convienently anywhere
Halogen	Energy efficient	10-50% improvement

Using the preceding as an example, please complete a table that describes the features, advantages, and benefits of your product. A final version of this table will also be placed in your business plan.

Feature	Advantage	Benefit

3) **Value Proposition:** The phrase "value proposition" is defined in various ways. However, the definition that I find to be of greatest utility is offered by Yahoo[4]. The value proposition summarizes what benefits you offer, to whom, and at what relative price. In order to draft the value proposition, you must first clarify who will ultimately use this product (i.e. the end-user). In addition, you will need to clarify the price. At this point in the planning process, you may not have settled on the ultimate price. However, you should be able to generate an approximation.

The value proposition will be a summary statement such as the one suggested below.

"The value proposition for instrument manufacturers looking to better serve the needs of the counter-terrorism market is that this new THz generation method will provide higher resolution and fewer false alarms, at a price that is comparable to existing x-ray methods."

Reality Check: Have I answered this question adequately

When you have completed this section, you will have drafted (1) a product description (text and images) that differentiates your product(s), (2) a table that contrasts the features, advantages, and benefits, and (3) a value proposition. Once refined each of these items can be used directly in your business plan.

Question 9-3: What forms of intellectual property will you use to reinforce your competitive position?

Relevant Section of Plan

Business plan – Section 2.3.1.

Why is this important and how does this relate to risk mitigation?

Intellectual property protection (IP) is an essential tool for limiting competition by erecting barriers to entry. Irrespective of which form of IP you choose, such intangible assets can accrue significant value for you, your partners, and potential licensees. Failure to protect one's intellectual property increases risk, as there is nothing to preclude competitors from taking advantage of the efforts you have made to develop a product or service to fulfill a need.

Background

When a scientist or engineer thinks of intellectual property the first thing that comes to mind is patents. However, there are four classes of intellectual property which should be considered for enhancing your company's value. These include (1) *copyrights,* (2) *trademarks,* (3) *trade secrets*, and (4) *patents*. The laws which regulate these forms of IP vary.

Copyrights: Copyright protection is extended to original works of authorship expressed in a tangible medium. Copyrights do not protect ideas, systems, procedures, or discoveries. Protection is extended to original expressions whether the expression be an architectural drawing, multimedia, a motion picture, sound recording, databases, software used to create and navigate information, books, musical compositions, choreographic work, and the like.[5]

For works created on or after July 1, 1978 copyright protection lasts for the life of the author plus fifty years after the author's death. Although an item is considered copyrighted at the time it is created, it is best to register the copyright with the Library of Congress.[6] Registration is a very simple and inexpensive procedure (under $50). However, it can be invaluable when you wish to license a work or in cases of infringement. A useful text, written in layman's language is the Patent, Copyright, and Trademark: An Intellectual Property Desk Reference. [7]

Trademarks: Trademarks can be extremely valuable and tend to be underutilized by technologists. However, a name, logo, or expression associated with your product or company can acquire goodwill and become a valuable asset. Trademarks can extend to words such as Kodak", distinctive packaging such as "McDonald's arches", number or letters such as "IBM" and pictures such as the rainbow colored apple associated with Apple Computer.

One can register a trademark through the Patent and Trademark Office (PTO)[8], the registered trademark, designated by the symbol ® after the mark, is effective for 10 years and my be renewed subsequently. The trademark holder has the responsibility to monitor the use of the trademark and follow certain procedures to assure that the trademark is used appropriately. Failure to do so can result in the trademark status being revoked. Prior to trademark registration being granted, one can use the symbol ™ after the mark. The ™ puts others on notice that the owner considers this word, phrase, or symbol to be a trademark, even though this has no legal status. The advent of the internet and domain names, has given rise to many issues with respect to trademarks. One can consult the Multimedia Legal Handbook[9] for information on this issue.

It is fairly inexpensive to register a trademark. One can do this on their own for less than $400 or utilize the services of an attorney. Due to the backlog at the PTO, it may take up to 12 months for the trademark status to be determined and designated.

Trade Secret: A trade secret is defined as "information including a formula, pattern, compilation, device, method, technique or process that:

(i) derives independent economic value, actual or potential, from not being generally known to, and not being readily ascertainable by proper mans by, other persons who can obtain economic value from its disclosure or use, and

(ii) is the subject of efforts that are reasonable under the circumstances to maintain its secrecy." (United Trade Secrets Act, Section 1(4),14 U.L.A. 372)

If one follows appropriate procedures to keep the information confidential, the following types of items could be considered trade secrets: financial statement, marketing plans, employee records, customer lists, ingredients in formulations, computer programs, manufacturing and other processes.[10]

One does not need to file registration forms to maintain something as a trade secret. However, it is important to consult with appropriate sources to determine what policies and procedures you need to put in place to provide oneself with trade secret protection.

Patents: The form of intellectual property protection with which most scientists and engineers are familiar is patents. Nevertheless, some of the more recent changes in patent law are still underutilized by inventors. One of the most significant modifications to patent law relates to provisional patents. For more information on provisional patent applications and how these differ from regular patent applications or disclosure documents, please see Patent It Yourself (10th edition) by Attorney David Pressman.[11]

Activities - Question 9-3

There are two activities associated with your intellectual property strategy that can be developed for inclusion in your business plan.

1) Competitive IP strategy

The purpose of this section is to demonstrate to the reader that you do have an over-arching intellectual property strategy. It is recommended that you do this by including a paragraph in your business plan which identifies your intellectual property counsel and indicates how frequently your counsel is consulted; what considerations trigger the filing of various forms of intellectual property protection; and how this works together to provide you with competitive advantage and to erect barriers to entry for your competition.

2) Intellectual Property Assets

Relative to this technology/product, provide a listing of relevant IP that has been issued and/or applied for. The following table pertains to patents only.

Filing date	Patent name	Issue date	Patent number	Countries

Reality Check: Have I answered this question adequately

This section will have been adequately addressed when your strategy is clearly articulated and relevant forms of protection have been identified.

Question 9-4: What milestones need to be funded and what is your preferred commercialization strategy?

Relevant Section of Plan

Business plan – Section 2.4

Why is this important and how does this relate to risk mitigation?

Advanced technology firms have a voracious appetite for money. Not only technology development, but also the protection of IP, the acquisition of appropriate certifications, market assessments, financial analysis, and production all cost far more money than most entrepreneurs anticipate. When used for external purposes, the overall intent of a business plan is to raise the funding required. Therefore, it is important that you anticipate how much funding you will need and the potential sources of funding that you could realistically approach, given the vision for your firm. The amount of funding that you will need, will be clarified during the process of developing operational plans. However, at this point the intent is to consider the activities that need to be funded and potential, generic funding sources that you could approach. Together these considerations give rise to what is called your commercialization strategy.

Background

The phrase "commercialization strategy" refers to the series of financing options that a company entertains to move its technology/product from concept to the marketplace. This strategy is highly dynamic and is affected by considerations that are both internal and external to your company. Internal considerations include: (1) your vision, (2) your business philosophy (3) and the stage of technology development; while external factors include (4) changes in market risk, and (5) your competitor's activities. Although a strategy is defined by a series of milestones and potential funding sources identified in the financing roadmap (Chapter 4), the protocol that we adopted was to name the commercialization strategy by the last financing choice usually associated with production and/or market launch. Sample strategies identified in Chapter 5 included Licensing, Strategic Alliance, Equity Investment (parent company or spin-off), or Initial Public Offering.

Activities - Question 9-4

1) Using the typology of visions identified in Table 4-1, start by identifying the vision that is most closely aligned with your vision for the future (lifestyle firm, high potential venture, foundation company). Describe your business philosophy below, borrowing ideas from the strategies articulated in chapter 5. Then, modify the list of key activities associated with new product development, so that it includes milestones that may be unique to your business, such as FDA approval, FAA approval, EPA approval, etc. Also, exclude those steps that have already been completed. In the right hand column, identify types of financing that you would most likely approach, selecting options from Figure 4-2. For each milestone identified in the left column, identify the type of financing source you are likely to approach. When you have completed the table, define the overall strategy by the decision that you make regarding how production and/or market launch will be handled.

   Please note that at this point, you are not identifying how much money you need, but are merely considering the type of funding you would approach.

2) After you have completed this table, draft a simple paragraph that clarifies the overall approach you will take to commercialize or fund the activities to be discussed in the business plan.

Vision:

Business Philosophy:

Milestone	Type of funding source
Initial screening	
Preliminary market assessment	
Preliminary technical assessment	
Detailed market study	
Predeveloped Business analysis/ financial analysis	
Product development	
in-house product tests	
Customer tests of products	
Trial sell	
Trial production	
Pre-commercialization Business analysis	
Production start-up	
Market launch	

Commercialization strategy selected:

Reality Check/ Have I answered this question adequately.

This question contains a table that you will complete and a paragraph that you will draft, describing your overall strategy. You will have answered this adequately when you have a one paragraph description of your strategy that can be included in your business plan in section 2.4

Summary and Conclusions

The objective of the activities in this chapter was to assist you in thinking about issues related to your technology, product(s), intellectual property strategy, and commercialization strategy. After you have completed these activities and received feedback from your business coach, revised items can be moved into the evolving business plan.

Chapter 9 Endnotes

[1] Cooper, Robert. Winning at New Products: Accelerating the Process form Idea to Launch, Basic Books, 2001.

[2] Ries, Al and Trout, Jack. Positioning: The battle for your mind. Warner Bros, 1986.

[3] White, Sarah. The Complete Idiot's Guide to Marketing. Alpha, 2003

[4] http://smallbusiness.yahoo.com/resources/business_plans/marketing_planning_guide.html?f=4.3.1

[5] Smedinghoff, Thomas. Multimedia Legal Handbook: A Guide from the Software Publisher's Association. New York, NY: Aspen Law and Business, 1998

[6] http://www.copyright.gov/

[7] Elias, Stephen and Stim, Richard. Patent Copyright, & Trademark: An Intellectual Property Desk Reference (7th edition). Nolo, 2004

[8] http://www.uspto.gov/main/trademarks.htm

[9] Smedinghoff, Thomas. Multimedia Legal Handbook: A Guide from the Software Publisher's Association. New York, NY: Aspen Law and Business, 1998

[10] Epstein, Michael and Politano, Frank. Drafting Licensing Agreements. Englewood Cliffs, NJ: Aspen Law & Business, 1994

[11] Pressman, David. Patent It Yourself (10th edition). Nolo, 2004

Industry, Customers and End-Users

"The relationship between the man and the customer, their mutual trust, the importance of reputation, the idea of putting the customer first – always. All of these things, if carried out with real conviction by the company, can make a great deal of difference in its destiny."

- Thomas Watson, Jr., Chairman IBM Corporation. The 1962 McKinsey Lectures, Graduate School of Business, Columbia University

Chapter 10

What is helpful at the outset is to take a broad brush, to paint the panorama, to draw some features on the map, and to place yourself on the road.

Introduction

The jacket selected for this book, depicts a vast expanse devoid of landmarks, fueling stations, and other travelers. A lonely and untamed region, the expanse is desolate until the traveler encounters signs that help transform the undifferentiated region into familiar space.

More often than not, an entrepreneur, like the lonely traveler does not know or understand the industry in which his or her enterprise operates. What is therefore helpful at the outset is to take a broad brush, to paint the panorama, to draw some features on the map, and to place yourself on the road.

Figure 10-1

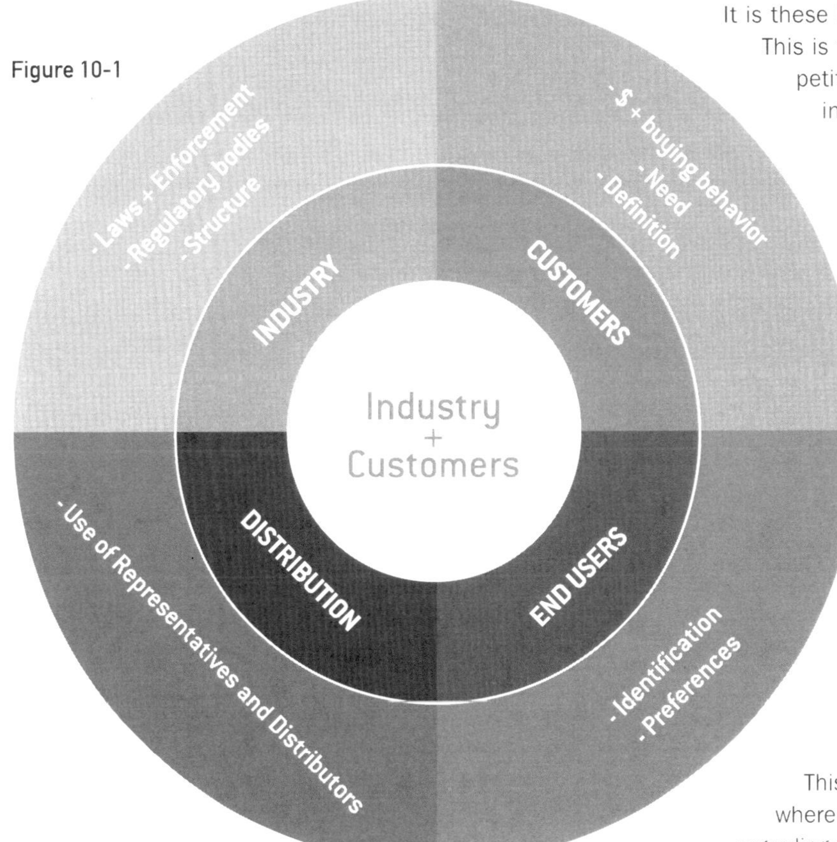

Figure 10-1: Overview of Topics covered in Chapter 10

It is these broadest strokes that define the industry. This is the context in which your company, competitors, customers, and markets operate. An industry can be identified by various attributes and labeled with a North American Industrial Classification Code (NAICS). Industry associations and regulating bodies provide useful statistics, and often identify rules and regulations that dictate how members of this industry must play together.

This chapter provides guidance on how to explore the structure of your industry. With the context thus defined, it is then important and instructive to take a molecular view in which you identify and speak with potential customers and end-users. We start then with the broadest perspective and then zoom in, so that you can understand needs and preferences on a micro level.

This is where your business research begins, where you begin to test hypotheses made earlier regarding needs, the basis for purchase decisions, the availability of funds, and purchasing power. Go back to questions 7-4 and 7-5 in your Mind Map and see what you hypothesized your customer needs to be. With these planning activities, you will test the hypotheses made.

Business Plan Outline

After completing primary research in which you speak directly with potential customers and end-users, and after having reviewed secondary information regarding the relevant industry, you will be ready to draft sections 3 and 4 of your business plan. The outline for these sections can be found below. Remember that the italicized items in the outline are suggestions regarding topics to discuss in that section of the plan. The sequence in which such information is presented is dictated by what makes the best case. In addition, more or less information can be included in these sections, depending on the nature of the information gathered. However, it should always be made abundantly clear to the reader that the information that you have included on customers and end-users comes from your direct interaction with members of these two groups. A method of reducing risk is to demonstrate direct experience with these fundamentally important groups.

3. Industry Overview

3.1. Industry definition and description

» ***Diagram representing the structure of the industry***
» ***Major players within the industry factor driving dynamics***
» ***New products and developments within the industry***

3.2. Legislation and policies

» ***Future and historical trends***

4. Customers

4.1. Customers and end-users

» ***Need addressed by the technology/product/service***
» ***How the need is currently filled***
» ***Need of end-users and customers***
» ***Distribution channels used by customers and end-users***

4.2. Buying behavior

Decision makers

» ***Who makes the decision to buy***
» ***Who influences the purchase decision***
» ***Characterization of decision makers***

Basis for purchase decision

» ***Frequency of purchase decisions***
» ***Basis for purchase decisions***

Question 10-1: What industry does your business operate in? What is the structure of this industry and what trends may affect related customers, competitors, and markets?

Relevant Section of Plan

Business plan – Section 3.1

Why is this important and how does this relate to risk mitigation?

It's very easy to become myopic and miss changes occurring at the broadest industry level which may have a profound impact on the buying behavior and preferences of potential customers and end-users. Such changes include a shift in dominant technology, a change in standards, consolidation of fragmented markets, and the like. This activity is designed to help you take a broader perspective, while at the same time completing other activities which bring focus on specific customer groups.

Background

There are several ways in which one can develop a broad industry perspective. These include:

» mapping out the supply chain from raw materials through finished product and then analyzing what is occurring with major players which dominate different parts of the chain. By contrast, if you are monitoring a waste stream, one would map out the processes which give rise to the waste and then analyze the pressures and constraints brought to bear on the processing and disposal of the waste. The EPA Sector Notebook Reports are excellent sources of such information[1].

» conducting literature searches using the phrases "industry analysis" (or variations thereof) in combination with the name of the industry (or a variant). It is also useful to find the appropriate North American Industrial Classification Code (NAICS)[2] or the older Standard Industrial Classification Code (SIC)[3].

» contacting various government agencies to see what kind of studies they have conducted on specific industry trends. A useful starting point is publications of the US Department of Commerce.[4]

Activities – Question 10-1

1) Locate an image or draw a supply chain from raw materials to finished product for your industry (In some industries, you may want to start at different starting points). Clarify the relative position of your firm relative to the distribution channel.

2) After reviewing literature related to your industry, draft a paragraph which summarizes relevant trends occurring within this industry being certain to address technology changes, as well as the structure of the business environment. If you can find an article that talks about industry drivers and constraints such information is important to include in your discussion. When searching for such a diagram, you may want to use search terms such as "food chain", "industry overview", "distribution chain", or "supply chain" in combination with a descriptor for the industry such as Semiconductor Food Chain

3) Find the appropriate NAICS code, as well as the appropriate industry definition. Indicate whether or not you can fulfill all the needs of the industry as defined.

Reality check: Have I answered this question adequately?

Deliverables: You will have addressed this issue adequately if you can draw a conceptual diagram of the supply chain in the relevant industry and provide a summary of major trends, industry drivers and constraints. This section can then be transferred to the draft of your business plan.

Question 10-2: What regulatory agencies and other certification bodies have an impact on this industry?

Relevant Section of Plan

Business plan – Section 3.2

Why is this important and how does this relate to risk mitigation?

Time and expense are incurred in meeting required government approvals and in acquiring certifications expected by the industry from organization such as the American Society for Testing and Materials (ASTM), Underwriters Laboratories (UL) and the like. Given the associated costs and the significant hurdles that this often poses, it is important in considering your commercialization strategy to anticipate the amount of funding that will be required to comply with these regulations and standards. Being unaware of important regulations can bring a project to a screeching halt. In addition, once you have a better understanding of the hurdles, it might effect your choice of a potential partner or other aspects of your commercialization strategy.

Background

Both Federal and State legislation may have an impact on the market for your technology/products. Government initiatives that are important to consider are not always related to regulations. New tax incentives for example could be provided which spur the growth of an industry. De-regulation, as opposed to regulation, can also drastically change industry dynamics.

Prior to acting upon proposed legislation, Congress holds hearings, calling upon the advice of experts before making their decisions. Numerous standing committees associated with the House of Representatives are involved with the preparation of such information. These committees include Agriculture, Energy and Commerce, and Transportation. A March 2004 publication, called "Looking Fit" includes an updated directory of House and Senate bill status telephone numbers by state – See Legislative Hot line Numbers. You can call the numbers provided and they will advise you which Committee is sponsoring pertinent bills.

Important federal organizations include:

Environmental protection Agency
http://www.epa.gov/epahome/rules.html

Federal Aviation Security
http://cas.faa.gov

Food and Drug Administration
http://www.fda.gov/

Industry Associations: various Industry Associations have a significant impact on the structure of an industry. A sample of such standards organizations is listed below:

American Society for Testing and Materials (ASTM)
http://www.astm.org

American National Standards Institute (ANSI)
http://www.ansi.org

National Resource for Global Standards
http://www.nssn.org

Underwriters Laboratories, Inc.
http://www.ul.com

Activities – Question 10-2

1) How does government regulation, de-regulation, or new policies effect the industry in which your business operates?

After having gathered information that relates to regulation, de-regulation, new policies /procedures, and certifications in your industry, draft the section 3.2 of the draft plan.

2) If additional expenses will be incurred to address regulations and certifications, make note of the anticipated expenses below and the time frame for securing.

Reality check: Have I answered this question adequately?

You will have addressed this section correctly, if after having gathered and considered appropriate information, you have drafted answers to the questions posed that can be readily transferred to the draft business plan.

Question 10-3: Does our technology fill a real or imagined need?

Relevant Section of Plan

Business plan – Section 4.1

Why is this important and how does this relate to risk mitigation?

Many technology-driven companies fail to talk to potential customers early in the technology/product development process. The tendency is to assume that there is a large pool of potential customers who will want the product under development and that the need addressed is genuine and wide-spread. As the ultimate survival of your business depends, however, upon actual purchases made by customers, it is vital to ask the customer what they want early in the development process.

For the technology-driven company, the customer must quickly shift from being a hypothetical construct to a tangible entity. The earlier you talk to potential customers, the quicker you can begin to articulate customer specifications and thereby save development time and dollars.

To demonstrate how important customer contact is - the Malcolm Baldridge Quality Award gives "customer satisfaction" the highest single weighting. Key areas that a company is expected to address relative to "customer satisfaction" include:

» process for identifying potential customers and their needs and expectations,
» frequency and types of data collected through interviews, surveys, and other contacts,
» relative importance of various features - "customer specifications"

The only way that you or an investor will realize a return from an investment is from the sale of your technology or product. Considerable emphasis is therefore placed upon trying to understand the "buyers" or "customers" for your technology/product. It is common for technologists and inventors alike to assume that the customers are there and that they will buy. This is the "Field of Dreams" approach. However, this fundamental assumption needs to be tested.

Background

Talking with potential end-users and customers is vital to successful commercialization. Early contact is not only important in product definition, but also helps you determine if the targeted customers have the means to purchase your product. If someone thinks that your product is the greatest thing since sliced bread, but doesn't have the funds to purchase it, their interest in your product is of little value.

Customers and end-users are often mentioned in the same breath, leading entrepreneurs to the faulty conclusion that these are synonyms. They are not. An *end-user* is the entity that utilizes the item produced (individual, organization); whereas a *customer* is the party which purchases it. The major difference then between customers and end-users is purchasing power. Customers make the purchase decision, whereas end-users do not. If you reflect upon this for a moment, it soon becomes apparent that there is often a chain of customers between you and the ultimate end-user.

Both customers and end-users are important. As you will discover in the next section, if no qualified customers exist, then you have no market - no matter how great the need. A qualified customer is one with desire, money, and access. The acronym *MAD* is sometimes used as short-hand to describe qualified customers. Your goal is to find customers who have *Money*, *Access*, and *Desire*. The latter is determined by need and the ability of what you offer to address that need. Access is determined by the channels that you use for sales and distribution. Money must exist in order for the interested party to qualify as a customer of interest to you. This point cannot be underestimated. Often entrepreneurs are blinded by the issue of need and confound need with purchasing power - however, these are two distinct issues. You must first qualify potential customers on the basis of need and money and then design your marketing and sales plan to maximize access.

Example 1: MRI components

Assume that your firm manufactures a component for a magnetic resonance imaging machine (MRI) and that you are contemplating who is your customer and who is the end-user. It becomes apparent that hospital technicians who use the MRI are the end-users. How easy or difficult it is for the technicians to use the MRI is important and affects the quality of the images produced. However, technicians do not make the decision to purchase the MRI. This decision is most likely made by a board of hospital administrators and/or doctors. The hospital administrators are customers - but not your customers. Indeed if you are the manufacturer of an MRI component, your customer is the system integrator who makes the decision to purchase your component. You need to understand your immediate potential customers; the frequency with which they purchase these components; what issues are important to them; price sensitivities; and the features, advantages, and benefits they seek. The ultimate customers in the chain (hospital administrators) are also important in understanding market size and the derived demand for this component. Problems that the technicians have in using the MRI affects the decision makers at the hospital level. It quickly becomes apparent that understanding the needs and concerns of this chain are important.

Example 2: Software for handicapped children

Assume that you design software for handicapped children. The end-users are clearly the handicapped children. However, those with purchasing power are parents, teachers, and librarians. It is unlikely that children will directly purchase the software. However, the children certainly influence the decision makers. If your commercialization strategy is to license to a software publisher, then your immediate customer is the publisher, not the parent who may actually purchase the software from a re-seller.

Again, in order to understand the size of the market opportunity, you must examine the chain of customers and end-users that exist between you and the end of the chain. Understanding the needs and limitations of the end-users affects software design; understanding the purchasing behavior of the ultimate customer effects your understanding of market size and growth; understanding the needs of your immediate customer allows you to position what you have relative to their needs.

Example 3: Exporting rice

To make this point blatantly clear let's assume that you grow rice and are looking to export to an overseas market. You know that thousands of individuals die each year from famine. Clearly there is a need for your agricultural product. However, the starving masses have no purchasing power. They are end-users, but lacking the money to purchase what you have, they are not customers. If no relief organization steps forward to purchase the food on their behalf, no customers exist. Without qualified customers no market exists, even though there is a need. However, if CARE or another relief organization steps forward to purchase the rice, a market is born. An absurd example? Not really.

Technologists frequently confound the need of end-users with market potential. A classic example involves the clean-up of US nuclear sites. Economists study the problem and conclude that it will cost somewhere between two hundred billion and a trillion dollars to clean up these sites. As with the previous example (rice), there is clearly a need. However, if the federal government does not provide the funds to clean up the sites, there is no market - in the same fashion that there was no market for selling rice to famine-ridden countries without qualified customers. End-users AND potential customers are important, but for you, qualified customers that are MAD are vital!

Activities – Question 10-3

1) What assumptions have you made regarding the purchasing power/behavior and the urgency of need as defined by customers and end-users?

2) What process could you use to locate end-users and/or customers to query?

3) Relative to each assumption that you have made regarding purchasing power/behavior and the urgency of need, what questions could you ask to obtain the desired information?

Preparation for talking with potential customers and end-users must begin with a clarification of your objectives. For example, if your objective is to determine features which affect a purchase decision, you might ask:

» When buying a solution to Problem Y, what features do you look for?

» When comparing similar products, what do you compare?

» What are the key criteria you consider when deciding to purchase a solution for problem Y?

» How frequently do you purchase X?

» What is the average price range of solutions that you entertain?

» Who is involved in the decision to purchase X?

4) What method will you use to gather information, how will you introduce yourself, and what is the timeframe for gathering information.

There are many methods that one can use to collect information from potential customers, end-users, and industry experts. You should ultimately use a method which conveniently fits with planned activities and your style. For example, if you will be attending a trade show you could develop a survey form and ask people to complete it. If you are traveling, you might collect anecdotal, in-depth information through person-to-person interviews. Other alternatives include phone interviews, e-mail and mailed surveys. Irrespective of which method you use to gather information, you must always begin by clarifying your objectives. The objectives, in turn relate to the hypotheses or assumptions you have posed regarding customers and end-users.

5) After reviewing the outline for sections 4-1 and 4-2 of the business plan outline, summarize the results of your primary research (talking directly with potential customers and end-users), in such a way that you can add the information directly to your business plan.

Reality check: Have I answered this question adequately?

The customer section is one of the most important. Do not draft this section of your business plan until you have spoken with at least 5-10 individuals who are end-users or customers. Work with your business coach on the development of objectives and questions. Ask him or her for assistance with locating people to contact. It is highly suggested that you speak with end-users and customers, as opposed to assigning this task to someone else; otherwise you may be less inclined to part with preconceptions.

When you draft section 4 of the business plan, make sure that it is abundantly clear that you have spoken with customers and/or end-users; describe the method used; the questions asked and most importantly the implications for your business model. You may elect to include the methodology, questions, and some raw data in an appendix.

Question 10-4: What are the pros and cons of the distribution channels used within this industry?

Relevant Section of Plan

Business plan – Section 4.1

Why is this important and how does this relate to risk mitigation?

Distribution refers to the method of delivering a product to customers and end-users. Business-to-business companies must decide how to best sell their product within the channel. Alternatives typically include direct sales, sales representatives and distributors. In preparing the operational plans for your business, you will need to make an informed decision about the best approach for you to use. In the event that you are licensing the opportunity to another company - you should also examine their distribution channel and pose any questions that you may have. Failure to utilize the appropriate distribution channel, can result in a failed sales initiative. [5]

Background

According to Don Debelak[6] there are five items which need to be considered in selection of the appropriate distribution channel. These include:

" 1. The amount of support your product needs
2. Your size versus the distribution channel's size
3. The percentage of customers that could buy the product
4. The degree of competition in the channel
5. The sales effort needed to get a positive response "

If your product needs a lot of support, consider using a direct sales force or smaller distributors. In situations like this - bigger is often not better. The larger distributors are often less inclined to take the time necessary to provide demonstrations and other kinds of support. In addition, larger distributors frequently carry a variety of products which possess many similarities. This creates more head-to-head competition in the eyes of the customer. Rather than selecting distributors based on what they sell, it is also recommended that you select distributors based on the market that they serve.

Activities – Question 10-4

1) What method will you use to distribute your product to targeted customers?
List the pros and cons of distributing your product or process through a direct sales force, manufacturers reps, or distributors. Present a detailed list of possible alternatives, using names of firms as appropriate, and then discussing the pros and cons based on an understanding of the properties of the product, your mission, and the strengths of the distribution alternatives.

(2) Draft a brief section to include in your business plan which identifies the distribution channel(s) to be used to effectively reach targeted customers (include supporting rationale).

Reality check: Have I answered this question adequately?

You will have addressed this question well, if you have started by securing the names of various reps and distributors, identified the products they carry now and then, after weighing the pros and cons have selected the best alternative for this stage of development.

Summary and Conclusions

A primary objective of this chapter was to highlight the importance of talking with potential customers and end-users. As mentioned throughout, one of the primary reasons for product failure is the absence of early and frequent conversations with potential end-users and customers regarding product specifications, purchasing decisions, and gauging the sense of urgency or need. An over-arching goal has been to increase your comfort level with this process.

Chapter 10 Endnotes

[1] EPA Sector Notebook Reports http:es.epa.gov/oeca/sector/

[2] North American Industrial Classification Code http://www.census.gov/epcd/www/naics.html

[3] NAICS and corresponding SIC tables http://www.census.gov/epcd/www/naicstab.htm

[4] US Industry and Trade Outlook http://www.ita.doc.gov/td/industry/otea/outlook/

[5] Kotler, Philip. Ten Deadly Marketing Sins: Signs and Solutions. John Wiley & Sons, 2004.

[6] Debelak, Don. Bringing Your Product to Market. New York: John Wiley and Sons, 1997.

Markets and Competitors

"If you can't stand the heat, get out of the kitchen!"

- Harry S. Truman

Chapter 11

The entrepreneur should make every effort to avoid self-delusion, and participate in a rigorous evaluation of the opportunity.

Introduction

Whether or not one should pursue an opportunity depends in large part on if there is money to be made. In making this statement, I recognize that this is often NOT the motivation of a scientist or inventor. However, when evaluating whether or not to put corporate resources behind a potential new product, the return on investment (ROI) should be a primary consideration.

If the entrepreneur is planning to use his or her own resources, he may be willing to pursue a smaller opportunity than an equity investor. Nonetheless, in making this decision, consideration should be given to the size of the potential opportunity, and an assessment made of the costs to be incurred in obtaining a desired level of market share. To the extent possible, the entrepreneur should make every effort to avoid self-delusion, and participate in a rigorous evaluation of the opportunity. Fundamental to such an assessment is consideration of: (1) the size of the market, (2) the existing and potential future competitors, and (3) the cost required to obtain the desired market share.

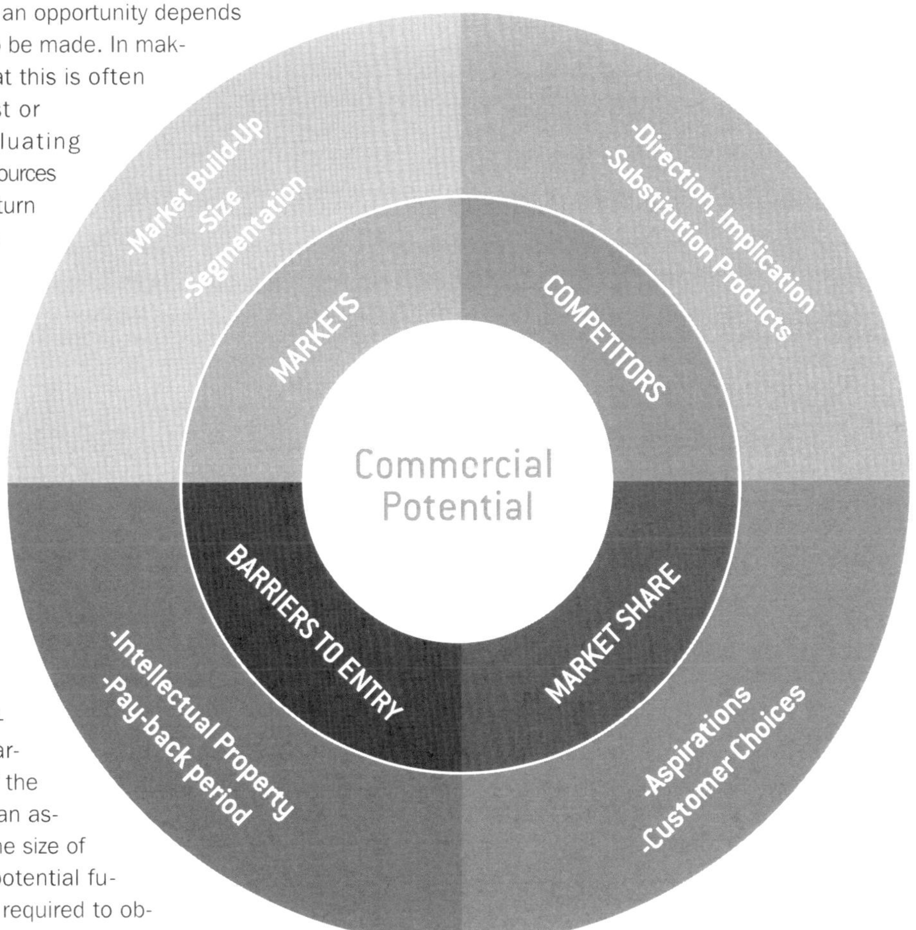

Figure 11-1: Overview of Topics covered in Chapter 11

Business Plan Outline

The purpose of this chapter is to assist in evaluating the true size of the opportunity (market), the likely actions of competitors to a perceived market threat (competitor analysis), and to determine if an opportunity exists. In conducting this analysis, you may find that the size of the opportunity does not merit further pursuit. In this case, you should curtail your business planning activities here. However, if you find that there is an opportunity worth pursuing, proceed with business planning and organize the information obtained in the general format recommended below.

The suggested outline is very broad, allowing plenty of latitude for you to take the description of the opportunity in the appropriate direction. Be sure to clarify how you have segmented the market, which market you consider *primary* (the market that you will pursue first) and which is considered secondary (markets to be pursued later). Be sure to clarify how you have sized the market if you have used a market build-up method, providing footnotes that reference the sources of information used. In drafting the competitor section differentiate between all methods of addressing a market need (indirect competitors) and direct competitors (competitors within the same technology space). Competitor analysis is often written from both a technology and a company perspective. It is fine to address both perspectives. However, do not shirk a good analysis of competitive firms.

5. Market
- **5.1. Market definition**
  - **5.1.1. Primary market**
  - **5.1.2. Secondary market**
- **5.2 Market size and trends – Primary market**
  - » ***Current total and served-available markets***
  - » ***Predicted annual growth rates***

6. Competitors
- **6.1. Indirect competitors**
- **6.2. Direct competitors**
  - » **Who are they?**
  - » **Market share of competitors**
- **6.3. SWOT analysis**

Illustration

One of the most difficult steps in this process is to conceptually define your market. Like so many aspects of business planning, this process is iterative. In other words, you start with a market definition and then as you examine the implications more closely, go back and either expand or restrict the definition used. The following is an example.

"Traintech" is a start-up company in Palo Alto, California that wishes to sell training seminars to industry. They have heard that training is becoming increasingly important and wish to develop a strategy to get a piece of the action. In their preliminary market research they discovered that sales of training to industry was a $19 billion market. They formulated the following mission statement:

"TrainTech is a training and consulting firm that designs and delivers negotiation training programs to industry, utilizing a unique combination of multimedia."

Traintech would have been wrong to assume that this total market of $19 billion (fictitious numbers used throughout) was their playing field. To size the market appropriately they had to examine the different types of training providers and examine what affects the purchasing decision of potential customers. Also, they would need to find a way to estimate how much was or could be spent on negotiations training by potential customers. Further research revealed that the major providers of training to industry included:

- » *small training firms (15%)*
- » *training programs associated with universities and colleges (45%)*
- » *training provided by major accounting firms (15%)*
- » *large training institutes (10%)*
- » *training franchises (15%)*

Traintech conducted further research and found that:

1) *Depending on the size of the company, purchasing decisions were either made by the human relations or personnel department, or individual managers.*

2) *In larger firms the sell cycle was usually 6-12 months. The individuals who evaluate training products do not usually have purchasing power. Companies tend to stick with known suppliers and only make a change if they are very unhappy with a vendor or if they are looking for a specialty product.*

3) *The primary reasons for purchasing training varies depending upon the size of the company. In large companies training is often a perk and is given to fast-track employees. These companies send their executives to Ivy League universities for their specialty training. Technical training was also preferred*

from university vendors. Trainers that would be invited into a large industry tended to be the "Guru of the month" — usually an academic with a new book on the Top 10 list.

4) *Training needs for secretaries and lower-level employees typically were fulfilled by training franchises that offered one day seminars for a $100 fee in a local hotel. In this fashion, large corporations were able to provide no-frills training for their lower level employees without paying the expense of travel, room and board.*

After gathering these data, Traintech took a long serious look at themselves. They were undercapitalized and therefore had a very limited marketing and sales budget. They had a small office; certainly not a beautiful facility where executives would want to hold retreats. They did not have a "guru of the month" on staff. They therefore made the following decisions, regarding their present market

1) *They were competing against other small training firms and not against the larger providers.*

2) *They also decided that they should probably sell their training programs to smaller companies, rather than large industrial firms. They didn't have the "guru of the month" to make sales to larger firms. Another option to entertain was to hire such a person. If they could, then they could tackle a larger piece of the market.*

(3) *Considering the length of the sell cycle and the cost of travel, TrainTech decided to limit its market scope to its immediate geographic location, thus decreasing the costs associated with sales. They gathered as much data as they could about their competition (i.e. small training firms going after the same market). They examined their competitors ' sales volumes and number of employees (data were available in a Book of Lists published in conjunction with the local Chambers of Commerce). They used the competitors' aggregate sales figures and assumed a 5% market growth rate and thus redefined the size of their market. The size of the market in which they were competing was a $10,000,000 market. This was their served available market, i.e., the part of the total available market in which they were going to compete. They had a list of names of all the companies to which they would like to sell their products, as well as a list of their competitors and comparative features, advantages, and benefits.*

After going through this entire process TrainTech revised its mission statement:

"TrainTech is a training and consulting firm that designs and delivers negotiations training programs to small high-tech firms in the San Francisco Bay area."

The activities that follow are designed to help you define and size the initial market for your product. Please keep in mind that there are various ways in which this can be done and that we will be using only one approach referred to as a Market Build-Up method. Before beginning with market and competitor analysis, a list of common misconceptions is provided.

Common misconceptions

In sizing markets, a number of misconceptions are rampant. The most common is to take the dollar value ascribed to an industry and then use that figure to represent the size of your market.

Example 1: A company that manufactures a sensor, quotes the dollar value of the entire instrumentation market as the size of its market. If you manufacture a component that can only be used in one family of instruments, you must conceptually limit your market to the dollar value associated with that component.

Example 2: If you have a device that can be used to remove heavy metals from a waste stream, do not cite the dollar value for the entire environmental remediation market as your market. The size of your market is that subset of actual and hypothetical customers which has the specific problem that you can address.

Example 3: If you produce a software package on topic X, do not cite the dollar value spent in the US on all software as the size of your market. Your market size is limited by the content scope of the software and the customers it targets.

Example 4: You have a combustor which can be used with generators of a certain size, do not indicate that the size of your market is equal to the entire power grid of the US x a certain price per kilowatt. Your market is limited to generators of a specific size.

Question 11-1 How is the market segmented?

Relevant section

Business plan: Section 5.1

Why is this important and how does this relate to risk mitigation?

Market segmentation is a method of targeting those markets where the Features, Advantages, and Benefits (FABs) of your product are important to the targeted customers and are available at a price they can afford. The process of segmenting your market provides focus that in turn will enable you to obtain a clearer understanding of how to proceed in efforts to penetrate the market.

Background

Segmenting the market appropriately is an art and takes considerable time and effort. Common ways of segmenting a market include:

- SIC/NAICS[1]
- Demographics
- Geographic
- Psychographic/Lifestyle characteristics
- Organizational Characteristics
- Attribute preference
- Buyer Behavior/Use
- Purchase Characteristics - Price
- Marketing Conditions
- Product Characteristics

Markets can be segmented in various ways. Therefore, it is important to have a method of determining if the approach you have taken is adequate. Taylor[2] provides three criteria for determining the appropriateness of market segmentation.

1) **Is the segment definable in some operational way?**

This criterion queries if you can accurately quantify the number of customers in this segment, as defined. For example, let's assume that you have a consumer product intended for children under five feet tall with freckles (conceptual definition of the market). Your next task would be to try and quantify this market to see if it makes sense to segment in this fashion. In all likelihood, you would have difficulty quantifying potential customers in this niche as it is unlikely that any organization would sort data this way. Instead, you might have to settle for a surrogate product for which data may be more readily available such as sales statistics on sunscreen packaged for children. If these data are available, it would make sense to modify your conceptual definition making it "*children with sensitive skin*", instead of "*children under five feet with freckles*."

2) **Can you reach this segment effectively through affordable advertising?**

The objective of the second criterion is to alert you to the fact that when segmenting the market, you should concurrently consider how easy it will be for you to reach the target market through affordable advertising. The advertising medium selected must be one that the customers use. It could include approaches such as face-to-face meetings, direct mail, internet communication, trade shows, phone calls, and the like. If you can use the same marketing communication materials with market segments that you have considered to be distinct, combine them into one segment instead.

3) Is the market segment small enough for you to dominate and large enough to provide good profits? You will make the most headway with sales if you appropriately segment your market and then communicate effectively with the customer, emphasizing benefits in terms that are meaningful to them. In so doing, you will need to determine whether it is the end-user or the customer who is the most influential in the buying decision. [3]

The most common error that companies make is to segment their market inappropriately. Seek a market that is large enough to be worth the effort and in which you can become a significant player within three to five years. Expect that you will step from one target market to another over time. This is a very common strategy to use with products that are initially very expensive to produce and which therefore have limited initial market potential. In such instances, one targets a market for initial entry which can afford to pay a higher price for the advantages that the product offers and then makes strategic decisions to also enter other markets as the price drops. For more information on market segmentation, consult Competitive Marketing Strategies [4] and The Successful Marketing Plan [5].

Activities – Question 11-1

1) What is the best way to segment your market and why (Please refer to the list of frequent options)?

2) What trade shows does this segment attend and what professional journals do they read?

Reality check: Have I answered this question adequately?

Before one can begin to size a market, it needs to be segmented conceptually. Before deciding on the segmentation, it would be instructive to see if one can find data collected in the fashion described. If data are NOT collected in this fashion by associations or industry groups, the segmentation criteria chosen will not be useful.

Question 11-2: What is the size of the market?

Relevant Section of Plan

Business Plan – Section 5.1

Why is this important and how does this relate to risk mitigation?

The phrase "size of the market" or "market size" refers to the potential of a market expressed in dollars, units, or both. This concept is applied to all segments for which the product is appropriate. The "size of the market" is the limit that one can hope to obtain. Keeping in mind Taylor's comment about competing in market niches in which one can become a dominant player, how the market is sized is very important. If the size of the market is too small, a potential investor will not be interested in investing as the return on investment may not be attractive. If the market size is fairly small, the entrepreneur should reconsider if the technology/product is worthwhile pursuing or if he should reconsider how the market is segmented. Market segmentation is fluid and has profound "decision implications" for everyone involved.

Background

There are many distinct, but related concepts used when discussing a market. Key concepts are defined below.

A **market** is a set of actual and potential buyers. The concept of potential buyer is vital to sizing an emerging markets and using the market build-up method.

A **potential market** is a set of actual and potential buyers that have money and desire to purchase a product with a specific set of price and performance characteristics. Please note the relationship between this concept and the definition of qualified customer.

The concept of **available market** adds one more descriptor to this definition - that of access. **Access** is determined by your marketing communication plan. If there are plenty of fish in pond X, but you fish in Dead Pond Y, your catch will be nonexistent, not because there are no fish - but because you have limited access. **An available market is a set of actual and potential buyers that have money, desire, and access.** It is the set of actual and potential MAD (money, access, desire) customers.

The **served available market** is the available market that you decide to serve. It is your niche. As indicated by Reis and Trout[6]" the essence of positioning is sacrifice. You must be willing to give up something in order to establish that unique position". One of the most difficult things for companies with a rich technology base is focus. Technologists tend to be overwhelmed by and sometimes enamored with the possibilities of their technology, and feel that by focusing something will be missed. However, it is important to keep in mind that a niche marketing approach is a sequential process, not a permanently exclusionary one. This approach leads to better use of resources and greater success. "Just because there are a lot of targets and you've got a lot of shot, doesn't mean that you don't have to take aim."[7]

The concept of **penetrated market** is different in kind and relates to the extent that the opportunity has already been addressed by yourself and others.

Total market demand is an expression of the volume that could be purchased by a specified group of real and hypothetical customers within a defined period of time under certain conditions.

If one represents the relationship between these markets visually, you will see that the result is that the size of the market niche is winnowed down to a more tightly defined and smaller niche. It is represented in dollars or units, on an annualized or total basis. However, annualized figures need to be based on verified data or known trends in that market, rather than as a straight average of the total market demand.

Relating back to the issue at hand, commercial potential increases with a niche marketing approach and if the total market size is above a certain threshold ($250 million or more is a common minimum). You should be cautioned that statements such as "The market is multibillions", make it apparent that you are not using a niche marketing approach. To say that the market is "unknown", betrays that you have not tried to assess the market potential. By contrast, if you have rigorously examined the market potential and it appears that the total market demand is less than a $10 million opportunity, it will be of little interest to most investors and corporate partners and should lead you to re-evaluate the market you are addressing, and may serve as a catalyst to re-examine the product definition.

Activities – Question 11-2

1) Has someone else already defined the size of the target market? If so what is the size of the market; how is the market defined, and what is the source material for these data?

Frequently, it is difficult to obtain the size of emerging markets. However, it is always worthwhile to see if the desired statistics have already been compiled by someone else. Keep in mind however that the reported figures may be at an industry level; be a reflection of the current volume of sales within a specific SIC/NAIC code; or a forecast based on various modeling techniques. It is unlikely that you will find information reported at the niche level. Therefore, after determining what is available from others, you will, in all likelihood need to refine the approach. To determine if this redefinition is necessary, ask yourself if your product/service meets all the needs that constitute the market as defined by the other source. If it does not, then you will need to further refine the size of the market so it reflects the need that your product can fulfill.

Listed below are some of the more common resources one can approach. Bob Berkman, the author of Find It Fast[8], has various tips for talking with experts and for gaining access to specialty libraries.

Government Statistics: Data on market size might be available from the Department of Commerce or other government agencies.

Associations: The *Encyclopedia of Associations* is an extremely valuable resource found in most libraries. This three volume set is produced annually and contains an index and two accompanying volumes. There are associations for almost every item imaginable. Every entry contains the name of the Association, its services, membership and a contact person. The Associations will indicate if they collect statistics. If they do collect statistics, call the contact person and inquire if they can sort the data in the manner of interest to you (your segmentation technique).

Journalists and Futurists: Another way to obtain information is to contact journalists and futurists who have written articles on the industry in question. When you find a valuable article, contact the editor and ask him to provide you with the phone number of the author. Contact the author and see if he has come across any information on "market size."

Findex: The Directory of Market Research Reports, Studies, and Surveys: This resource is found in large libraries and lists published market research reports. For the most part the reports are quite expensive. However, if you find the name of a research report of interest, you can contact specialty libraries in your area and see if they have a copy that they will let you see. Corporate libraries are most likely to have such reports. You may also see if you can obtain a copy of the Abstract from a Findex report as the abstracts themselves often contain very useful information.

Professional Associations: Be sure to contact the professional associations appropriate for the industry in question to determine if they have commissioned any studies on the market of interest.

Reality check: Have I answered this question adequately?

You will have answered this question correctly, if you have obtained information on the relevant market, understand what products/services were included in the definition of the market sized, and have recorded the appropriate references.

Question 11-3: Using the market build-up method to determine the size of your NICHE market

Relevant section

Business plan - Section 5.2

Why is this important and how does this relate to risk mitigation?

During the past thirty years there has been a steady migration away from the concept of mass market and towards the concept of niche markets. With mass markets the premise was to produce product in large quantities so that there were economies of scale and to provide the mass produced product to the greatest number of customers. Most customers received a little of what they wanted, and few were totally satisfied. By comparison, the concept of 'niche market' focuses on customization and meeting very specific needs of customers. In a study conducted by the Strategic Planning Institute in 1987 they concluded that the return on investment from addressing larger markets averaged eleven percent; whereas the return on investment from smaller niche markets was twenty-seven percent. Focusing on tightly defined market niches is more profitable.

The shift then is away from generic products, to customer defined products. The task that every company faces is to determine which market niche(s) it will serve. Companies grow their business by focusing on customers and then stepping from one niche to another. Furthermore, "Customer choice shapes the business, which is why customer choice is such a critical strategic decision."[9]

Earlier we spoke about a chain of customers (distribution channel), starting with the entity that purchases directly from you and ending with the customer that makes the ultimate purchase decision. The first question to address then is which level of customer do we focus on when sizing the market? To shed some light on this question, let's begin by differentiating between consumer and industrial markets.[10] Industrial markets consist of all individuals and organizations that acquire goods and services that are used in the production of other products and services that are supplied to the ultimate customer. Industrial markets are larger than consumer markets.

Industrial markets share a number of characteristics:

1) There are fewer buyers than in the consumer market. For example, if you make a component that can be used in automobiles, there are but a handful of major automobile manufacturers or automotive assembly manufacturers which would be your direct customers.

2) The buyers are larger. The quantity of items that a customer such as Boeing or Motorola might buy could be sizable i.e. hundreds of thousands of units versus dozens.

3) There is a geographical concentration of industrial buyers, with 50% being in ten states (California, Massachusetts, Ohio, and others).

4) Demand is derived from the purchasing behavior of other customers in the chain. This is an important point in sizing markets as you need to size the market from which your immediate customer's need is derived.

5) Demand is inelastic which means that short-term price changes do not produce disproportionate demand changes.

6) The demand is more volatile. This means that small changes in consumer demand can result in large changes in industrial demand.

7) There are professionals involved with the purchasing function.

With respect to industrial customer buying behavior, there are three major types of buying situations: (1) **a straight rebuy,** (2) **modified rebuy**, and (3) **new tasks**. The latter is the arena in which most new technology firms will find their opportunities. The greatest number of decision makers are involved in such purchase decisions, therefore it is important to interact with the variety of people that influence the purchase decision. These include the users of the technology/product; the influencers, such as design engineers, regulators, and the like, and the decision makers. Factors which are known to affect the ultimate buying decision include product specifications, price, terms and delivery times, service terms, order quantities, payment terms, and whether the suppliers are approved.

Thus, if you have a component that you wish to license, sell, or distribute to an industrial customer it will be important to understand not only who is involved in the decision making process, but what issues are of importance to them. As their demand for what you have will be derived from other customers and end-users in the chain, you will need to size the market as it pertains to the ultimate customer at the end of the chain. In other words, lets assume that you are looking to sell an MRI component to a company in the manufacturing sector and you are trying to assess the size of the market opportunity for you. In this case, you will size the market based on the ultimate customer in the chain (the hospital administrators). Likewise, if you sell a software tool that can be used to interface more effectively with the internet, you would size the market opportunity based on the ultimate customer in the chain - i.e. the individuals who make the decision to purchase the software for themselves or their organization. If you sell a device that can be used in clean-up of nuclear sites, you size the market based on the ultimate customer in the chain that makes the decision to purchase the technology to be used in the clean-up.

Thus, you will need to understand your industrial customers and then size the market based on the ultimate customer in the chain.

Background

The approach you will use to size your niche market is referred to as a market build up method, also referred to as a bottom-up method. Successful use of this approach requires that you utilize the information gathered previously regarding customers - their need, their degree of interest in your solution, their price point, their ability to pay for the product, and accessibility. In addition, you will need to combine this information with some assumptions which seem reasonable to make given your knowledge of the field. Engineers are often most uncomfortable with sizing markets as it is not exact. However, this approach can provide a good approximation upon which you can make decisions.

A Market build-up approach: An example

There are many methods which can be used to derive the size of emerging markets. The method preferred by Dawnbreaker is referred to as a market build-up method. This method yields a hypothetical construct which defines the size of an available market. The data and assumptions used in building the model are clearly articulated, so that anyone can see the method used to derive market size. One starts with commonly available data points and then looks for or collects more difficult information to refine the model. In the example which follows information from a resource called Statistical Abstract of the United States[11] was used as the starting point and then used in combination with other information gathered from industry experts by phone and from potential end-users (who were also potential customers) in a mall intercept.

One begins the market build-up method with a product concept. In the example which follows the product is a “warm suit for stranded motorists”, a lightweight piece of outerwear that could be tightly rolled and conveniently stored under one's car seat in a vacuum sealed bag. The concept was that in a cold weather emergency situation, the driver could pull this out, put it on, and remain warm for an extended period of time. The need addressed was protection from the cold in remote areas. It was assumed that the selling price would be $25.95.

The obvious potential market for this product was the one for which is was designed - car owners that lived in snowy regions. However, after brainstorming regarding other potential end-users, other market segments were suggested including sports enthusiasts, military, and workers on oil rigs. However, in most of these cases, the product definition would need to be refined to serve these markets. The decision was made to size the market first for automobile use. The challenge was to define the available market based on money, access, and desire - the criteria mentioned earlier which qualify potential customers.

STEP 1: Obtain data from the Statistical Abstract of the United States regarding automobile registration by state and tally the number of automobiles registered to people in those states which have considerable snowfall.

> **Result:** 67,611,000 motor vehicle registrations.

STEP 2: Determine what percentage of this group would have a desire for this product.
It would be wrong to conclude that by virtue of owning a car and living in a cold climate that one would have a desire for a warm suit. The premise adopted was that those individuals who carry some sort of emergency gear in their car have demonstrated an interest in protection from the cold and would be a potential customer. Various approaches were used to try and get a handle on the size of this subset including contacting Triple A, various associations, and editors of journals and catalogs which specialize in emergency situations. Ultimately the decision was to conduct a mall intercept in a number of cities. In the mall intercept, a table was set up at an exhibit and men and women of driving age were asked if they kept cold weather emergency gear in their car. 10% of the sample did. Using this data point, we reduced the size of the potential market, currently discussed in terms of registered vehicles in cold climates to 10% of 67,611,000 or 6,761,100.

> **Result:** 6,761,000 were inferred to have a desire for product.

STEP 3: Determine what % of this group had the money to spend on this product.
The Statistical Abstract of the United States includes information on car registration broken down by age , income, and gender. Given the initial conceptualization of the product - retailing for $25.95, it was assumed that this would be of greatest interest to those which had an income above $35,000 - others would just use a blanket. 45% of the sample fit into this category.

The figure obtained previously (6,761,000) was further reduced to reflect income.
6,761,000 x 45% = 3,042,450

> **Result:** 3,042,450 was inferred to have the disposable income to spend. Thus, the potential market size for this niche was 3,042,450 units over the life of the product.

STEP 4: Determine the size of the available market, by taking into account access, which is determined by marketing communication strategy selected by the company.

The decision was made to market this product strictly through catalogs. After talking with industry experts it was determined that 40% of this income group make purchases from catalogs. The market size was further reduced to take into account the distribution channel selected. 3,042,450 x 40% = 1,216,980 units.

> **Result:** 1,216,980 people were inferred to have access to this product through widespread use of catalogs. Thus, the available market size was 1,216,980 units. Translating this into a dollar value was accomplished by multiplying the total number of potential purchasers by the selling price of $25.95 = $31,580,631. Realize that the marketer of this product would then need to determine what might be the annual market for the warm suit and any current or potential competing products. The actual market demand in any given year would be substantially less than $31.5 million, the figure which would exhaust all current, potential buyers in the US market.

Conclusion

The market build up method uses a combination of data and assumptions which are reasonable and clearly articulated to determine the size of a market niche. As you can see, the conclusion is as good as the assumptions made, the product definition, pricing, and the marketing communication plan. A different configuration would yield a different result. However, in all cases the conclusion drawn needs to be reasonable, defensible, and clear.

This approach is to be contrasted with the common mistake made by most entrepreneurs which would begin and end with finding the number of people that have cars in areas with heavy snow (67,611,000) and falsely concluding that the market size was $25.95 x 67,611,000 = $1,754,505,450. The market build up method requires that the user examine the issues of desire, money, and access, and size the market in light of those.

Activities - Question 11-3:

1) Use the market build-up method to estimate the size of your served available market. Be sure to differentiate between assumptions and data points in this model.

Please keep in mind that it is often difficult to find the information that will allow you to use this method. Often the approach needs to be modified, using surrogates.

2) Draft section 5-1 of your business plan, being sure to clarify how the market was segmented and sized. Using a pie chart, differentiate between potential market and served available market.

Reality check: Have I answered this question adequately?

Deliverable: You will have answered this question adequately, when you have obtained data and used methods, such as the market-build up method to size the market that you can serve. If the market size is for an associated market that is larger than the need you can address, then it is sized inappropriately. For example, if you offer negotiations training and you define your market as the training industry this would be incorrect – as your product does not meet all training needs of all learners in this industry.

Question 11-4: What are substitution products?

Relevant Section of Plan

Business Plan – Section 6.1

Why is this important and how does this relate to risk mitigation?

It is not uncommon to hear technology entrepreneurs emphatically state that they have no competition. They quickly follow by saying *"There is no other university professor doing this." or "There is no other company in California that makes this product."* or *"No one else uses this technology and its patented."* Rest assured, if there is genuine need for your product, there is competition. Competition consists of the myriad of alternative ways to address the targeted need. The methods of fulfilling the need may be low-tech, no-tech, or advanced technology with approaches reminiscent of your own. To be prepared for competition, it is important to start by asking "What are substitution products?" In other words, what are the alternative ways of addressing a given need.

Background

In order to assess competition at its most fundamental level, you must pursue "the need" or as some people put it "the pain". Once you have isolated the need, then ask yourself what are the variety of ways in which that need is currently being addressed. For example, if you are making an IR intrusion detection system for use in warehouses - the competition may be watchdogs. Potential customers evaluate alternative ways of addressing a need. For the most part, they are not attached to the solution being high tech or low tech - they want an effective solution; and often have a particular price point in mind.

Competition is in the eye of the customer. In other words, you may think that your product is significantly different than that of your competitors, however, if your customer thinks you provide the same offering, you must differentiate further in order to show your product's value. Customers think in terms of their need and not in terms of your solution. Therefore, think broadly about the competition and differentiate between indirect and direct competitors. Indirect competitors are alternative ways of addressing a need. Direct competitors operate in same technology space.

Activities – Question 11-4

1) Use the table below to organize your thoughts.

The Need: Please describe

Approach	Provider	Product Name	Price

Start by defining the need that you and your competitors are addressing. Be sure to describe the problem in layman's language. Then, using the column labeled approach, generate a list of the alternative ways of addressing that need. In subsequent columns provide an example of key competitors that utilize that approach and clarify the product name and price.

2) Draft section 6.1 of the business plan entitled Indirect competitors

The information provided should clarify the need addressed and the alternative ways of addressing the need. It would be appropriate to mention the shortcomings of the various techniques, setting the stage for why your solution is needed.

Reality check: Have I answered this question adequately?

You will have answered this question adequately when you have described three or more methods of addressing the stated need that vary in technical sophistication.

Question 11-5: Who are the competitors in this market and what provides them with their competitive advantage?

Relevant Section of Plan

Business Plan – Section 6.2

Why is this important and how does this relate to risk mitigation?

The market place is dynamic and filled with competitive actions and reactions. When product development is complete and you successfully enter the market with a new product, the status quo will be disrupted. Often, the growth of your company is at the expense of another. In order to prevent erosion of their business, competitors will take actions that put your firm on the defensive. They may decrease price; increase quality; provide greater service; provide greater margins to their distributors; attend more conferences and the like. In order to determine your strategy, it is best to examine the competitive landscape and see where you most readily can obtain a toe-hold.

Background

Every company has competitors that are already operating within the market segment of interest. Your resources and skills relative to the other players will affect how profitable your business will be. The types of information that you can obtain on your competitors depends to a large extent on whether they are privately-owned or publicly traded. Considerably more information is available on publicly traded companies. Leonard Fuld's book entitled Monitoring the Competition[12] provides many helpful hints on how to build up good data files on your competitors.

If the company is publicly-owned you can request an annual report, 10-K, 8-K, and 10-Q, from the Securities Exchange. If the company is privately owned the task is more difficult. However, you can develop good data from news articles, product literature and catalogs, price lists, and market studies.

Other resources which can be consulted to gather information on your competitors include:

» Industry journals, local newspapers, customers, suppliers, and trade associations.

» The Thomas Register of American Manufacturers is a large comprehensive set owned by most major libraries. It is updated annually and lists manufacturers' names, addresses, and phone numbers. Information is organized alphabetically by product. This is an excellent starting place.

» Ward's Business Directory of US Private and Public Companies provides a listing of the public companies with largest sales sorted by SIC code.

» Dialog. When looking for more obscure information and/or information on a global basis, Dialog is extremely useful.

Often technology entrepreneurs examine competitors because they are required to do so, but miss the true value that comes from conducting a thorough competitor analysis. In looking to the future, assess the strategies that your competitors currently use to expand and also look for commentaries by upper management and analysts regarding the future direction of these firms. Often times they are very revealing. A careful examination of the information that you gather on your competitors will help you to understand how to position your product and your company; will prepare you to anticipate competitive responses to your market entry; and will affect your final choice of a commercialization strategy. A historical perspective on your competitors also has great value in understanding what is required to grow a business in the targeted industry – especially costs associated with marketing and sales.

Activities: Question 11-5

1) After reviewing competitor information, generate a table which summarizes key competitor information

	Company A	Company B	Company C	Company D	Your company
Product Name					
Price					
-					
-					
-					
-					
Markets Targeted					

Please modify the table by filling in the names of the companies instead of referring to them as company A, company B, etc. and including important product attributes on the vertical access instead of "-"

2) After reviewing available competitor information, write a paragraph for each key competitor indicating who their customers are and what approach they appear to be using to increase market share. If a publicly traded company, indicate the percentage of revenue spent on marketing/sales.

3) Look at your competitors websites. Then, after analyzing their approach to marketing and customer support, write an additional paragraph for each competitor that indicates how they position their company and product(s); what you anticipate their likely response will be to your market entry; and the implications that this has for your commercialization strategy.

Reality check: Have I answered this question adequately

You will have answered this question well, if after collecting information on competitors, you can analyze their strategic direction and reflect upon the implications for your strategy.

Business Plan

Question 11-6: Conduct a SWOTT analysis

Relevant Section of Plan

Business Plan – Section 6.2

Why is this important and how does this relate to risk mitigation?
SWOTT stands for Strengths, Weaknesses, Opportunities, Threats, and Trends. SWOTT analyses can be conducted for many purposes - including corporate self-analysis and competitor analysis. When used for corporate self-analysis, the team reflects upon its own strengths and weaknesses, and also examines market trends, looking for opportunities for and threats to one's business. This information is then used to fuel one's strategic planning.

Background

Your objective in conducting a SWOTT analysis is somewhat different. In this activity, you will look at the strengths and weaknesses of your competitors as well as trends that are apparent in how they conduct their business. With that information in hand, you will then examine Opportunities for your company, in light of their competitive weaknesses, and also examine Threats in light of their strengths. The objective in conducting this SWOTT analysis is to enable you to make better decisions regarding your choice of a commercialization strategy.

As indicated previously, the commercialization strategy that a company selects should be shaped by both internal and external factors. Internal factors such as a company's mission, vision, and sustainable competitive advantage affect initial choices, but external factors such as actions of your competitors and windows of opportunity should also influence your thinking.

Activities – Question 11.6

1) After reviewing competitor information, generate a list of competitor strengths. Items to consider include things such as market position, brand name, value added to products through warranties and extra care rendered customers, product performance, ability to raise money, distribution network, patents, strategic alliances, productivity, product price, management, reputation, consistent quality, customer loyalty, and international capabilities.

2) Consider analysts comments regarding weaknesses of competitors (if analyst comments are available). Also, consider the absence of certain strengths (see list above), as weaknesses. Then, generate a list of competitor weaknesses.

3) In light of both competitor strengths and weaknesses, articulate where the opportunities lie for your firm. Also indicate where the threats for your firm lie, from your competitors.

4) Draft Section 6.2 of your business plan

Reality check: Have I answered this question adequately?

A SWOTT analysis is a good way to represent the dynamics of the market place and to draw conclusions regarding the implications for your firm. You will have addressed this question well, if your analysis extends to at least 3 key competitors and if you clearly draw strategic implications for your firm.

Summary and Conclusion

The work of Jeffry Timmons[13] provides a useful way to examine the magnitude of an opportunity. Highlights of such an analysis are summarized in the table below. These criteria constitute a partial list of those that can be used in evaluating venture opportunities and are presented here as a means of looking at high and low potential of a business opportunity.

As the information in the preceding table indicates, if you have an identified niche, are entering an emerging market with a minimum total threshold of $250 million, aspire to be a significant player in that tightly defined niche, and if the market is growing at 30-50% per year, your commercial potential is high. By contrast, if you have not yet defined a niche, are entering a mature market; have not sized the market, commercial potential decreases. If your statements regarding market share take the form "We should be able to get 2-3% of this market within 5 years", your potential from the perspective of a potential ally or investor is greatly decreased. Such statements show a lack of understanding of niche markets and betray a lackluster approach and a poor appetite for business.

The purpose of this chapter was to help you assess the size of the market opportunity, as well as the strengths and weaknesses of your competitors, so that you are better able to determine if an opportunity exists for the product(s) under development.

Table 11-1: Measuring Commercial Potential

Important Variables	Important Variables	High Potential	Low Potential
Customers	Meets customer need	Yes	No
	Customers are receptive	Yes	No
	Customers loyal to other suppliers	No	Yes
Market	Identified niche	Yes- customer's reachable	No
	Market size	$250M+	Unknown, less than $10M, multibillions
	Market growth	30-50% or more	Contracting or less than 10%
	Market structure	Emerging	Mature
	Market share	At least 20% in 5 years	Less than 5% in 5 years
Competitive Advantage	Barriers to entry	Yes	No
	Well established networks	Yes	No
	Top talent	Yes	No
	Value added potential	High strategic value	Low strategic value

Chapter 11 Endnotes

[1] SIC= Standard Industrial Classification Code. NAICS= North American Industry Classification System.

[2] Taylor, James W. Competitive Marketing Strategies: An action plan for achieving market leadership. Radnor, PA. Chilton Book Co, 1986.

[3] Linneman, Robert E. and Stanton, John L. Jr. Making Niche Marketing Work. McGraw-Hill, Inc., 1991.

[4] Taylor, James W. Competitive Marketing Strategies: An action plan for achieving market leadership. Radnor, PA. Chilton Book Co, 1986.

[5] Hiebing, Roman Jr. and Cooper, Scott. The Successful Marketing Plan, Chicago, Il: NTC Business books, 1997.

[6] Ries, Al and Trout, Jack. Positioning: The battle for your mind. Warner Bros, 1986.

[7] Linneman, Robert E. and Stanton, John L., Jr. Making Niche Marketing Work. McGraw-Hill, Inc., 1991, page 7.

[8] Berkman, Robert. Find it fast (5th edition). Harper Resource Book, 2000.

[9] Webster, Frederick. Market-Driven Management: Using the new Marketing Concept to Create a Customer-Oriented Company. New York: John Wiley and Sons, 1994, page 96.

[10] Sandhusen, Richard L. Marketing. Barron's Educational Series, Inc. New York, 1987.

[11] http://www.census.gov/statab/www/

[12] Fuld, Leonard M. Monitoring the Competition: Find Out What's Really Going on Over There. New York: John Wiley & Sons, 1994.

[13] Timmons, Jeffry A. New Venture Creation (4th Edition). Irwin, 1994.

Operational Plans

"If you can't get paid for it, don't sell it!"

- Benjamin Franklin

Chapter 12

Opportunities exist... because of the synergy between great ideas and the capabilities of a team to exploit them.

Introduction

Chapters 8 through 11 focused on the description of your company, your technology, and the opportunity itself. Irrespective of your strategy for bringing a technology to market, the opportunity must be amply described in the first sections of a business plan, referred to jointly as the "Business Opportunity Preview". In the last chapters of this workbook our focus shifts to "how" you will realize the opportunity. In the diagram below, these operational plans are described as "risk pools".

Figure 12-1: An Overview of Operational Plans

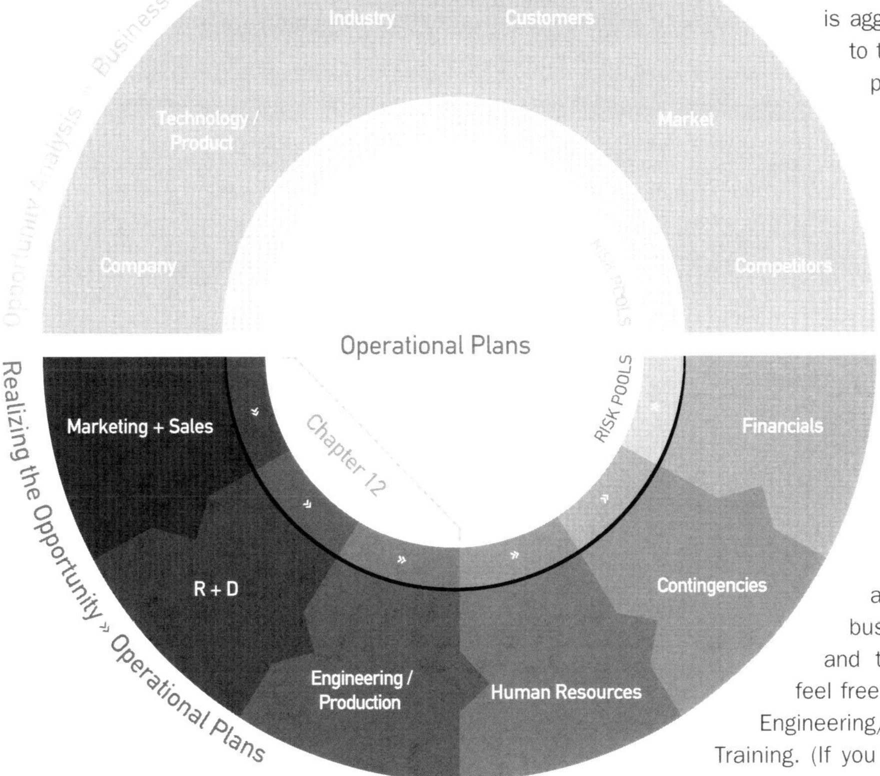

Opportunities exist not merely because of the presence of a great idea or a magic moment, but because of the synergy between these and the capabilities of a team to exploit them. It is for this reason that you often hear venture capitalists say that given the choice between a *"Grade A team with a Grade B plan"* or a *"Grade A Plan with a Grade B team"*, they would take the former. One can see an opportunity, but be afraid to go after it. One can see an opportunity, and not know what to do with it. One can see an opportunity and not have the means to exploit it. The purpose of this chapter is to help you to do all three: prepare to see an opportunity, understand what is needed to exploit it, and revisit your commercialization strategy.

In determining the best way to exploit an opportunity, it is vital that the founder be mindful of his or her own aspirations. It is possible that a significant opportunity exists if it is aggressively pursued, but you may not be up to the task.Therefore, you may initially dismiss pursuit of the opportunity as you cannot see yourself growing your company rapidly. However, recognizing your concerns, you might instead pursue the opportunity by licensing to another entity and/or forming a joint venture with a firm that could fully exploit the opportunity. The choice of a strategy is not done in a vacuum. A choice is made in consideration of what it will require to exploit the opportunity from the perspective of those that will be lead the charge.

In this chapter we will address three risk pools: Marketing and Sales, R&D, and Engineering/Production (or an appropriate surrogate). Depending on the business functions your company performs and the commercialization strategy preferred, feel free to substitute other business functions for Engineering/Production such as Customer Support/ Training. (If you will be using a licensing strategy please refer to the discussion of a licensing package in Chapter 6 and to appropriate financials in Chapter 13). The driving force for the operational plans is marketing and sales. Thus, the first risk and indeed the primary one comes from over or under-estimating projected sales. Great care must be taken to minimize risk in your business planning. Your potential partners and investors will look at the opportunity from a risk perspective and you should do the same. Be sure to spend sufficient time and energy developing sales projections that are defensible. The projections that you develop DO matter. This is not just an exercise. Decisions that you make regarding the rate of scale up, financing resources required, and other commitments will depend upon these projections. It is for this reason that during the due diligence process performed by potential investors and partners they will linger on market development and customer feedback.

The various operational plans share an emphasis on quantified objectives that enable one to measure performance, garner the resources required, and develop financial projections. An **objective** is a statement that is both quantifiable and time-bound. The objectives for the various business functions are related, with all ultimately being connected to a company's sales objectives. In order to develop sales objectives, you must be specific about what you are selling (i.e. Product Model 1000 with XYZ features); the product's price ($1,000 per unit) and the target market (i.e early responders). In the statement of your sales objectives you must specify the number of units you will attempt to sell; as well as the time frame in which those sales are to be made. The objectives for all other business functions - research and development, manufacturing, customer support, human resources, and finance - must be consistent with the sales projections. In other words, you must have a plan to deliver manufactured products at a rate consistent with your sales projections. You must have the human resources required at the appropriate time to perform the various business functions that support the infrastructure that is delivering product on the timetable outlined.

Although there is no guarantee that you will be successful in achieving the sales projections articulated in your objectives, your marketing plan needs to be sufficient to deliver the level of response you are looking to achieve. When utilizing the plan, review your sales objectives every couple of months and track your performance relative to these. As a result of your analysis, you may decide to adjust your objectives and/or increase the amount of resources dedicated to their attainment.

As a business plan has a 3-5 year horizon, you must develop sales objectives which span this time frame. The implications of this statement are that you need to articulate the series of products or models you will introduce over time; and clarify the sequence of markets you will attack - as a function of time, price, and positioning.

Business Plan Outline

The purpose of this chapter is to assist you in the preliminary development of the operational plans you will implement to realize the opportunity you have articulated to date.

7. Marketing / Sales Plan

- 7.1. Opportunity statement
- 7.2. Sales Objectives
- 7.3. Current customers (if appropriate)
- 7.4. Potential customers
  - » *Customers targeted for intensive selling efforts*
  - » *How other customers will be identified and qualified*
  - » *Product features emphasized and contrasted with competitors*
- 7.5. Pricing
  - » *Basis for targeted price point*
  - » *Margins & levels of profitability at various levels of production & sales*
- 7.6. Sales Plan
  - » *Sales force analysis (reps, distributors, direct)*
  - » *Sales expectations for each salesperson & each distribution channel*
  - » *Margins given to intermediaries*
  - » *Service and warranties*
  - » *Organizational chart for sales/marketing staff, indicating planned growth for 3 - 5 years*
- 7.7. Marketing Communications Plan
  - » *Year 1- Detailed Marketing Communications plan*
  - » *Years 2-5 (general)*
- 7.8. Sales/Marketing Budget
  - » *Assumptions*

8. R&D Plan

- 8.1. R&D Objectives
- 8.2. Milestones and current status
  - » *What remains to be done to make the product marketable?*
- 8.3. Difficulties and risks
- 8.4. Staffing
- 8.5. R&D Budget
  - » *Assumptions*

9. Manufacturing/Engineering Plan

- 9.1. Objectives
- 9.2. Use of Subcontractors
- 9.3. Quality control
- 9.4. Staffing
- 9.5. Manufacturing/Engineering budget
  - » *Assumptions*

Question 12-1: Develop an Opportunity Statement

Relevant Section of Plan

Business plan – Section 7.1

Why is this important and how does this relate to risk mitigation?
In activities completed to date, you have conducted strategic planning and analyzed data regarding the market opportunity and competitive landscape. Before beginning work on business plan financials, it is recommended that you develop an opportunity statement that highlights the market opportunity; clarifies why your firm is in a position to take advantage of this opportunity; and clearly states your revenue objective for the next 5 years. From a risk perspective, such a statement requires that you sort through and highlight those factors that provide you with sustainable competitive advantage.

The following is an example of a resulting opportunity statement.
"An examination of the pharmaceutical market indicates that there is a clear opportunity for specialty manufacturing firms which can perform chemical synthesis, formulation, pilot and large scale production of pharmaceuticals. Such an opportunity exists because of the increasing pressure to reduce the cost of pharmaceuticals to the consumer. In response, the larger pharmaceutical firms are increasingly becoming more narrowly focused on discovery and are outsourcing "scale-up" and in some instances larger scale production to specialty manufacturing firms. It is estimated that the size of the opportunity for outsourcing of all classes of pharmaceuticals in the US is $100 billion (fictitious number). In order for a specialty manufacturer to be competitive, it must be GMP certified, have an outstanding reputation, and be able to provide this service at X% of the cost which would be required for the larger pharmaceutical companies to do the work themselves. Our goal is to become a $60 million company within 5 years in the microbial fermentation segment of the $2 billion biopharmaceutical market."

Background

"I was seldom able to see an opportunity until it had ceased to be one.' – Mark Twain

Hindsight is one thing, but for those looking to develop high-potential ventures, the ability to predict if an opportunity exists is essential. These future opportunities are often referred to as "windows of opportunity" and according to Timmons, they must be open long enough for a company to take advantage of them. However, it is important to also keep in mind that the presence of a window of opportunity is a necessary, but insufficient condition for a company to be successful. The company addressing the opportunity must have their wherewithal from a financial, management, and business culture perspective in order to reap the potential benefits. One becomes skilled at finding opportunities, if they continue to canvas the market and attend to the cues provided by customers and competitors.

Activities – Question 12 - 1

1) Clarify the nature of the opportunity and what conditions give rise to this?

2) Indicate the size of the opportunity and how long it is likely to last.

3) Clarify why your firm is in a position to take advantage of this opportunity?

4) Utilizing the information from questions 1-3, draft an opportunity statement that can be used in the business plan.

Reality check: Have I answered this question adequately?
You will have answered this question well, if you have developed a clearly defensible opportunity statement. You should be able to defend with data the reasons for indicating that a market opportunity exists and will last for a given period of time. You should also be able to demonstrate through your corporate behavior, the ability to take advantage of the opportunity.

Business Plan

Question 12-2: What approach will you take to revenue generation?

Relevant section

Business Plan – Section 12.1

Why is this important and how does it relate to risk mitigation?

Before discussing revenue generation, it is instructive to revisit the concept of commercialization. There is much confusion about the definition of "commercialization". Some seemingly view this as a synonym for sales; while others view commercialization as the process of bringing a product to market which bridges all stages from concept development to market sales.

If one accepts that commercialization is a process, then it is also clear that when one is engaged in concept development, product development, and ultimately sales, that they are all participating in the commercialization process, al beit, at different points. However, what changes over time is the need for a company to obtain financing to fund these development activities. Examples of financing methods to underwrite development activities include reinvestment of company profit; equity investment by business angels, institutional venture capitalists, and investment bankers; debt financing by banks and other lending institutions; participation in science for hire programs offered through government and state agencies, and sweat equity. These financing methods were discussed earlier in Chapter 5.

As can be readily seen in the following Figure, during the Technology Creation stage financing was required. As one would expect, no revenue was generated from product/technology sales during this same period. However, during the Market Focused Biz and Produce Development Stage, when product sales began, the need for financing increased.

Figure 12-2: The Valley of Death Relative to Commercialization

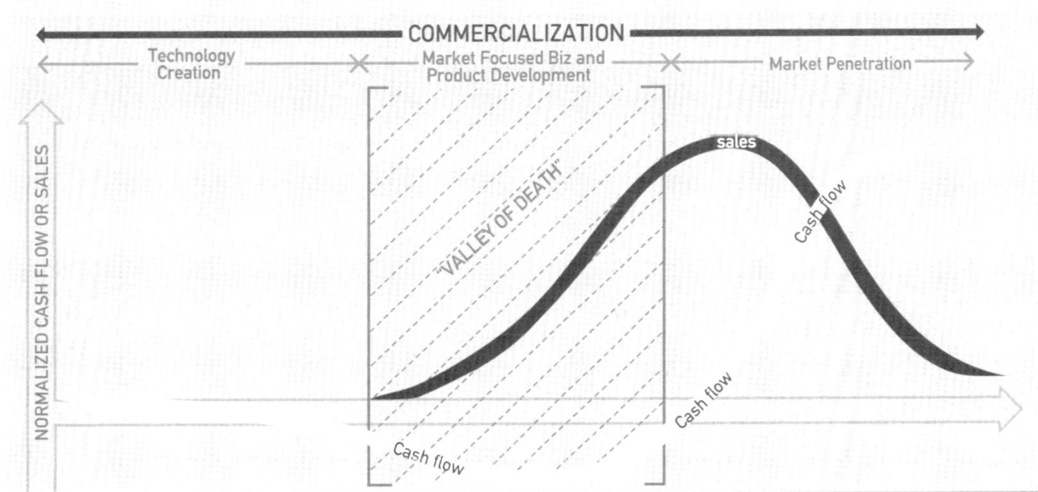

Ultimately, after traversing what is referred to as "The Valley of Death", revenue generation from sales, outstripped the need financing.

The Valley of Death is the most treacherous point for a company engaged in new product/technology, as it is the point when the demands for cash are at its highest, and so is the risk aversion of many potential financing sources. In an excellent report by the National Renewable Energy Laboratory (NREL)[1], the differences in perspectives of public and private sector sources of financing are highlighted. In this text, we have addressed the issue of financing through discussions of commercialization strategies which marries various technical and business milestones with sources of financing.

At this point in the business planning process our objective is to revisit your commercialization strategy to determine if that has changed during the business plan development process and to begin to shift our focus to the topic of revenue generation (from sales) in preparation for the development of pro forma financials.

Background

Although there is a clear distinction between financing and revenue generation, these activities overlap. In other words, a company may be generating revenue from one line of business while they are concurrently seeking methods of financing other lines of business. A company may be selling and producing product, but still need significant investment to be able to do this on a larger scale. Various examples of revenue generation from products, technologies, and services are listed below

Your firm is responsible for
- manufacture, marketing, and direct sales
- customer support /training

Your firm subcontracts these functions to others that do it in your name
- sales through value added resellers or other distributors
- utilize contract manufacturers

You give the rights to another entity to perform these functions in their name
- joint venture
- spin-off
- licensing

When considering approaches to revenue generation, at its simplest you are clarifying who will manufacture the product; market and sell it; and provide customer support. You can opt to have your firm perform these business functions directly or be one removed and have other entities do this on your behalf and derive revenue from their actions (licensees, joint ventures). When discussing the revenue generation approaches that you will take, in essence you are identifying if specific roles that will be completed by your firm or by another entity. If you reflect upon this, you will clearly see a relationship with the earlier activities on mission and vision.

Activities – Question 12 - 2

In mapping out your pro forma financials you will need to concurrently consider who will play roles in revenue generation from sales, and what type of financing you will need to seek to traverse the cash flow "valley of death". Therefore, before completing this activity, review what you said earlier regarding your company's mission and vision, as well as the commercialization strategy. In the mission activity you indicated business functions that your firm would perform and in the commercialization strategy activity, you clarified types of organizations that might be involved with sales.

1) Please use the table below to indicate your current intent regarding the near and long term approaches to revenue generation. Start by defining as year 1 the year in which you will begin to sell product in the upper left hand corner. Then, place an x in the appropriate column to indicate who will perform the different business functions near and long term. This table will serve as a stepping stone to the creation of your pro forma financials.

Table 12-1: Near and Long Term Approaches to Revenue Gerneration

Year 1 = ????	Your company	Contract manufacture	Distributor/ Rep	Licensee	Joint Venture
Manufacture					
Near Term (1-2)					
Long Term (3-5)					
Market					
Near Term (1-2)					
Long Term (3-5)					
Sales					
Near Term (1-2)					
Long Term (3-5)					
Customer Service					
Near Term (1-2)					
Long Term (3-5)					
Quality Control					
Near Term (1-2)					
Long Term (3-5)					

Reality check: Have I answered this question adequately?

This table will not appear in the business plan, but is a preliminary activity aimed at helping you think through the timing and approach to revenue generation.

Question 12-3: Begin to formulate your sales projections

Relevant section

Business Plan – Sections 7.2, 7.4, and 7.5

Why is this important and how does it relate to risk mitigation?
The engine for any company's growth is sales. Therefore, the first operational plan to be crafted will be the sales plan. One of the most difficult tasks is to be realistic about sales projections. Two extremes are common - over-optimism resulting from lack of information and inexperience, as well as meager sales projections resulting from lack of information and fear. The challenge then is to obtain the best information possible upon which to project realistic sales goals.

Background

Five approaches are described that could be used to estimate sales:

1) **Talk to your customers.** If you have a close relationship with a key customer, ask them how many units of X they will need for each of the following 1-5 years. Be sure to also probe what will be necessary to assure these sales are made; who the decision makers are; as well as the sell cycle. This approach can most readily be used when you produce a component and your customer is an established system integrator, interested in the advantages that your component will bring.

2) **Look for a benchmark.** A second approach to approximating the rate of sales is to find an appropriate surrogate and use that as a benchmark. In other words, examine what it took for a surrogate product to enter the market place. If you can find a surrogate in a publicly traded company - then the record of what occurred with that product's introduction will be a matter of public record. By studying the material, you will also be able to determine the costs associated with that products launch from this same source.

3) **Survey and extrapolate.** A third approach is to systematically collect data from potential customers regarding their intent to purchase X during the near future. Also be sure to find out how much they would expect to pay for the item and what are the characteristics of the vendor that they are most likely to buy from. Knowing that customers intend to buy X is different than feeling confident that they will purchase X from you. To increase the likelihood that you will be the vendor of choice will require considerable marketing and sales effort. Your sales projections will therefore need to be tempered by a recognition of the degree of effort required to assure these sales. You would then extrapolate from these data to form projections.

4) **Professional Associations.** On occasion you may find that professional associations serving a discipline may have gathered some data of this nature to assist their membership. Also, there are associations of distributors and sales reps that may also be contacted on such matters.

5) **Advisory Board and Consultants.** If you have made the decision to penetrate a specific market, it would be invaluable to seek the guidance of individuals who have worked in that market as members of your advisory board. You can also consider hiring consultants who have worked in this field to provide assistance.

Activities – Question 12 - 3

1) List your sales projections (in units) for each of the next five years. Indicate what sources you consulted or gathered which support that these projections are reasonable. Also be sure to indicate the

Table 12-2: Sales Projection by year

	Year 1	Year 2	Year 3	Year 4	Year 5
Product Name					
Sales projection in units					
How estimated					
Target market					
Sales Price					
Profit margin					
Type of sales force					

If you have multiple products, please complete a comparable table for each product. The table should be completed with the intent to include in Section 7.2 of your business plan with supporting narrative which expands the discussion of the condensed information included in the summary table. If you amply discuss the issue of pricing in Section 7.2, feel free to omit section 7.5 of the draft plan

2) If you have existing customers to whom you are selling or delivering product, please be sure to discuss this in Section 7.3. The purpose of so doing is to demonstrate to potential partners and/or investors that there has been preliminary market acceptance.

Question 12-4: Market Penetration

Relevant section

Business Plan – Sections 7.5, 7.8

Why is this important and how does it relate to risk mitigation?
As a technology entrepreneur begins to prepare the financials, a number of surprises lurk around the corner. The disparate pieces of the puzzle come together and the entrepreneur often finds him or herself surprised by the implications of the goals set. Suddenly, one can see that if they wish to exploit the market opportunity at the rate projected, they must sell far more product than anticipated in the near term. Often, when confronted by the implications of the financial model, the entrepreneur begins to reassess their commercialization strategy and/or their goals. Both considerations are appropriate.

Background

One can develop financials using a *bottom-up* or a *top-down* approach. It is actually instructive to use both approaches. In preparing pro forma (forward looking) financials, the starting point is sales, the revenue engine for the company. In a top down approach, one starts by looking at the size of the market and the company's market penetration goal (i.e. the amount of that market that the entrepreneur wishes to capture for themselves as sales). When you insert the sales price (NOT cost) of your product into the model, you can readily deduce how many units you will need to sell by year in order to achieve the desired level of market penetration. This is where the element of surprise comes in – Is it reasonable to sell the number of units the model spits out?

By contrast, when using the bottom-up approach, one starts with a reasoned assessment of the number of units that could realistically be sold by year, given your understanding of the sell cycle, as well the extent to which the development and production processes could be accelerated if appropriately funded. If you input both the number of units and the sales price, the model will indicate the company's degree of market penetration by year. A potential partner and investor in reviewing your plan will examine the projections to see how aggressive or conservative your market penetration goals are.

Activities – Question 12 - 4

Two models are provided below for examining market penetration – the first model represents a top-down approach and the second, a bottom-up model. In order to use either model you must start with the unit sales price. Please be sure NOT to use unit cost, but unit sales price in the model. The best way to determine sales price is through interaction with your customers. However, an alternative is to survey the price of products/services that your targeted customers consider to be comparable. Depending on the nature of your pricing strategy, you could opt to then use an average price in your model, or a price that reflects the high or low end of the continuum.

Top- Down Model

A spreadsheet is available which contains formulas in the background and explanatory comments. In this top-down model, you plug in the market penetration goal, and the model will generate the estimated sales revenue and the number of units that must be sold to achieve that level of market penetration. Surprise! Can you sell 2,000 units in Year 1, given what you know about the sell cycle for this type of product?

Table 12-3: Market-Penetration Goals and Sensibility Check

	Year 1	Year 2	Year 3	year 4	year 5
Market Size	$100,000,000	$102,000,000	$104,040,000	$106,120,800	$108,243,216
Rate of Market Growth	NA	2%	2%	2%	2%
Market Penetration Goal	2%	3%	4%	5%	6%
Sales goal	**$2,000,000**	**$3,060,000**	**$4,161,600**	**$5,306,040**	**$6,494,593**
Selling Price Per Unit	$1,000	$1,000	$900	$900	$800
Number of Units	**2000**	**3060**	**4624**	**5896**	**8118**

Figures calculated for you

Bottom-Up Model

In the bottom – up model, input the number of units that you have reason to believe could be sold into this target market, GIVEN that you had the appropriate resources, and GIVEN that the product could be available in this time frame. The challenge here is to focus on customer receptivity, rather than your company's past production experience. If your firm has classically been an R&D firm, any projections that reflect more than a slow ramp in product sales may be dismissed as unreasonable, if they are outside your experience to date. However, your experience is not the issue when looking at sales projections – the issue is reasoned and tested customer receptivity. Again, let me stress the importance of having good guidance from sources that are experienced with sales into the targeted market when developing sales projections. The projections used should be well-reasoned estimates. In the following model, market penetration goals decreased when well reasoned sales projections were inserted.

Table 12-4: Bottom-Up Comparison of Market Penatration Goals

	Year 1	Year 2	Year 3	year 4	year 5
Served available market size	$100,000,000	$102,000,000	$104,040,000	$106,120,800	$108,243,216
Rate market growth	NA	2%	2%	2%	2%
Sales overall					
Units expected to be sold	5	50	100	250	500
$ avg selling price of total product	$1000	$1,000	$1,000	$1000	$1,000
New product sales	$5,000	$50,000	$100,00	$250,000	$500,000
Consulting or aftersale service	$10,000	$10,000	$10,000	$10,000	$10,000
Total sales	$10,500	$60,000	$110,000	$260,000	$510,000
$ market share - total market	0%	0%	0%	0%	0%

Figures calculated for you

If you look at the two tables (top-down and bottom-up), you can readily see the difference in sales and % market share that results from applying the two models. In the bottom-up approach, the rate of projected sales will not even reach the 1% market share point by year 5. There is a clear performance gap between the two models. The challenge is to decide what to do; to determine how you can minimize your risk, yet still successfully move to a sales goal that is a stretch that is achievable. In considering that stretch you should consider:

- Who will actually make the sales?
- How many calls or contacts with a customer will be required to convert the contact to a sale?
- What amount of sales per sales person is reasonable?
- If you are using distributors or reps, ask them to provide you with their sales forecasts

Reality check: Have I answered this question adequately?

In this chapter and the next, we begin development of pro forma financials in a cumulative fashion. As "sales" drives company growth, we have started the process of developing pro formas by considering the relationship between sales projections and market penetration. You will have addressed this task adequately, if you have defensible assumptions regarding price and sales projections that extend beyond your fears and experience base. However, the projections must reflect reasoned estimates based on expert opinion, as well as information that you have gathered from direct interaction with potential customers and/or end-users.

Question 12-5: Developing a marketing communications (advertising) plan?

Relevant section

Section 7.7

Why is this important and how does this relate to risk mitigation?
Technology doesn't sell itself and "word of mouth" doesn't travel nearly as fast, nor as far as you would like. Indeed, you must develop a "marketing communications plan" as a companion to your sales projections. Having carefully selected your sales objectives, now you must develop a marketing communications plan that will result in the targeted level of sales.

As an R&D firm morphs into a product company, the technology founders are often amazed at how much money is actually required for marketing and sales. There is the well-recognized tendency to under-estimate the cost of marketing and sales. To avoid this pitfall, it is important to keep a number of points in mind.

- It is more expensive (%) to get on someone's "radar screen" than it is to stay there.
  - *When initiating sales of any new product or service, you should expect that considerable time and effort will be required to obtain that first sale (maybe 7 repeat calls and numerous visits over an extended period). However, once the initial order is obtained and assuming that you perform well, repeat sales will require less effort.*

- As a company transitions from being an R&D firm to a product company, marketing and sales expenses should outstrip R&D expenses. This change would be reflected in a ratio of R&D as a % of sales.
  - *R&D $ spent as a % of sales is, to a large extent, the result of a product life cycle. If the product life cycle is 10-15 years, the product is more likely to be treated as a commodity and there will be great pressure to keep prices low. The result is low investment in R&D (less than 5% of sales). By contrast, where the product life cycle is very short (3-5 years) money is continually invested in R&D at a higher rate (15-20% sales) to create the replacement products. R&D firms start with high R&D expenses, but over time, these should decrease.*

- A useful ratio to watch over time and to benchmark against industry standards is Sales and Marketing Expenses as a function of Sales
  - *Sometimes Sales and Marketing expenses are each tracked separately, but more often that not they are combined and includes the costs of your sales force (direct, distributor, reps) and all marketing expenses (trade shows, print media). A prototypical sales and marketing ratio is 15-20% of sales. However, when starting to develop a market presence for the first time, sales and marketing will be a larger and more significant investment than this benchmark.*

If you don't have a good understanding of the type of advertising that will be effective with targeted customers, and/or don't understand the costs of marketing communications, you run the risk of wasting both time and money. Careful planning is therefore required.

Background

Marketing communications is commonly referred to as "advertising". However, the phrase "marketing communications" tends to more fully convey the objective of communicating effectively with your target market. Communication implies that you, the sender, intentionally convey a specific message about your product and your company that is received and understood by your customer. Previous discussions of positioning, product differentiation, and value proposition, all come into play in determining the message to be conveyed. An understanding of your customers and the most effective way to reach them is also important. In determining the best way to reach targeted customers and to estimate costs, it is suggested that you explore you competitors websites and/or consult with professional associations that also serve your targeted customers

A marketing communications plan refers to the materials that you will use to support your sales objective, coupled with the timeline indicating when the promotion materials will be used. Common promotional materials/events include:

- a web-site
- brochures
- conference presentations
- trade show displays
- press releases
- advertisements in selected trade journals
- direct mail
- seminars
- radio or television appearance

The time and frequency with which you use these materials depends upon your objectives and how your company fits into the market structure. In the activity that follows, indicate which promotional activities/ materials you will conduct/use in support of each of your sales objectives for the next two years. Be sure to consult with experienced advisors or examine the reports of publicly traded companies to determine the cost of their product launch. This can then be adjusted for your goals and used as a benchmark.

Activities: Question 12-5

Complete the following table for the first two years, provide a timeline for market roll out, and estimate the associated expenses. Keep in mind that the marketing associated with the roll out of a new product should precede sales by several months and should have a clear start date and a coordinated timeline involving everyone in the company[2].

1) Complete the spreadsheet provided in order to outline the elements of your marketing communication plan. Information has been added below as an example.

Table 12-5: Relationship between Sales Objectives and Marketing Communication Plan

YEAR 1				
Sales Objective	Targeted Customers	Promotional Approaches	Rationale for use	Payback
Sell 100 seats to new CFD software to product designers in aerospace industry	Product designers at Boeing, Lockheed Martin	• Participate in Paris Air Show • Participate in Sea, Air, and Space • Develop new product literature • Develop trade show booth	• This is THE place to be. Attendance by high ranking members of targeted companies • New literature with spec sheets and price sheets are essential • These are prestigious events and we need to be appropriately showcased	• Number of leads (Expectation = 50) • Number of leads that result in sales (Expectation is that 4% of leads would turn to sales)
Sell 10 seats to universities with aerospace engineering programs	Purdue Cornell	• Add applications section to website • Special pricing for university • Visit key faculty	• New application ideas will be sparked by such a section • University pricing is usually less	• Combination is expected to result in sales of 10 seats at discounted pricing. Loss leader - sets the stage for sales to new graduates
YEAR 2				

2) For the initial product roll-out, develop a visual which plots promotional activities over time. The following is a simple example created in PowerPoint.

Figure 12-3: Sample Marketing Communication Timeline

TradeShows	Sales Call	Journal Ad	Direct Mail
Sea, Air & Space	Boeing	Janes Defence Weekly	Promotional brochure on new product
Paris Air Show	Lockheed Martin	Aviation Week	Postcard announcing presence at trade show
NDIA Conference	Cornell	Computational Fluid Dynamics	
	Purdue	Aerospace	

3) Develop an itemized budget for all out of pocket expenses associated with the marketing communication plan. Be sure that the budgeted items coincide with your sales objectives. An excel workbook is provided that contains separate worksheets for Trade Shows, Personal Sales Calls, and Print Media.

4) Calculate the head count and cost of your sales force by year. Keep in mind that the costs will vary greatly depending on your sales goals.

During the start-up of your sales force, it is recommended that you structure your sales staff salary such that 80% of the person's income would be guaranteed and the balance from commission. The reason for this recommendation is two-fold: (1) the sales person will primarily be doing " missionary work" while developing the market and will not make that many sales; (2) if you are paying more of the person's salary, they will be more available to become engaged in other activities within the company. By contrast, when most of a person's salary comes from commission, they are incentivized to be on the road and will be less available inside the firm. It is also recommended that at the outset, you mention to new hires, that your plan is to re-evaluate the commission structure as the market is developed and shift the percentage of their salaried income down and increase the % contribution from commissions. Once the missionary work has been done, this approach provides a good incentive for the sales team.

Reality check: have I answered this question adequately
This question contained a number of important activities. Be sure that you gather actual price quotes for all items and expand the excel spreadsheet as necessary to meet your unique needs. Also, consider whether it is more appropriate to use sales representatives or distributors.

Sales representatives work strictly on commission. Therefore, in your planning you must allow sufficient margin (often 5-15% depending on value of the item) to serve as an incentive for the rep to sell your product. For planning purposes, it is advisable to plan for the higher percent. Also, if using reps you will need to provide them with sales tools and aides to help them do a better job in representing you.

Distributors actually purchase goods from you. They own the receivables and are totally responsible for sales, delivery of product, collections. Distributors receive a bigger margin (average 20-25%). However, with some items such as parts, they could receive up to 30-35% margin.

A number of associations that may be helpful in learning more about working with reps and distribibutors are listed below.

Manufacturers' Agents National Association
www.manaonline.org

United Association of Manufacturers' Representatives
www.uamr.com

Association of Independent Manufacturers'/Representatives, Inc.
www.aimr.net

Question 12-6: How much additional R&D will be required?

Relevant Section of Plan

Business Plan – Section 8

Why is this important and how does this relate to risk mitigation?

The best way to determine both the amount and nature of research and development activities that remain is to contrast existing performance with price and performance that meets your customers' expectations. The delta between existing and expected performance defines the domain of research that has yet to be accomplished. As scientists and engineers often run the risk of over-engineering a product, defining the end point in terms of customer expectations can be most helpful. When time is of the essence, an alternative to consider is potentially licensing-in technology to achieve a pressing goal.

Background

In the following activities you will be asked to address the degree of technology risk. It may seem strange that this is requested and will become a component of the business plan. However, the discussion shows that considerable forethought has been applied.

Activities – Question 12-6

1) For product X, which customer specifications have not been filled? Which research tasks are implied by the delta between the current and desired performance and price?

2) Are there specific R&D milestones that may be more difficult to address? Assuming that there are, please complete the following table and provide an accompanying narrative. (Section 8.3)

Table 12-6: Difficulties and Risks

Milestone	Degree of potential risk	Alternative path
Maintain sustained temperature for 10 hours	50% chance of failure	Change fuel

3) Indicate the headcount required to complete the projected research and develop a budget which reflects labor categories, number of employees, and salary.

Reality check: have I answered this question adequately

Question 12-7: What are your manufacturing objectives and your staffing needs?

Relevant Section

Business Plan – Section 9

For some companies a production plan is not merited (i.e. software). In such instances please substitute another appropriate section such as Customer Support.

Why is this section important and how does this relate to risk mitigation?

All parts of an organization must act in consort to assure that new products are brought to market on a timely basis. If marketing and sales are gearing up to roll out a new product and deliver it on a specified schedule, then manufacturing must be able to deliver. Manufacturing objectives must coincide precisely with the sales objectives. In other words, if you indicate that you will sell X number of units at Y price, with Z profit margin in a given year - then, you must be able to produce that quantity within those price constraints in that time frame. One turns a sales objective into a manufacturing objective simply by substituting the word "produce" for "sell". i.e. *In year 1 our objective is to produce Y quantity of product XYZ at Z price and X profit margin.*

Overzealous scale-up of production facilities is to be avoided. As a risk mitigation strategy many companies start by outsourcing production to contract manufacturers. While volumes are small, it is common to "farm-out" some or all of production and to retain assembly and quality control functions in-house. Later, if market potential is sufficiently large and market risk reduced, companies often find it more profitable to develop their own-in-house production capabilities. Over time, as demand increases, companies increase the sophistication of their means of production in order to increase through-put and reduce manufacturing costs.

Background

Activities – Question 12-7

» Develop a flow diagram showing the production steps required to produce the orders targeted for years 1-5. Indicate the quality control steps throughout. Use different colors to indicate which parts of this process may be outsourced. In narrative form, describe the quality control process in detail. (Section 9.3)

» Describe your existing production capabilities (include a photo) and discuss when additional space and equipment will be required to meet the increasing production objectives. (Section 9)

» Identify specialized equipment required by your firm to meet this production goal (specify type of equipment, price, and lease/buy decision).

» If you will be using contract manufacturers indicate who the suppliers are (will be), your experience with them to date, and the names of alternative vendors that could fulfill that role. (Section 9.2)

» Indicate the staffing requirements by year to meet the targeted production goals. Indicate labor categories; numbers of employees within each category, and average salary. Also, be sure to discuss the timing of new hires with the appropriate level of expertise.(Section 9.4)

» Indicate cost of production as a function of volume.

Reality check: Have I answered this question adequately?

In preparing the manufacturing objectives, gather and provide as much detail as possible, irrespective of whether production will be accomplished in-house or through the use of contract manufacturer's. Keep in mind that if manufacturing is a new business function for your firm, it represents a significant source of risk. In writing this section of the plan, it is therefore important to present sufficient detail to reflect that appropriate attention has been given to the addition of this new business function.

Summary and Conclusions

In Chapter 12 we began the process of developing detailed operational plans, all of which revolve around defensible sales projections. Operational plans should be developed for each business function and be coordinated with sales projections and with one other. The business plan outline included in this book is for a manufacturing firm. However, it is understood that not all companies will perform all business functions represented in the outline. In addition, some companies may require an emphasis on other business functions such as Customer Service. Please feel free to modify the plan outline to reflect your business, keeping in mind that any plan should involve all business functions and must be coordinated with sales projections and with one another.

In developing the preliminary draft of the plan, it is recommended that you put staffing requirements and budgets within each operational plan in order to see the relationship between what needs to be accomplished and the resources required. After you receive feedback on your draft plan, it is recommended that before you use it that you move all of the staffing needs to the Human Resources Section, and all of the budget elements to the Pro Formas.

Chapter 12 Endnotes

[1] Murphy, L.M and Edwards, P.L. Bridging the Valley of Death: Transitioning from Public to Private Sector Financing. NREL, May 2003 NREL/MP-720-34036

[2] Your product roll out is a big deal. One false move and you've lost millions http://www.impactmarketing1.com/pages/mhtl.html

Financials

" Happiness is not in the mere possession of money; it lies in the joy of achievement, in the thrill of creative effort. "

- Franklin D. Roosevelt

Chapter 13

... communicate to a targeted audience the benefit of their collaboration or investment in the business case presented.

Introduction

In previous activities you developed operational plans for discrete business functions - all anchored to sales projections. In Chapter 13 we will bring together previously developed financials and assumptions to incorporate in the Human Resources, Financials, and Contingencies sections of your plan. Emphasis in this chapter is clearly placed upon financials. We start by examining various ratios and applying them to pro forma financials that represent your business opportunity. A generic financial template has been developed for your use. This spreadsheet should make the process of compiling the financials for R&D firms much easier.

It is recognized that every firm "pools" financial information in different ways. Therefore, a discussion of this topic at the micro level has been avoided. Depending upon the specific audience for your business plan and their requirements, anticipate that you may need to expand the financials to meet their specifications. This chapter also includes information on preparation of financials for those pursuing a licensing strategy.

Please note that this is the last chapter containing planning activities. Sections of the business plan addressed in this chapter are highlighted below. Once the activities associated with Chapter 13 are complete, you will begin the process of drafting the business plan. In preparation for that task remember that a business plan

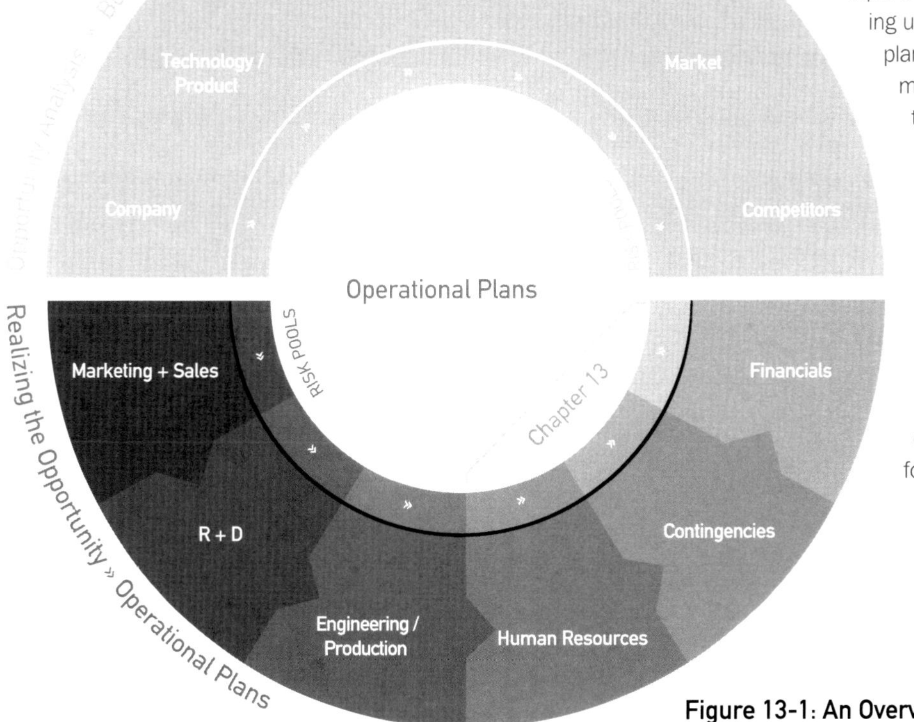

Figure 13-1: An Overview of Operational Plans

10. Human Resource Plan

- 10.1. Staffing Objectives
- 10.2. Organizational structure - phased over 3-5 years
  - *Introduction of management team*
  - *Key individuals to be recruited and plans for doing so*
  - *Board of Directors, Advisory Board*
  - *Incentives for commitment*
- 10.3. Human Resource Budget
  - *Assumptions*

11. Contingencies

- 11.1. Potential Risks
  - *Impact and responses*

12. Financials

- 12.1. Financial Objectives
  - *Commercialization strategy (elaborated)*
  - *Use of funds*
  - *Terms and conditions of any previous financing arrangements*
- 12.2. Plans for obtaining investors or strategic alliance
  - *Profile of investor or partner sought*
  - *Leveraging advantage for investor/partner*
  - *Detailed plans for obtaining investor/partner*
  - *Costs and time associated with securing investor/partner*
- 12.3. Pro Forma Financials

is more than a collection of information. This document should present a compelling case that effectively communicates the benefit of potential collaboration or investment in your opportunity to others. If you lack clarity regarding the audience, the business case will not be hard-hitting. Potential licensees, strategic partners, equity investors, debt lending institutions, and your own management have different needs – that should be uniquely addressed by your plan. Irrespective of your audience the purpose of the plan is to convey the strategic benefit to them of investing or teaming with you. The plan should not be presented as a case for why you need money, but as a vehicle for jointly creating wealth.

Business Plan

Question 13-1: Human Resources – Preparing for growth

Relevant section

Business Plan – Section 10

Why is this important and how does it relate to risk mitigation?

A friend showed me a wonderful image of a person walking on a tightrope strung between two buildings. Upon closer examination, you could see that the tightrope was a gossamer thread being laid in mid-air as the individual stepped forward. It wasn't attached to the other building at all – Well?! Timing the growth of a company has much in common with this image. The trick is to avoid falling - by not getting ahead of yourself or lagging too far behind. The *"build and they will come"* philosophy is to be avoided.

To be successful during periods of rapid growth, you must be closely attuned to the needs of your customer and concurrently communicate constantly and effectively with all parts of your organization. You must anticipate the need for good staff and develop relationships with universities, industry, and professional associations so that when the time is right, you can hire and retain good people. You must develop good relationships with your community banks and Departments of Economic Development, so that when you need a new building or equipment, there are others to which you can turn. Above all, constantly redefine your role and become a *"transformational entrepreneur"*, one who grows, changes, and evolves with the needs of your company.

Background

As noted earlier, all business functions revolve around sales. When you see that your company has successfully met projections, it provides the confidence needed to step out a little further and to bring others in. To avoid over-hiring, assure that your existing team is exceeding capacity before hiring additional personnel. Recognize that as you add different business functions to your firm, the importance of recruiting those with complimentary skills is heightened. It will take time and considerable resources to find and retain management for these new business functions. Consult with human resource organizations to gather benchmarks on pay scales as a function of position, training, experience, and geographic location. In your draft plan, you will need to clearly articulate a plan for assembling the best team to accomplish the objectives set forth.

Activities: Question 13-1

1) Draft a section that can be used in your business plan to introduce the members of your management team, highlighting the experience base of each which makes him or her an excellent candidate for that role. (Section 10.2)

2) Indicate your plans for recruiting and hiring key individuals to your team, and expanding your Board of Directors and/or Advisory Board. (Section 10.2)

3) Draw an organizational chart that shows when various functions will be added (section 10.2)

4) Provide a Table which indicates headcount by department by year.

5) Develop a detailed financial budget for staff by department, including head count, salaries, and commissions as appropriate. (Section 10.3)

Reality check: Have I answered this question adequately
You will have addressed this question well, if you have benchmarked the salaries of the various individuals in your HR plan and if the plan is tightly related to your sales projections.

Question 13-2: Using ratios to evaluate your financial health

Relevant section

Business Plan – Section 12.3

Why is this important and how does it relate to risk mitigation?

The ultimate success of a company is measured by its financial success. Therefore, in looking forward, it is important to develop a financial plan that matches revenue expectations against the costs to implement your venture. Such planning should increase the likelihood that you can obtain the cash flow required to sustain your business through product development to market entry.

For potential investors and partners, the most important elements of your business plan are the financial projections, the assumptions which underlie them, and their assessment of the risk associated with achieving those projections. The will evaluate the expertise of your company's management, the size of the opportunity, the strength of your intellectual property, and the prevailing market conditions. If you are not seeking external investment, but are looking to develop a new product line utilizing your own financial resources, it is highly recommended that you adopt a similar perspective.

Background

In looking at an opportunity, a potential investor will explore a series of ratios and benchmark them against industry standards for comparable firms. The ratios that are most commonly examined are various *profitability ratios, efficiency ratios, liquidity ratios,* and *debt management ratios*. Sources that can be consulted for industry ratios (for a fee) include:

- **BizMiner** www.bizminer.com/about.asp
- **VentureLine** www.ventureline.com/

General Information about industry ratios can be found at the following sites, each of which is affiliated with a university. NAICS (or SIC) codes discussed earlier, are required before one can conduct this type of analysis.

- www.mlb.ilstu.edu/ressubj/subject/business/ratio.htm#norms
- http://newarkwww.rutgers.edu/guides/business/com-ratios.htm
- www.uni.edu/lyle/ratios/ratios.htm

Primary classes of ratios are defined below.

liquidity ratios: A liquidity ratio is a measure of a company's ability to pay its debts (short and long term) and serves as an indicator of financial risk. Two common liquidity ratios are *current ratio* and *quick ratio*. To determine the goodness of these ratios, they need to be compared with industry standards. A liquidity ratio that is lower than the industry standard may suggest that the company has liquidity problems; whereas a liquidity ratio higher than the industry standard might indicate that it is not efficiently using its funds. The goal is to have a liquidity ratio that approximates the industry norm.

profitability ratios: Profitability Ratios show how successful a company is in terms of generating returns or profits on the investment that it has made in the business. Internally, such ratios enable a firm to see if profit is stable or changes over time (increases or decreases). Change in trends is a sign of management's activities. Profitability ratios can also be compared with industry standards in order to determine how the company fares relative to its cohorts. It is important to take age of the firm into account when conducting such comparisons. Common profitability ratios include *% gross profit, net profit %,* and *% return on assets.*

efficiency ratios: Efficiency ratios measure the efficiency of a company in either turning their inventory, sales, assets, accounts receivables or payables. It also ties into the ability of a company to meet both its short term and long term obligations.

Efficiency ratios, sometimes referred to as asset ratios provide a quick indication of how well a company's credit policy is working. Common ratios include collection period (days outstanding) and payables period (days outstanding). It is important to assure that your customers are not using you as their unpaid bank. In other words, some customers, will delay payment for 60 – 120 days which puts tremendous pressure the company that is being forced to play this role and negatively effects your cash flow. Sometimes delayed payment may be the result of the presence of many intermediaries in the approval process. In such cases, when you first notice that terms of payment do not coincide with what was agreed, contact the organization and determine if things are in order.

Activities – Question 13-2

The intent of this activity is to assist you in increasing your comfort level with ratios. Potential partners and investors will use ratios in evaluating your pro formas and there's no reason why you cannot become just as comfortable with the ratios and their implications. The activity associated with this question consists of studying and understanding the significance of the ratios.

» ***Liquidity Ratios:*** Current ratio, quick ratio

The current ratio is used to evaluate the liquidity, or ability to meet short term debts. High current ratios are needed for companies that have difficulty borrowing on short term notice. The generally acceptable current ratio is 2:1. The quick ratio is used to evaluate liquidity. Higher quick ratios are needed when a company has difficulty borrowing on short term notice. A quick ratio of over 1:1 indicates that the business could meet its current obligations with the readily available "quick" funds on hand.

Bankers look at liquidity ratios as an index of your ability to pay your debts. With current ratios, a score higher than 2 is considered good and means that you have sufficient liquidity. With the quick ratios a score of 1 or higher is desirable.

» ***Profitability Ratios:*** Return on assets, Return on equity, Gross Profit Margin (%)

In general, Return on Equity and Return on Investments in excess of 25% is considered acceptable. To the extent that the percentage is higher than this benchmark, the health of the company is viewed as being superior.

» ***Efficiency Ratios***: Collection period, Payables period & Inventory turns

The Days Sales Outstanding ratio shows the average time it takes to turn the receivables into cash. The ratio is regarded as a test of the effectiveness with which it converts its receivables into cash. This ratio is of particular importance to credit and collection associates. *Accounts Payable Days Sales Outstanding:* Outstanding ratio shows the average time it takes pay your suppliers. This ratio gives you an indication as to how much of their suppliers money does this company use in order to fund its Sales. Higher the ratio means that the company is using its suppliers as a source of cheap financing. Inventory Turnover ratio: This ratio is obtained by dividing the 'Total Cost Sales' of a company by its 'Total Inventory'. The ratio is regarded as a test of Efficiency and indicates the rapiditity with which the company is able to move its merchandise.

Your goal is to have your Payables period exceed your collection period. For example, if the average collection period for your company is 45 days and the average payables period is 47 days, this condition would exist. This will assure that you have sufficient cash flow and are not acting as your customer's banker. If you find that the reverse is true and that you are paying your creditors before your customers pay you, you need to change your collection procedures and interact forcefully with the accounts payable departments of delinquent customers.

» ***Other ratios:*** % sales growth, Sales per total employees, Marketing as a % of sales, Sales & Marketing as % of sales, G&A as a % of sales

The significance of these ratios will vary by industry and point in company growth. However, some general benchmarks of reasonableness at steady state are that marketing as a % of sales = 5%, sales as a % of sales =10-15%, G&A as a % sales =5%, sales and marketing as a % of sales = 15-20%, and sales, marketing, and G&A as a % of sales = 25%. To the extent that numbers are smaller than this it reflects insufficient attention to these efforts.

If you would like to have more background on financials and ratios, a number of sites can be consulted. Also, please keep in mind the sites for industry standards cited earlier.

D&B: Understanding Financial Statements
www.dnb.ca/community/unfinstate.html

Income Statement Analysis
www.ameritrade.com/education/html/encyclopedia/tutorial2/t2_s8.html

Reality check: Have I answered this question adequately?
You will have received the intended value from this activity if you can define each of the ratios listed above and discuss the implications with respect to your historical data.

Question 13-3: Developing pro forma financials

Relevant section:

Business plan - Section 12

Why is this important?

On the surface, the answer to this question seems obvious --- you need to know the financial requirements of your company so that you can determine how much capital you need to operate your business profitably and then select the best method to raise the required funds. What is less obvious, is the manner in which to accurately calculate your financial requirements.

Few companies are started by individuals with a strong financial background. Instead companies tend to be started by founders with strong scientific, marketing, sales, or manufacturing expertise. The frame of reference needed to assess financial requirements is foreign to most entrepreneurs. Lacking the right tools, the tendency is to use other approaches including "pulling a number out of thin air", providing unrealistic numbers which reflect the cash available to you, rather than the cash you need; plugging numbers into a software program that generate desired outcomes, or by simply ignoring the question. However, these approaches need to be set aside. As you plan for growth, it is important to take calculated, well considered risks, not those based on unrealistic and unfounded assumptions. If you fail to consider the assumptions adequately, you may make financial choices that have profound and negative implications for you and your firm.

The manner that is recommended for determining your company's financial requirements is to build a model based on an understanding of:

» The size of the opportunity and your ability to take advantage of it,

» Your competitors strategies for market penetration,

» the tasks to be accomplished by function (R & D, Engineering, Manufacturing, Marketing, Sales, Customer Service),

» the time associated with these functions,

» the cost of skilled labor; and

» other operating expenses

Background

Three Pro Forma (forward looking) financials for a strategic business unit engaged in production are described below, The Pro Formas are organized around Profit and Loss, Balance Sheet, and Cash Flow with explanations provided so that you can begin to gauge the goodness of the numbers.

Pro Forma Profit and Loss

The accompanying Pro Forma Profit and Loss, Balance Sheet, and Cash flow have been developed for a strategic business unit (as opposed to an entire company). You can however, expand the approach and use it with an entire company if you wish. As these three pro formas are associated, the anchor is the Profit and Loss statement. A set of assumptions is clearly articulated and accompanies the Profit and Loss Statement.

Please review the P&L, looking carefully at the accompanying assumptions. Assure that you understand the P&L model that has been divided into 9 sections:

Market
The market section clearly identifies the market niche being pursued with this product and the rate of market growth. Other activities leading up to the preparation of the financials should be drawn upon.

Production Revenue
Clear assumptions need to be articulated to indicate why this sales projection is reasonable as well as the basis for the selling price of the product. In this example, consulting or aftersale services are also sold. Market share is calculated automatically, as a function of your sales projections and product selling price. Please note that SBIR/STTR Contract R&D was placed under production revenue in this model. As this is considered income to the company, and is associated with this product, placing this here, allowed the ratios to be more meaningful.

Cost of Goods Sold (COGS)
The expenses listed under cost of goods sold are strictly associated with this product. In other words, the materials and production labor costs associated with this product only are clearly identified, as well as any royalties that may need to paid out, assuming that you have licensed in technology that is the basis for production. The COGS per unit does not include the consulting or after sales service. All of the cost associated with SBIR/STTR Contract R&D for this product are listed on a separate line in the cost of goods sold section.

Gross Margin
Note that the gross margin for the product and consulting are calculated separately.

Expenses
Expenses include all other expenses other than COGS that are associated with bringing this product to market. This includes sales, marketing, G&A, internal R&D (not under contract), legal and facilities. Please note that these are NOT all the expenses for the company, but just that proportion that supports the forward looking commercialization of that product.

Operating Earnings or Earnings before Interest and Taxes (EBIT)
The Earnings before Interest and Taxes takes into account the expenses that have supported that product using the formula Total gross margin – Total Expenses

Other Income/Expenses
In the example provided, assume that the company has also licensed-out production rights in a market the company has chosen not to pursue. The royalty is income from that license. Other expenses may include items such as deferred expenses, interest expense and miscellaneous expenses not included in general and administrative expenses.

Income before Taxes
Income before taxes, takes into account the other income/expenses before calculating the taxes. Although, you don't pay the government, negative taxes, companies can opt to book that against profit from another part of the company. The calculated "~~Net~~ income before taxes as a % of sales" is a useful index. 6% would be considered poor performance. 15% is OK and 20-25% would be considered outstanding.

Other Measures
The other measures contains head count that is important in estimating the various expenses, and also contains a number of ratios which utilize headcount and sales. Please note that all staff entered, is again staff working strictly on this project. Note that in the model provided, sales staff was added in year 3. If you trace performance over time you will be able to see the impact of adding sales staff and increasing the funds spent on marketing.

Pro Forma Profit and Loss - Scenario 1

XYZ Corporation
For years A to Z

[ ] = figures calculated for you

Market	Year 1	Year 2	Year 3	Year 4	Year 5
Served available Market size	$100,000,000	$102,000,000	$104,040,000	$106,120,800	$108,243,216
Rate Market growth	NA	2%	2%	2%	2%
Production Revenue (Sales - Product)					
Units expected to be sold	10	50	100	250	500
$ avg selling price of total product	$6,000	$5,500	$5,000	$5,000	$5,000
New product sales	$60,000	$275,000	$500,000	$1,250,000	$2,500,000
Consulting or aftersale services	$5,000	$25,000	$50,000	$125,000	$250,000
Total Production sales (Revenue)	$65,000	$300,000	$550,000	$1,375,000	$2,750,000
$ market share - total market	0.1%	0.3%	0.5%	1.3%	2.5%
SBIR/STTR Contract R&D	400,000	0	0	0	0
Total revenue	465,000	300,000	550,000	1,375,000	2,750,000
Cost of Goods Sold (COGS)					
Material	$20,000	$85,000	$135,000	$312,500	$625,000
Labor	$10,000	$50,000	$100,000	$250,000	$500,000
Licensing & Royalties	$2,500	$12,500	$25,000	$62,500	$125,000
Total COGS new product	$32,500	$147,500	$260,000	$625,000	$1,250,000
COGS (per unit)	$3,250	$2,950	$2,600	$2,500	$2,500
COGS consulting or after sale service	$3,000	$15,000	$30,000	$75,000	$150,000
Direct SBIR/STTR Contract Expenses	$400,000	$0	$0	$0	$0
Total COGS	$435,500	$162,500	$290,000	$700,000	$1,400,000
Gross Margin					
Total GM$	29,500	137,500	260,000	675,000	1,350,000
Total Gross Margin %	6%	46%	47%	49%	49%
GM$ (Per Unit)	$2,750	$2,550	$2,400	$2,500	$2,500
GM% (per unit)	46%	46%	48%	50%	50%
GM% consulting or after sale service	40%	40%	40%	40%	40%
Expenses					
Sales	0	0	75,000	85,000	192,500
Marketing	5,000	10,000	20,000	$35,000	40,000
Sales/Marketing	$5,000	$10,000	$95,000	$120,000	$232,500
Administrative (G&A)	$10,000	$10,000	$30,000	$50,000	$70,000
Internal R&D	$60,000	$60,000	$60,000	$60,000	$60,000
Legal	$15,000	$10,000	$20,000	$15,000	$15,000
Facilities	$30,000	$30,000	$45,000	$30,000	$30,000
Total Expenses	$120,000	$120,000	$250,000	$275,000	$407,500
Operating Earnings (EBIT)	($90,500)	$17,500	$10,000	$400,000	$942,500
EBIT Margin %	-139%	6%	2%	29%	34%
Other Income/expense					
Royalty	0	50,000	50,000	75,000	100,000
Other expenses					
Total Other Income	0	50,000	50,000	75,000	100,000
Income before tax	-90,500	67,500	60,000	475,000	1,042,500
Tax rate	35%	35%	35%	35%	35%
Taxes	-31,675	6,125	3,500	140,000	329,875
Net income	-58,825	43,875	39,000	308,750	677,625
Net income as %/sales	-12.7%	14.6%	7.1%	22.5%	24.6%
Company Cash Flow	(74,835)	12,956	(7,244)	118,136	357,937
Other Measures					
Admin Staff	0.5	0.5	1.5	2.0	3.0
Sales Staff	0.0	0.0	1.0	1.0	2.0
Production	0.5	1.0	2.0	2.0	3.0
R&D staff	6.0	1.0	1.0	1.0	1.0
Total Employees supporting product	7.0	2.5	5.5	6.0	9.0
% Sales Growth		-35.5%	83.3%	150.0%	100.0%
Sales per Total product Employees	66,429	120,000	100,000	229,167	305,556
Sales & Marketing as a % of Sales	1.1%	3.3%	17.3%	8.7%	8.5%
General Admin.as a % of Sales	2.2%	3.3%	5.5%	3.6%	2.5%

* Earnings before interest, taxes. Excludes venture capital funds.

The following is an example of the assumptions associated with the example provided.

Assumptions accompanying financials, organized by section		
Section 1	Market	The served available market for the product (GenPro) was previously calculated and information found to reasonably project the rate of market growth.
Section 2	Production Revenue	XYZ Corporation has historically been a contract R&D firm and has never been involved with either manufacturing or sales. XYZ wants to test the waters with this product (their first). GenPro (stands for Generic Product), a manufactured item that will be sold directly to the power generation market. The selling price of the product is based on market comparisons. The company has a machine shop and can do small quantity production in-house. Therefore, their goal is to start small and use their existing resources. XYZ corporation has had significant SBIR/STTR/ATP investment in the technology platform. Their intent is to commercialize other products from this technology platform using a variety of commercialization strategies.
Section 3	Cost of Goods Sold (COGS)	The company is 8 years old and prior to this time had 90% of its income come from science-for-hire contracts from the federal government. For this reason the company's accounting system was set up for government accounting and was divided into Direct Labor, G&A, OH, and Fee. XYZ recognizes that as it shifts to being a commercial product company, it must also represent its financials in a manner consistent with commercial practices. The COGS calculation is based on the expenses associated with this particular product. These costs are highlighted below
	Material	Assumptions accompanying financials, organized by section
	Labor	During Year 1: The GenPro products were produced in-house by the engineers who had worked on the design during the SBIR contract work. Production of the first 5 units was NOT done with SBIR funding and required about 20% of their time. XYZ quickly recognized that it would be too expensive to use these engineers during scale up. Therefore, a mechanic and a production engineer were hired during year 2, who were 50% engaged in this product. During year 3, this same team would work 100% time on production of this product. In year 5 an additional production engineer and machine shop personnel were added (all working 100% time).
	Royalties	In the production of GenPro a process was used that was exclusively licensed(in) from the unversity with which the company had an on-going relationship.
Section 5	Other Expenses	The other expenses are a % of the total company expenses associated with this product, and represent the proportion spent on support of the GenPro product. Sales were initially done exclusively by the company President who did not spend a lot of time on this endeavor. Support staff also spent some of their time supporting this initiative. The expenses on the sales/marketing line in Year 1 are the costs associated with attending 1 trade show and producing a short-run of publicity materials. In year 3, a VP of Sales was added. His salary, anticipated commission and marketing expenses were added to the Sales/Marketing line in year 3. With respect to internal R&D, as the number of units to be sold increased, the amount invested in development of new processes to produce the product in a more cost effective way increased and then dropped. Contract R&D associated with this product ended at the end of Year 1, and the company increased its IR&D Legal fees include patent filings in Year 1 and 3 estimated to be $15,000 each and other costs associated with related commercial contracts. With respect to facility costs, the company did not outgrow its existing space but did need to add new equipment in year 3.

Sales Head Count Requirements							
	Direct	Headcount	Base Salary	Incentive %	Incentive $	Total cost
Year 1	President	1	$80,000	President is G&A: assume 5% time on sales		
Year 2	President	1	$83,000	Same		
Year 3	VP, Sales	1	$65,000	20%	$16,250	$81,250
	President	1	$83,000	Assume 10% time spent on sales		
Year 4	VP, Sales	1	$68,000	20%	$17,000	$85,000
	President	1	$86,000	Assume 15% time on relationships and bonus for corporate growth		
Year 5	VP, Sales	1	$70,000	20%	$17,500	$87,500
	Sales men	1	$84,000	20%	$17,500	$105,000

Please note that headcount, salary and commission considerations, all effect the financials

Pro Forma Balance Sheet

In putting together the pro forma balance sheet, the method used to develop the balance sheet is instructive. Listed below is the model used, with an explanation provided.

			Model Inputs				
Cash as % of sales			3%	3%	3%	3%	3%
Cash$			13,950	9,000	16,500	41,250	82,500
Avg days sales			178	822	1,507	3,767	7,534
Collection period (days)			45	45	45	45	45
Receivables			8,014	36,986	67,808	169,521	339,041
Inventory turnover x			6	6	6	6	6
inventory $			5,917	27,083	48,333	116,667	233,333
Change in sales			65,000	235,000	250,000	825,000	1,375,000
capital investment rate as % of sales change			3%	3%	3%	5%	5%
capital investment			1,950	7,050	7,050	41,250	68,750
	% dep	2%	8,000	8,000	8,000	8,000	8,000
	% dep	20%	390	390	390	390	390
	% dep	20%		1,410	1,410	1,410	1,410
	% dep	20%			1,500	1,500	1,500
	% dep	20%				8,250	8,250
	% dep	20%					13,750
	depreciation		8,390	9,800	11,300	19,550	33,300
	Cum depreciation		8,390	18,190	29,490	49,040	82,340
Avg days purchases			55	233	370	856	1,712
Payables period (days)			47	47	47	47	47
Payables			2,575	10,945	17,384	40,240	80,479

The model began with making the following assumptions, which are identified in the clear rows, as well as the deprecation percentages. Starting at the top with *"Cash as % of sales"* – 3% was selected because that was a reasonable amount of cash to have on time at anyone time. The 3% was then applied to the Total revenue line in the Pro Forma Income and Expenses statement to generate the specific amount of cash on hand. The *"average day sales"* was derived by dividing the Total revenue from the Pro Forma Income and Expense statement by 365 days to provide the average income per day. An *average collection period* of 45 days was selected and the average daily sales multiplied by 45 to generate the average *receivables* during the collection period. *"Inventory turns"* is an indication of the number of times during a 12 month period you restock an item. The higher the number of turns the more frequently you are replenishing stock and conversely don't have product sitting around for a long time before it is sold. Six turns is good. By comparison 1 or 2 inventory turns would be poor. The "inventory dollars" is the total cost of goods served divided by the number of turns. Please note that the contract SBIR R&D dollars was removed before calculating the $value of the inventory.

In order to calculate how much should be reinvested in the company in capital equipment, the delta or difference in sales between the preceding year and the current year and then multiplied by 3%. This percentage was chosen as it was a reasonable on-going amount to spend on capital improvements. To then calculate how much should be invested each year the % was multiplied by the delta in revenue.

A Depreciation schedule is used to collect annual depreciation charges. Typically each asset is depreciated according to its expected life or Federal guide line. In this model the buildings are expected to have a very long life of 50 yrs and the first line of the depreciation schedule is for the buildings and had a rate of 2% per year. The remaining lines (one line for each year) in the schedule had a 20% annual straight line depreciation rate reflecting a five year period.

The *average day purchases* is the cost of materials (from COGS) divided by 365. Payables period was 47 days and when multiplied by the "average day purchases" yielded the amount that needed to be paid to suppliers during each period as *payables*.

This model was then used to populate the blue areas in the balance sheet below. The balance sheet is broadly divided into *assets, liabilities, shareholder's equity,* and *ratios*. In terms of *fixed assets*, if you are leasing, entering the annual dollar value of the lease through its duration on the building line. If you are leasing equipment, you would do the same. With respect to liabilities, *short term liabilities* are those that need to be paid off within a year; while others are long term liabilities. In all cases, these are NOI companies assets and liabilities, but the % of those assets and liabilities applied to this strategic business unit.

Next, if you look at the key ratios: *the profitability, efficiency,* and *liquidity ratios* are telling. In terms of ROI or ROE, this product line begins to become very good in year 4. If in excess of 25% is viewed as very favorable, both indices are excellent in years 4 and 5. With respect to efficiency ratios, the number of inventory turns is good and the payables period, exceeds the receivables period which means that the company has cash with which to pay its bills. In looking at the liquidity ratios, the quick ratio is less conservative than the current ratio. According to the quick ratio where a score of 1 or higher is good, in Year 2 the company has achieved this ratio. With using the current ratio where 2 or more is considered good, the liquidity ratio reaches good form in year 4

Balance Sheet Dec 31st	Actual			Pro Forma				
	YR-2	YR-1	YR0	YR1	YR2	YR3	YR4	YR5
Assets								
Cash				13,950	9,000	16,500	41,250	82,500
Accounts receivable				8,014	36,986	67,808	169,521	339,041
Inventory				5,917	27,083	48,333	116,667	233,333
Other current assets								
Total current assets	0	0	0	27,880	73,070	132,642	327,437	654,874
Fixed Assets								
Land				100,000	100,000	100,000	100,000	100,000
Buildings				400,000	400,000	400,000	400,000	400,000
Equipment				300,000	307,050	314,550	355,800	424,550
Subtotal				800,000	807,050	814,550	855,800	924,550
accumulated depreciation				8,390	18,190	29,490	49,040	82,340
Net Property Plant and Equip.	0	0	0	791,610	788,860	785,060	806,760	842,210
Other assets				100	100	100	100	100
Total fixed Assets				791,710	788,960	785,160	806,860	842,310
Total Assets				819,590	862,030	917,802	1,134,297	1,497,184
Liabilities and Shareholders' Equity								
Current Liabilities								
Short term debt				30,000	32,000	32,000	50,000	60,000
Account payables				2,575	10,945	17,834	40,240	80,479
Other current liabilities				0	0	0	0	0
Total Current Liabilities	0	0	0	32,575	42,945	49,384	90,240	140,479
Long -Term Debt				300,000	350,000	350,000	500,000	550,000
Other long term liabilities				0	0	0	0	0
Deferred income taxes				0	0	0	0	0
Total long term liabilities				300,000	350,000	350,000	500,000	550,000
Total Liabilities	0	0	0	332,575	392,945	399,384	590,240	690,479
value of initial stock at time of issue	0	0	0	100	100	100	100	100
Retained earnings				486,915	468,984	518,318	543,957	806,605
Stock Holder's Equity	0	0	0	487,015	469,084	518,418	544,057	806,705
Total Liabilities and Equity	0	0	0	819,590	862,030	917,802	1,134,297	1,497,184
Key ratios								
Profitability ratios:								
Return on equity %				-12.1%	9.4%	7.5%	56.7%	84.0%
ROI (EBIT/Total Assets)				-11.0%	2.0%	1.1%	35.3%	63.0%
Efficiency Ratios								
Inventory turnover x				6	6	6	6	6
Collection period (days)				45	45	45	45	45
Payables period (days)				47	47	47	47	47
Liquidity Ratio								
Current Ratio				0.9	1.7	2.7	3.6	4.7
Quick Ratio				0.7	1.1	1.7	2.3	3.0

Pro forma Cash Flow

Much of the information in the Pro Forma income and Expenses Statement and Balance Sheet are automatically linked to the Pro Forma Income and Expense and the Pro Forma Balance Sheet. The analysis of cash flow can show you where investment may be needed and can be used in analyses of the impact of various decisions.

Cash Flow Sheet (indirect method)								
	Actual			Pro Forma				
	YR-2	YR-1	YR-0	YR1	YR2	YR3	YR4	YR5
Cash from operations								
Net income				(58,825)	43,875	39,000	308,750	677,625
Add-depreciation				8,390	9,800	11,300	19,550	33,300
Net cash flow from income	0	0	0	(50,435)	53,675	50,300	328,300	710,925
Cash provided (used) by operating activities								
Operating cash (1)				(13,950)	4,950	(7,500)	(24,750)	(41,250)
Accounts receivable (1)				(8,014)	(28,973)	(30,822)	(101,712)	(169,521)
Inventory (1)				(5,917)	(21,167)	(21,250)	(68,333)	(116,667)
Other current assets (1)				0	0	0	0	0
Account payables (2)				2,575	8,370	6,438	22,856	40,240
Other current liabilities (2)				2,955	3,150	3,090	3,026	2,959
Total change in working capital	0	0	0	(22,350)	(33,669)	(50,044)	(168,914)	(284,238)
Net cash flow from operations	0	0	0	(72,785)	20,006	256	159,386	426,687
Investment transactions Increases (decreases)								
Capital spend (building & equip)				1,950	7,050	7,500	41,250	68,750
Other assets				100	0	0	0	0
Net cash used in investments	0	0	0	2,050	7,050	7,500	41,250	68,750
Free cash flow from operations	0	0	0	(74,835)	12,956	(7,244)	118,136	357,937
Cumulative cash flow	0	0	0	(74,835)	(61,880)	(69,124)	49,013	406,949

1) Delta increase in these balance sheet accounts from prior year is a use of cash.

2) Delta increase in these balance sheet accounts from prior year is a source of cash.

Activities: 13-3

1) Prepare a **Pro Forma Profit and Loss statement** for a strategic business unit built around a product offering. Two spreadsheets are included: (1) the spreadsheet for this example, (2) a spreadsheet template for use in preparing your financials. It is recommended that you put in actuals for the current year, and if it is instructive for the past two years. In going forward, be sure that you clearly articulate all assumptions as they relate to pricing, staff, production, and associated costs.

2) Prepare a **Pro Forma Balance Sheet**, either using the assumptions provided in the model or through the development of a parallel model. Two spreadsheets are included: **1) the spreadsheet for this example, (2) a spreadsheet template for use in preparing your financials**

3) Prepare the **Pro forma Cash Flow** and discuss its implications from an investment perspective.

Reality check: Have I answered this question adequately?
You will have answered this question adequately if the assumptions used to build the Pro forma Income and Expenses statement are clearly articulated and are considered reasonable by others working with you.

Summary and Conclusions

The financial expression of the opportunity you have chosen to pursue, as well as your plans for pursuing it – constitute the "bottom line." From an investor's perspective this is the raison d'etre for your business. Although the scientist in you may wish to pursue an opportunity because of its technical challenge or the contribution it may make, the businessman or woman in you, must come to the surface and look at the cost-benefit of different alternatives. As you work with the numbers, and explore different scenarios, make sure that you tightly tether numerical abstractions to the reality of what will be required to realize the opportunity. For example, if you set a market penetration goal of 5% that requires that you produce 1,000 units a year, you must get inside the numbers and test the likelihood that this could be realized. Decide what will change – how you do business or the numbers? By clarifying assumptions and evaluating their likelihood, you will be better able to address and meet your financial objectives.

Putting it all Together

"You gain strength, courage, and confidence by every experience in which you really stop and look fear in the face."

- Eleanor Roosevelt

Chapter 14

Emphasize the strategic benefit for others of investing in your vision to jointly create wealth.

Drafting the Plan

Now that you have completed the planning process, you are ready to begin drafting the business plan. To assist in this endeavor, another copy of the suggested business plan outline is included. In the margins, next to the outline, you will find a description of what you need to accomplish in each section. In all cases, we are assuming that the reader for your business plan is a potential investor or strategic ally. In drafting the plan you should assume that the business decision maker will not be an expert in your technology, therefore, do not use jargon without first introducing key concepts. The decision maker is reading the business plan to evaluate the business case you present for creating value (wealth). He or she will view the technology as a means to that end and NOT the end in itself. Therefore, do not go overboard when describing the technology. If you succeed in getting your reader's attention, then expect that during the due diligence process, technology experts will be consulted. The phrase **due diligence** indicates that an independent evaluation is being conducted. Due diligence is commonly performed on the technology, market, competition, and opportunity. However, as due diligence in itself requires an investment of time and resources, this is not done lightly. You must first present a compelling business case which gets the reader's attention.

The first time you draft the business plan, do not worry about page limits, but instead focus on being comprehensive. It is assumed that you will revise the business plan and at that time you can decrease the number of pages (See page 180). Use the suggested subheadings (numbered items) to make it easy for the reader to quickly maneuver around the document. The bulleted items, under each section heading are intended to serve as prompts and can be addressed in any order. These prompts are not intended to be comprehensive, but illustrative. There indeed may be additional items which you must include to present your business case.

In terms of mechanics, the document should be double spaced or at minimum spaced one and one- half lines apart. This protocol leaves space for people to write notes and makes it more inviting. You can place more information on a page by using a smaller and legible font, such as times roman (point 12). Other good font alternatives are optima, arial and palatino.

The Executive Summary should be drafted last, but not when you are tired. Many times busy investors will read only the Executive summary and the financials. If it doesn't grab them, they won't go any further. A suggested outline for your executive summary is included after the business plan outline (page 177). Do not include any proprietary information in the Executive Summary. In this fashion, you will also be able to use this as a stand-alone document, that you can give out separately to pre-qualify the interest of potential partners and investors. When using the Executive Summary as a stand-alone document, we recommend that you dress-it up. The stand-alone document should have a cover page with a title that expresses the nature of the opportunity and includes information on the appropriate contact person. You may also add images to the cover.

Business Plan Outline (Detailed)

Cover Page
Table of Contents

1. Executive Summary

2. Company & Technology

- 2.1 Brief company introduction
  - » *Mission*
  - » *Location, size, history*
  - » *Overview of company capabilities*
  - » *Customers & past performance*
- 2.2 Technology
  - » *Brief description*
  - » *Applications*
- 2.3 Product/Service
  - » *Brief description*
    - 2.3.1. Intellectual property status
- 2.4 Commercialization strategy - brief overview

3. Industry Overview

- 3.1. Industry definition and description
  - » *New products and developments within the industry*
  - » *Major players within the industry, factors driving dynamics*
- 3.2. Legislation and policies driving the industry
  - » *Future and historical trends*

4. Customers

- 4.1 Customers & end-user
  - » *Need addressed by the technology/product/service*
  - » *How the need is currently filled?*
  - » *Features, Advantages, and Benefits; Price point*
  - » *Who has the need? - Differentiate between end-users and customer needs*
  - » *Distribution channels used by customers and end-users*
- 4.2 Buying behavior
  - » Decision makers
    - › *Who makes the decision to buy*
    - › *Who influences the purchase decision*
    - › *Characterization of decision makers*
  - » Basis for purchase decisions
    - › *Frequency of purchase decisions*
    - › *Basis for purchase decisions*

5. Market

- 5.1. Market definition
  - 5.1.1. Primary market
  - 5.1.2. Secondary markets
- 5.2. Market size and trends - Primary market
  - » *Current total and served-available markets*
  - » *Predicted annual growth rate*

6. Competitors

- 6.1. Indirect competitors
- 6.2. Direct competitors
  - » *Who are they?*
  - » *Strengths and weaknesses*
  - » *Market share of competitors*
- 6.3. SWOT analysis

7. Marketing / Sales Plan

- 7.1. Opportunity statement
- 7.2. Marketing & sales objectives
- 7.3. Current customers (if appropriate)
- 7.4. Potential customers
  - » *Customers targeted for intensive selling efforts*
  - » *How other customers will be identified and qualified*
  - » *Product features emphasized and contrasted with competitors*
- 7.5. Pricing
  - » *Basis for targeted price point*
  - » *Margins & levels of profitability at various levels of production & sales*
- 7.6. Sales Plan
  - » *Sales force analysis (reps, distributors, direct)*
  - » *Sales expectations for each salesperson & each distribution channel*
  - » *Margins given to intermediaries*
  - » *Service and warranties*
  - » *Organizational chart for sales/marketing staff, indicating planned growth for 3 - 5 years*
- 7.7. Advertising
  - » *Year 1- Detailed Marketing Communications plan*
  - » *Years 2-5 (general)*
- 7.8. Sales/Marketing Budget
  - » *Assumptions*

8. R&D Plan

- 8.1. R&D Objectives
- 8.2. Milestones and current status
  - » *What remains to be done to make the product marketable?*
- 8.3. Difficulties and risks
- 8.4. Staffing
- 8.5. R&D Budget
  - » *Assumptions*

9. Manufacturing/Engineering Plan

- 9.1. Objectives
- 9.2. Use of Subcontractors
- 9.3. Quality control
- 9.4. Staffing
- 9.5. Manufacturing/Engineering budget
  - » *Assumptions*

10. Human Resource Plan

10.1. Staffing Objectives

10.2. Organizational structure - phased over 3-5 years

» *Introduction of management team*

» *Key individuals to be recruited and plans for doing so*

» *Board of Directors, Advisory Board*

» *Incentives for commitment*

10.3. Human Resource Budget

» *Assumptions*

11. Contingencies

11.1. Potential Risks

» *Impact and responses*

12. Financials

12.1. Financial Objectives

» *Commercialization strategy (elaborated)*

» *Use of funds*

» *Terms and conditions of any previous financing arrangements*

12.2. Plans for obtaining investors or strategic alliance

» *Profile of investor or partner sought*

» *Leveraging advantage for investor/partner*

» *Detailed plans for obtaining investor/partner*

» *Costs and time associated with securing investor/partner*

12.3. Pro Forma Financials

This detailed outline is included as a preview of the end product. It is organized in a way that builds a logical business case, both for internal and external use.

Executive Summary

Many times investors read ONLY the executive summary and your financials and then make a decision about proceeding to read the document. Listed below is a suggested outline for the Executive Summary. This should be no longer than 5 pages in length (including the cover) and may include figures and tables.

Company & Background

» company location & mission statement, sustainable competitive advantage

» provide background on core technology

» commercialization strategy

The Market Opportunity

» describe market need

» market size & trends

Management Team

» key players and relevant background

» highlights and accomplishments

Investment Highlights

» what level of financing are you seeking?

» how funds will be used

» what type of partner/investor you seek

» why this is a good opportunity for them.

Get Feedback on the Plan

Once you have completed your first draft of the plan, do NOT give it to a potential investor to read. First drafts tend to be too long and cumbersome. However, do give it to other members of your team, board members, and significant others to provide you with feedback on the content. Tell them that you know it is too long - but that you value their reaction to the content, with specific attention to all of the action plans that you have mapped out for the company. Gather their feedback and again re-evaluate your course of action based on their feedback.

Revising the Plan

The next draft of the business plan, should be prepared for its ultimate use. Here you must pay attention to page limits. The way to reduce the size of your plan is to use graphics, tables, and charts wherever you can and relegate other information to appendices. In this final iteration - form becomes vital. As you draft your business plan, you should keep in mind an old Marshall McLuhan, cliche "The medium is the message". In other words, the appearance of the document, the form in which the business plan is presented, tells the potential investor something about you. Furthermore, it affects the attitude with which he or she will read your document and makes it stand out above the hundreds of others the investor has and will see. The message that you wish to leave with the investor is that you have a technology of value; you are an excellent technologist; you are also a business person and are sensitive to market issues, design, engineering, and production costs; you have an opportunity for them to consider; and your company would be a good firm with which to work.

Some general guidelines are listed below:

- Adopt a style that you will use throughout.
- Use a type font and point that are easy to read.
- Whenever possible represent market data by use of pie charts, tables, and other figures.
- Represent development time lines with Gantt and PERT charts.
- If you have too much data for some sections of the plan, include them in the Appendices. The document should read smoothly and not appear to go off on tangents.
- Make sure duplicated copies photocopy well.
- Consider the use of color.

It is not possible for us to include a copy of a completed business plan as all of those which we have developed or have assisted in developing are proprietary. However, the guidelines that we have presented throughout should be of assistance.

Guidelines for Business Plan Revisions

Listed below are some general guidelines regarding page lengths

1. Executive summary	2 - 3 pages
2. Company & Technology	3 pages
3. Industry overview	1 page
4. Customers	2 - 3 pages
5. Market	2 - 3 pages
6. Competitors	2 - 3 pages
7. Marketing/sales plan	3 - 4 pages
8. R & D plan	2 - 3 pages
9. Manufacturing/Engineering plan	2 - 3 pages
10. Human resource plan	2 - 3 pages
11. Contingencies	1 page
12. Financials	3 - 4 pages

How to use your Business Plan

As mentioned at the outset, your business plan has both internal and external value. As the external value is the purpose for which you have presently developed this plan, we will discuss its external application first. Your business plan should be valid for approximately one year. At the end of that period, you should reassess the situation and revise the plan. During this year your business plan will serve as a very important selling document. However, as it contains very complete information on your business, you should distribute it with great care. Listed below are some general guidelines for distribution:

Distribution protocols

1) Do not distribute your plan to anyone who has not demonstrated a sincere interest in your technology/product. Gauge their sincerity by the confidence and trust they engender in you, as well as by their reputation.

2) Keep track of all your business plans by number, recording their distribution in a log. Request their return within 30 days. Extend on an exception basis only.

3) Clearly mark each business plan in the following manner: Proprietary, Confidential, Not to be Duplicated.

4) Ask the person to sign a confidentiality agreement with you before sharing the business plan with them. Ask if they have any problem with this. If they do, you can remove sections of your plan that you consider to be particularly sensitive.

On the following page you will find a sample confidentiality agreement. This is not meant to be a template, but an example. Please consult an attorney in drafting the one which you will use. This agreement should be the first item in your business plan.

Summary and Conclusions

Putting a business plan together is a unique challenge, requiring that the author remains focused on the plan's intended audience and communicates effectively the nature of the opportunity it presents for them. The best plans are those that look like they are written specifically to address the needs of a potential strategic partner, equity investor, or licensee. In other words, the ideal plan maps out how they can leverage an investment in or partnership with your firm into a significant return on investment. In this scenario, the entrepreneurs' personal needs and aspirations become subsumed under the greater goal of generating a significant return. A challenge indeed!

If you are developing a business plan strictly for internal purposes, there is much to be learned from assuming a more objective stance and looking at what you wish to accomplish from a businessman or woman's perspective. Conveying clarity of vision, can help empower your team.

XYZ CORPORATION'S CONFIDENTIALITY AGREEMENT

The information contained herein is the property of XYZ Corporation and is confidential. The recipient agrees that he will not release this plan or disclose information herein, or make reproductions or use it for any purpose other than this evaluation of a prospective investment. The recipient further agrees to return all proprietary materials to XYZ Corporation upon request.

By signing below the recipient acknowledges that the confidential information contains valuable concepts, of a business nature, of XYZ Corporation. The recipient further acknowledges that the confidential information constitutes a trade secret of XYZ Corporation, and loss or disclosure of such confidential information will result in irreparable financial harm to XYZ Corporation.

Information in the Plan is based upon the best available sources at the time of writing, but should not be taken as final. In particular, the forecasted financial information is estimated based on XYZ Corporation management's judgment, and actual results will vary from the information presented, and the variations may be material. This document is not an offer to sell, nor a solicitation of an offer to buy any securities, or other interest, in any corporation or other entity. The sale of any securities in and the making of any investment in any corporation or other entity would be solely under the terms of the applicable agreements, and subject to the laws of the appropriate jurisdiction.

Signature of Recipient Signature for XYZ

Date Date

Epilog

Business Planning for Scientists and Engineers was designed to serve as a useful guide in conducting business research and in drafting your initial business plan. Hopefully, the process of developing the plan should also strengthen your team, increase your confidence and assist in making well informed decisions regarding your future direction. Best wishes with your business endeavors.